学术英语写作与演讲

主编 张荔 盛越

清华大学出版社
北京

内 容 简 介

本教材专门为学术英语混合式教学而设计和编写。全书18个单元全面、系统阐述学术论文撰写与演讲的各要素和流程,包括研究题目的确定、学术文献的检索与管理、学术剽窃、学术论文各部分的撰写要点、语言表达的提升、语料库的利用、学术会议发言的准备、学术演讲与即兴问答的要略等。

每单元提供丰富的课前学习资源、课中活动和课后任务,将慕课资源、教材内容和网络多媒体素材完美融合,为开展学术英语线上线下混合式教学提供了方法和素材,也适合社会学习者自主学习。

本书附配教学资源请登录 http://www.ftp.tup.tsinghua.edu.cn/ 下载。

版权所有,侵权必究。举报: 010-62782989, beiqinquan@tup.tsinghua.edu.cn。

图书在版编目(CIP)数据

学术英语写作与演讲/张荔,盛越主编.—北京:清华大学出版社,2021.12(2023.1重印)
ISBN 978-7-302-59715-5

Ⅰ.①学⋯ Ⅱ.①张⋯ ②盛⋯ Ⅲ.①英语—写作②英语—演讲 Ⅳ.① H31

中国版本图书馆 CIP 数据核字(2021)第 276761 号

责任编辑:刘细珍
封面设计:子 一
责任校对:王凤芝
责任印制:宋 林

出版发行:清华大学出版社
网　　址:http://www.tup.com.cn, http://www.wqbook.com
地　　址:北京清华大学学研大厦 A 座　　邮　编:100084
社 总 机:010-83470000　　邮　购:010-62786544
投稿与读者服务:010-62776969, c-service@tup.tsinghua.edu.cn
质量反馈:010-62772015, zhiliang@tup.tsinghua.edu.cn

印 装 者:三河市铭诚印务有限公司
经　　销:全国新华书店
开　　本:185mm×260mm　　印　张:19.75　　字　数:373 千字
版　　次:2022 年 1 月第 1 版　　印　次:2023 年 1 月第 2 次印刷
定　　价:79.00 元

产品编号:091820-01

前　言

　　本教材是中国大学慕课"学术英语写作与演讲"课程配套教材，专门为混合式教学设计编写。全书共 18 个单元，系统体现了学术论文撰写与学术演讲的各个要素。每个单元提供了丰富的课前学习资源、课中活动设计和课后任务。该教材为高等院校开展学术英语线上线下混合式教学提供了方法和素材，也为广大在线慕课学习者提供了自主学习的辅助途径。

　　本教材体现了多要素融合的特点，具体表现为：

　　（1）教材的设计框架体现混合式教学课前、课中和课后的融合。每个章节包含三个混合式教学模块：

- 课前自学内容：MOOC/SPOC 知识点自主学习，包含视频、文字材料、问题讨论、测试。
- 课中教学活动：线上或智慧教室讨论活动，使知识点内在化，包含活动内容和实施步骤。
- 课后教学任务：借助学习管理平台（如 Canvas）的项目式学习任务，对知识点加以应用，包括课后任务设计和实施。

　　（2）教材的设计理念体现语言输入（文献阅读）和语言输出（写作与汇报）技能的融合以及书面语（学术写作）与口语（学术演讲）的融合。课程体系和教学内容符合从输入到输出的语言教学理论体系，并以成果为导向，模拟真实的论文发表和会议发言过程展开教学，将从文献阅读、论文写作到会议发言的全过程引入教学内容的组织和教学活动的实施。线下教学则通过论文的过程性写作而展开，充分体现了形成性评估与终结性评估相结合的方法。

　　（3）教学材料体现慕课资源、书面文字材料和网络多媒体链接相融合的立体式教材特色。慕课课程"学术英语写作与演讲"在中国大学慕课平台免费开放，为课前自学提供了帮助。教材中的文字材料，为自学提供了更多的内容阐述和实例分析，还包含了慕课中未涉及的内容。书中的二维码链接则提供了与课堂活动对应的论文文字材料和演讲视频资源。这些内容不仅为教师利用本教材组织课堂教学提供了方便，也为社会学习者自主学习提供了有效途径。

（4）教学目标体现了语言能力提升和综合素质培养相融合的特点。本教材融入了学术诚信、批判性思维、创新探索能力的培养目标，隐性体现了课程思政的元素。例如，在确定研究主题时，教材引导学生以联合国的17个议题，如平等、环境、公正、科技、教育、贫困等为基础展开研究，鼓励学生进行探索，培养他们的社会责任感和人文素养。在学习学术论文结构要素的同时，将特定主题的研究论文融入学习任务，帮助学生理解主题内容，潜移默化地实施"价值引领、知识探究、能力建设、人格养成"四位一体立德树人的思政教育，鼓励学生对这些主题展开进一步的学术研究。学术演讲教学视频主题则包括成功的要素、意志力的重要性、如何将压力转化为动力、如何调节身心健康等，着重考虑所选内容的科学性、思想性和学术性。

本教材可以根据教学实际需求灵活使用。一、某些内容的顺序可以有所调整。例如，学术诚信虽然出现在教材的第四单元，但是可以在第一次课就提出来以突出其重要性。二、可以根据教学学时长短对课中活动内容加以合并、删选或补充。例如，可以将某几个单元内容合并在一次课中完成；课前学习案例亦可作为课中活动；课中活动可加以挑选作为课后练习；甚至可以针对学生的学习能力，让学生自己根据教材和慕课进行学习，而课中则针对项目的推进情况组织和实施阶段性任务并对完成情况进行点评，以深入贯彻从"做"中"学"的理念。为了方便教师设计教学，我们提供了上海交通大学学术英语课程的教学大纲（见 Appendix 8）和 PPT 课件，教师可以根据本校学生的实际情况进行个性化设计。另外我们也提供了学术论文评分标准（Appendix 9）和学术演讲评分标准（Appendix 10），以作为对项目完成情况进行评估的参考。所有这些附配教学资源可登录 http://www.ftp.tup.tsinghua.edu.com 下载。

本教材是教育部人文社会科学研究项目"融入课程思政的学术英语线上线下混合式教学模式探究"（项目号 21YJA740051）和上海外国语大学外语教材研究院 2021 年外语教材研究重点项目"混合式学术英语教材设计、开发与评价研究"（项目号 2021SH0013）的部分成果，特此感谢教育部和研究院对项目的大力支持！

主编

上海交通大学外国语学院

2021 年 8 月

Contents

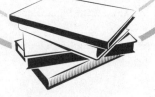

Unit 1　Topic 1
1.1 Objectives 2
1.2 Pre-Class Learning 2
1.3 In-Class Activities 6
1.4 After-Class Tasks 13

Unit 2　Sources 15
2.1 Objectives 16
2.2 Pre-Class Learning 16
2.3 In-Class Activities 24
2.4 After-Class Tasks 25

Unit 3　Academic Reading 27
3.1 Objectives 28
3.2 Pre-Class Learning 28
3.3 In-Class Activities 41
3.4 After-Class Tasks 46

Unit 4　Plagiarism, Paraphrase and Summary 49
4.1 Objectives 50
4.2 Pre-Class Learning 50
4.3 In-Class Activities 57
4.4 After-Class Tasks 63

Unit 5　Language Improvement 65
5.1 Objectives 66
5.2 Pre-Class Learning 66
5.3 In-Class Activities 92
5.4 After-Class Tasks 98

Unit 6　Title and Thesis 99
6.1 Objectives 100
6.2 Pre-Class Learning 100
6.3 In-Class Activities 107
6.4 After-Class Tasks 110

Unit 7　Outline 111
7.1 Objectives 112
7.2 Pre-Class Learning 112
7.3 In-Class Activities 119
7.4 After-Class Tasks 125

Unit 8　Abstract 127
8.1 Objectives 128
8.2 Pre-Class Learning 128

8.3 In-Class Activities 134
8.4 After-Class Tasks 139

Unit 9   Introduction 141
9.1 Objectives 142
9.2 Pre-Class Learning 142
9.3 In-Class Activities 149
9.4 After-Class Tasks 152

Unit 10   Literature Review 155
10.1 Objectives 156
10.2 Pre-Class Learning 156
10.3 In-Class Activities 174
10.4 After-Class Tasks 176

Unit 11   Methods 179
11.1 Objectives 180
11.2 Pre-Class Learning 180
11.3 In-Class Activities 192
11.4 After-Class Tasks 194

Unit 12   Results 197
12.1 Objectives 198
12.2 Pre-Class Learning 198
12.3 In-Class Activities 206
12.4 After-Class Tasks 210

Unit 13　Discussion 211

13.1 Objectives 212
13.2 Pre-Class Learning 212
13.3 In-Class Activities 221
13.4 After-Class Tasks 225

Unit 14　Conclusion 227

14.1 Objectives 228
14.2 Pre-Class Learning 228
14.3 In-Class Activities 234
14.4 After-Class Tasks 237

Unit 15　Citations and References 239

15.1 Objectives 240
15.2 Pre-Class Learning 240
15.3 In-Class Activities 245
15.4 After-Class Tasks 247

Unit 16　Peer-Review and Revision 249

16.1 Objectives 250
16.2 Pre-Class Learning 250
16.3 In-Class Activities 260
16.4 After-Class Tasks 261

Unit 17　Presentation Content 263

17.1 Objectives 264

17.2 Pre-Class Learning 264

17.3 In-Class Activities 275

17.4 After-Class Tasks 276

Unit 18   Speech Delivery 281

18.1 Objectives 282

18.2 Pre-Class Learning 282

18.3 In-Class Activities 294

18.4 After-Class Tasks 299

References & Example Sources 301

Unit 1

Topic

1.1 Objectives

Know what topic to choose.
Learn how to choose a topic.
Learn how to elaborate on a topic.

1.2 Pre-Class Learning

Watch the MOOC/SPOC videos and do the online exercises. The contents in the textbook will help you understand the lessons better.

Source: https://www.icourse163.org/

Course name: "学术英语写作与演讲" (Academic Writing and Presentation in English)

Unit 1 Topics and Sources

1.1 Topic choice and elaboration

You are now embarking on the journey of academic writing. First and foremost, you should choose an appropriate topic for you to do the research and write a paper in the next few months. The topic you choose will, to some extent, determine the value of the research and your experience in the process. It is therefore necessary that you know what topic to choose, how to choose a topic, and how to elaborate on a topic.

What topic to choose

Interesting. You are supposed to have interest in the topic that you are going to spend your time researching because interest is the best teacher and motivator. The more interested you are, the more devoted and absorbed you will be. Actually, you will feel very struggling and can hardly go on researching without interest.

Familiar. You also need to have some previous knowledge about the topic you choose, offering you some degree of familiarity. Your familiarity with the topic can lay a foundation for your research, which adds further to your current knowledge as a result of your new exploration. Actually, this is the purpose and process of doing research.

Original. It is advisable that the topic be new and updated. People tend to be attracted by fresh ideas and original explorations, so you'd better get access to the latest development of issues you are going to research. A topic involving new ideas can attract the interest of other people and make your research more valuable. Actually, a researcher, updated with the latest development in the discipline of study, is inclined to be more creative and more likely to come up with more valuable and original research findings.

Problem-oriented. The topic you choose is also supposed to deal with the problems of practical significance. You'd better take notice of what is happening around you, predict what problems might occur, and how to solve them. A research is usually a problem-solving process. In order to solve the problem, you read the related literature to obtain background knowledge, on the basis of which you do research to solve the problem.

For example, the United Nations aims to solve problems regarding poverty, hunger, health, education, equality, energy, economy, infrastructure, industrialization, sustainable consumption and production, climate change, peace, justice, partnerships, and so on (Figure 1.1). You can find out the one that you are most interested in and familiar with. Then, decide whether you are able to do additional research on it. Also try to relate it with what is happening around you so that you can come to a topic that is feasible and manageable. As a university student, you may like the topics related to university issues, such as university students' psychological health, campus study and life. You can also address the issues of online education, voluntary work, critical thinking, motivation of learning, etc.

Figure 1.1   Sustainable Development Goals of UN

(Source: https://www.un.org/sustainabledevelopment/)

How to choose a topic

Once you have decided on a topic, you can do the brainstorming by using mind-map or clusters (Figure 1.2). Brainstorming is an efficient way of generating ideas because the process of brainstorming is unrestrained and spontaneous. You can have free associations and develop ideas by listing any related matters that come into your mind.

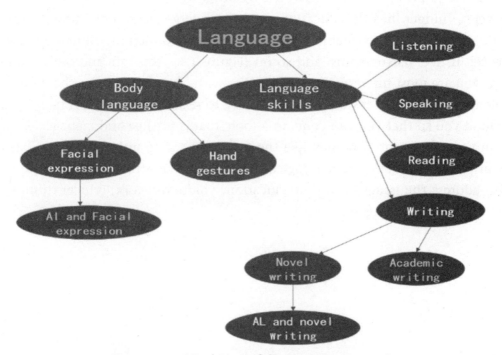

Figure 1.2   Mind-Map of the Topic "Language"

Besides, you can track down a list of books or periodicals in the library and read the table of contents or the bibliography for ideas. The books usually provide a comprehensive and systematic description of a certain subject while the periodicals are regularly published and may involve the most recent explorations of the subject. Both of them can be useful resources for you to find your topic for research.

A frequently adopted way of choosing a topic is browsing the Internet for information. For example, you may like to find information about a certain topic by reading Wikipedia, which may provide you with some general knowledge about the topic. But the information online may not be authoritative, you still need to read published journal articles to find out what researchers are actually doing.

How to elaborate on a topic

A topic that is too general can hardly be explored in depth within the length of your research paper. Therefore, you'd better elaborate on the topic to make it more specific and manageable.

- **Example 1**

General topic:	Writing
More specific topic:	Evaluation of writing
Elaborated topic:	Automated writing evaluation

In example 1, "writing" is too broad a topic to be addressed because there are many aspects involved in writing, such as writing instruction, writing methods, process of writing, evaluation of writing, etc. The topic "evaluation of writing" still covers a lot of subordinate topics such as summative evaluation, formative evaluation, teacher, peer, self-or automated evaluation, each of which involves aspects that are worth exploring at length. Thus, the topic can be elaborated further to "automated writing evaluation", which requires more research to achieve a deeper understanding.

- **Example 2**

General topic:	Computer
More specific topic:	Computer Games
More specific topic:	Computer Games and Its Influence on Behavior
Elaborated topic:	Computer Games and Aggressive Behavior

In this example, "computer" is too general a topic because it can hardly be covered completely. Therefore, it should be narrowed down to the more specific topic "computer games", which can further be elaborated as "computer games and its influence on behavior", and then to "computer games and the aggressive behavior". Such a topic can be addressed with the following research questions:

—What is aggressive behavior?

—How do computer games relate to aggressive behavior?

—What can we do to prevent the negative effect caused by computer games?

If you have decided on the general topic but find it hard to narrow it down to a specific topic for your research, try to get ideas by reading the sources so as to know what other researchers are concerned about. Reading the literature helps expand your knowledge and deepen your views on a certain topic.

1.3 In-Class Activities

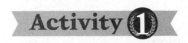

Please use the mind-map to do brainstorming on the topic of "education".

Education

Steps for organizing the activity:

1. Do brainstorming in groups of three and draw the mind-map together.
2. Exhibit the mind-map sheet in the whole class.
3. Walk around the classroom and tick on the sheet of the mind-map you think is the best.
4. Find out the mind-map most classmates think is the best by counting the ticks and tell why.

Activity 2

Scan the outline made by a student for the topic of "Artificial Intelligence" and find out the problem of the topic.

> Topic: Artificial Intelligence
>
> 1. Introduction
> 2. Basic concepts of artificial intelligence
>   2.1 Fundamentals of artificial intelligence
>   2.1.1 Reasoning and problem solving
>   2.1.2 Knowledge representation
>   2.1.3 Machine learning
>   2.1.4 Creativity by artificial intelligence
>   2.1.5 Artificial general intelligence
> 3. Application of artificial intelligence
>   3.1 Heavy Industry
>   3.1.1 Manufacturing
>   3.1.2 Automotive industry
>   3.2 Service sector
>   3.2.1 Automated driving
>   3.2.2 Healthcare
>   3.2.3 Customer service
>   3.3 Financial sector
>   3.3.1 Market analysis
>   3.3.2 Financial trading
>   3.4 Media
>   3.4.1 News publishing
>   3.4.2 Writing
> 4. Current situation of employment
>   4.1 Unemployment caused by technology
>   4.2 Decrease demand for human labor

    4.3 Job polarization
5. Prospective of artificial intelligence causing employment crisis
    5.1 Difference from the three previous industrial revolution
    5.2 Income inequality
    5.3 Proposed solution
6. Conclusion

Steps for organizing the activity:

1. Scan the outline.
2. Discuss with your group members to find out the problems of the content.
3. Think about how to narrow down the topic to make it researchable.
4. Generalize some researchable topics in class.

Activity 3

Please try to elaborate on the following topics. The first one is given as an example.

Core word	Elaborated	More elaborated	Much more elaborated	Research title
Education	College education	Performance in the college	Research experience and performance in the college	Can undergraduate research experience help students improve their performance in the college?
Health				

Unit 1 **Topic**

(Continued)

Core word	Elaborated	More elaborated	Much more elaborated	Research title
Love				
Occupation				
Environment				
Life				
Equality				
Development				
Technology				
Ethics				
Society				

Steps for organizing the activity:

1. Do the task in groups of three students.
2. Choose one of the topics all the group members are interested in.
3. Discuss and elaborate on the topic together.
4. Share the elaborated research topic with other groups, esp. the groups that work on the same topic.
5. Compare your topic with the following research topics taken from past students' research papers, which demonstrate students' interest and capability.

- **Education**

    Exploring the Factors Influencing Undergraduates' Selection of Major

    The Optimal Pedagogy to Improve Critical Thinking in Class

    Primary Education in Rural China: The Current Condition, Policies and Effects

    Exploring the Feasibility of Applying MOOC-Based Flipped Classroom to University Courses

    Exploring the Application of Mobile Phone in the Learning of Science in University Classroom

    Online Education's Impact on People with Little Educational Background

    Can Undergraduate Research Experience Help Students Improve Their Performance in the College?

    Understanding the Impact of Accent on Speaker and Audience: Based on College Students' Classroom Presentation in China

- **Health**

    Exploring a Health and Nutritional Quality Assessment Model of Delivered Food

    The Effects of Obesity on Adolescent's Physical and Mental Health

    Exploring the Relationship Between Eating Patterns and Dietary Problems Among Teenagers

A Review of Cognitive Behavior Therapy for Internet Addiction

Surveying Undergraduates' Mental Health and the Measures to Cope with Negative Emotions

COVID-19 Epidemic: Peoples' Mental Health Status and Associated Factors During Quarantine

- **Love and Marriage**

Exploring the Influence of Romantic Relationship on College Students' Academic Performance

Impacts of Romantic Relationship on College Students' Health

The Social Status Que of Sex, Love and Marriage and Its Impact on the Future Society

Investigation of Millennial College Students' View on Intimate Relationship and Marriage

- **Employment and Occupation**

The Impacts of Artificial Intelligence on Employment Market

The Relation Between China's GDP Growth and Unemployment—Based on Okun's Law

The Impact of the COVID-19 Pandemic on Medical Students' Academic and Occupational Motivation

- **Environment**

Relationship Between Energy Profile and Climate Change: Analysis of Different Regions

Wildlife Protection: Is China Going the Wrong Way?

A New Framework for Ecosystem Service Valuation Applied to Wetland

Exploring Impacts of Marine Debris in Coastal Ecosystems and Feasible Solutions

Exploring the Necessity and Feasibility of Waste Sorting in China: A Case Study in Shanghai

- **Campus Life**

    The Influence of Sleep Quality and Patterns on Chinese College Students' Academic Performance and Extracurricular Activities

    Predicting Academic Performance Among College Students Through Sleep Quality

    Space Syntax Analysis for Evaluating and Improving Road Systems of College Campuses: A Case Study

    The Correlation Between Self-Confidence and Mental, Physical Well-Being of Undergraduate EFL Students

- **Equality**

    Gender Inequalities in Workplace Considering Position, Enterprise and Rate of Employment

    Historic Development and Current Situations of Gender Equality in Universities

    Exploring Gender Inequality in Medicine: Obstacles in Female Doctors' Promotion

- **City Development**

    Optimizing the Distribution of Automated External Defibrillator in Shanghai: A Computer Simulation Method

    Exploring the Use of Quick Respond Codes to Build a Smart and Safe City

    Prediction of Electric Vehicle Market Based on Civic Opinion Valuation and Regional Market Expansion Gradient

- **Technology and Design**

    Improvement of a New Gene Regulator: Small Transcriptional Activating RNA

    Photovoltaic Power Generation Technology Applied to the Structure Design of Shutter

    Functional Analysis of Strawberry Fruit Development Related Genes

    Comparison of Corpus-Based Coh-Metrix and L2 Syntactic Complexity Analyzer

The Impact of the Linear or Nonlinear Interior Architecture Design on Work Performance: A Study on SJTU Students

- **Ethics**

  Exploring the Essential Reasons Behind International Discrimination During the COVID-19 Epidemic

  The Feasibility of Euthanasia in China from the Perspective of Ethics and Regulations

  Rethinking AI Ethics: An Exploration of Driverless Car

  A Review of School Bullying: Causes, Effects and Solutions

- **Society**

  Advancing Better Living for Elders: Exploring a Retirement Community to Help Elders Stay Independent, Mentally Engaged and Relevant

  The Influence of Social Norms on Chinese College Students' Self-Control of Mobile Phone Use

  Using Critical Thinking Skills to Distinguish Rumors During the Global COVID-19 Outbreak

  Factors Influencing People's Willingness to Volunteer in COVID-19 Pandemic

 After-Class Tasks

Find some researchable topics on the basis of the 17 goals of UN and relate them to the problems around you. Elaborate on the topics and compare your possible topics with the research topics that demonstrate students' interest and capability in Activity 3 in 1.3.

Task 2

Prepare for a presentation about one of your research topics. Your presentation should include:

1. What is the general topic?
2. What is the elaborated topic?
3. Why are you interested in this topic?
4. What problem(s) do you intend to solve?
5. Is this topic within your capability? / Is it feasible for you to do the research (e.g. finding literature and collecting data)?

(**Note:** *The presentation of the research topics can be an in-class activity in the next class.*)

Unit 2

Sources

2.1 Objectives

Learn how to find sources about your topic in the library.

Learn how to use EndNote to manage your source.

2.2 Pre-Class Learning

Watch the MOOC/SPOC videos and do the online exercises. The contents in the textbook will help you understand the lessons better.

Source: https://www.icourse163.org/

Course name: "学术英语写作与演讲" (Academic Writing and Presentation in English)

Unit 1 Topics and Sources

1.3 Literature search

1.4 EndNote bibliography management

After deciding on the topic for your research paper, the first thing you have to do is to read a large number of books and articles so that you can be equipped with some knowledge of the topic, on the basis of which you can generate your own ideas. No research can be done without reading other researchers' works because you need the knowledge base on which you build your own knowledge. In this unit, we are going to deal with how to make use of the library to search for source materials.

Searching library database

Many university libraries offer students free and ready access to databases, among which the most popular databases are EBSCO (Figure 2.1) and WOS (Web of Science) (Figure 2.2). They cover a comprehensive range of disciplines and provide both abstracts and full texts.

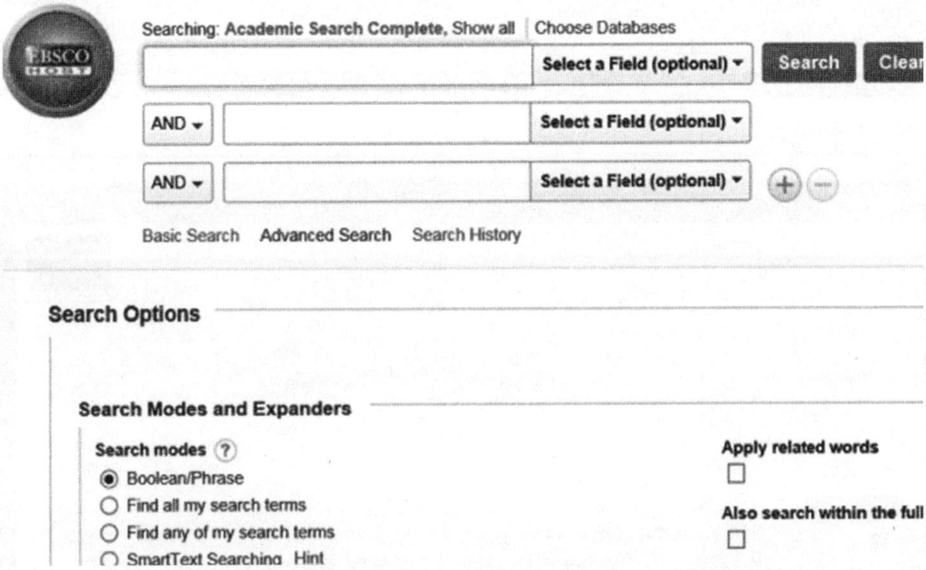

Figure 2.1   The Search Page of EBSCO Database

Figure 2.2   The Search Page of WOS Database

- **Example**

Let's take EBSCO as an example to illustrate how to use databases to search for information related to your topic.

1. Browse the university library online database list (e.g. Shanghai Jiao Tong University library database: http://www.lib.sjtu.edu.cn/f/main/index.shtml) and click on EBSCO (Figure 2.3).

Figure 2.3   Major Library Databases in Shanghai Jiao Tong University

2. After retrieving the EBSCO database, click on "Frontpage" (平台首页) (See Figure 2.4) and then select source, for example, "One-stop search for all EBSCOhost Databases" (Figure 2.5).

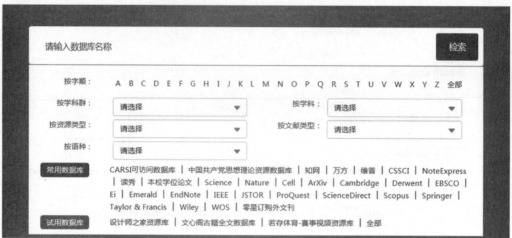

Figure 2.4   EBSCO Database

Unit 2 **Sources**

Figure 2.5   One-Stop Search for All EBSCO Databases

3. The advanced search page will immediately pop up (Figure 2.6), allowing users to choose from a number of search functions and limiting options when searching for information. At the top of the page are three search boxes which allow multiple, simultaneous keyword searches. Beside them are respective search limits to specify the searches in specific fields such as all text, author, title, keyword, source, abstract, etc. You can also narrow down the search results by ticking the choices below such as search modes, research results, or published dates, etc.

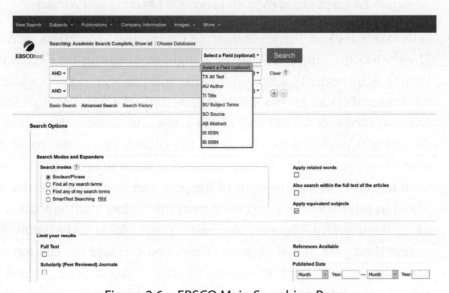

Figure 2.6   EBSCO Main Searching Page

4. Use search boxes by typing in a keyword or keywords and selecting a field. Suppose you are going to search for articles about the topic of "how to improve writing when learning a language", enter the keywords "language learning" and "writing" in the "TI Title" field, and the first 10 of the 305 articles show up below the search box (Figure 2.7). You can scroll through the listed articles to find those that appeal to you for your research purpose. If you need more articles, you can change the "TI Title" to "AB Abstract" or "TX All Text" and more articles can be accessed.

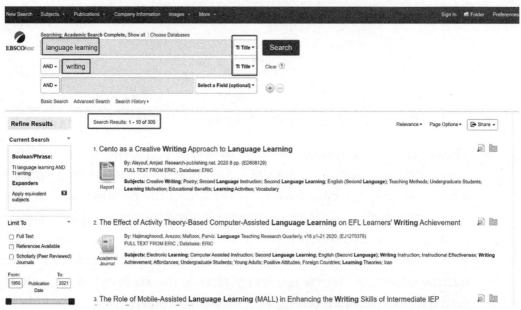

Figure 2.7　Searching Page for Language Learning and Writing

5. Let's take a look at the second paper on the list "The Effect of Activity Theory-Based Computer-Assisted Language Learning on EFL Learners' Writing Achievement". Click on the title and you will come to a page with full information about the article (Figure 2.8). The "Availability" link will give you access to the full text of the article. An abstract that summarizes the article is displayed for you to get the general idea of the paper. If you wish to save the article and keep on looking through other articles, use the "Add to folder" link at the right of the page and save the article. All articles placed in this folder can be accessed from the "Folder" button located at the top of the interface. There are also buttons that enable you to print, e-mail, or save the article. If you click on "Cite", you can find the citation of that particular article in kinds of citation formats. If you click on "Export", you can save the information of the article to the file management software, such as EndNote or Zotera (Figure 2.9). They are tools for you to organize all of your sources and manage their citations and references conveniently.

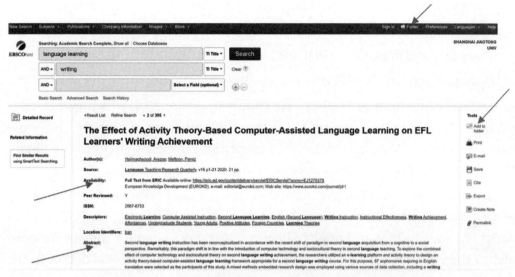

Figure 2.8 Information About the First Paper Generated

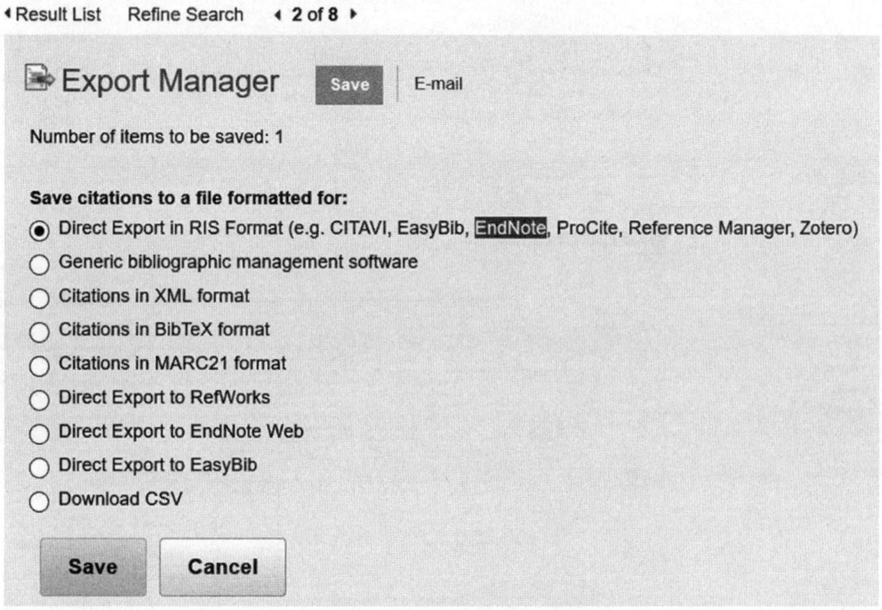

Figure 2.9 Export to EndNote

Using EndNote

You can use the file management software to arrange sources and insert citations in your article. Let's take EndNote for example. EndNote can serve a lot of functions, such as:

—creating a library for all your references;

—organizing your library to categorize references by topic or subject;

—automatically creating a bibliography that matches the in-text citations;

—reading and annotating PDF files; and

—sharing references with other researchers.

Different functions of EndNote are shown in Figure 2.10, which gives a clear picture of how they are represented using different icons. There are also more details of how EndNote can create your library and import sources to the library (Figure 2.11), and how to cite sources in the article (Figure 2.12).

There is a very detailed instruction of how to use EndNote in Unit 1 of our MOOC. You'd better learn how to use it at the very beginning so that you can export the sources to your EndNote library when you search for sources. You can refer to the video in our MOOC whenever you forget some specific details in the instruction.

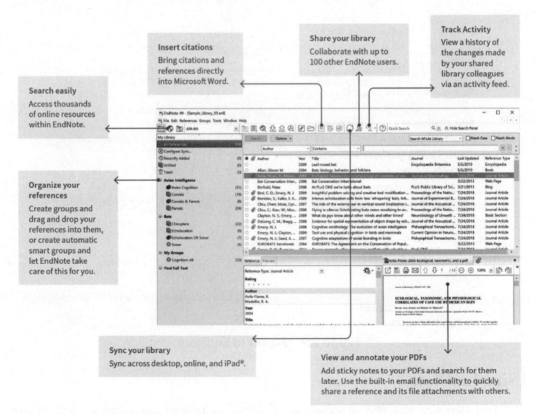

Figure 2.10　General Functions of EndNote (Web of Science Group, 2018)

Unit 2 **Sources**

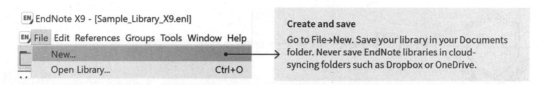

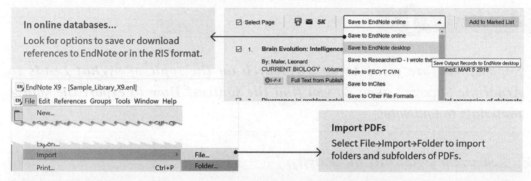

Figure 2.11   Create Your EndNote Library and Import Sources (Web of Science Group, 2018)

When you install EndNote, it will search for your word processor and install the appropriate Cite While You Write (CWYW) files to let EndNote and your word processor communicate. On Windows, Cite While You Write is available for Microsoft Word, Apache OpenOffice, and LibreOffice. With Microsoft Word, you will see the EndNote X9 tools shown below in Word.

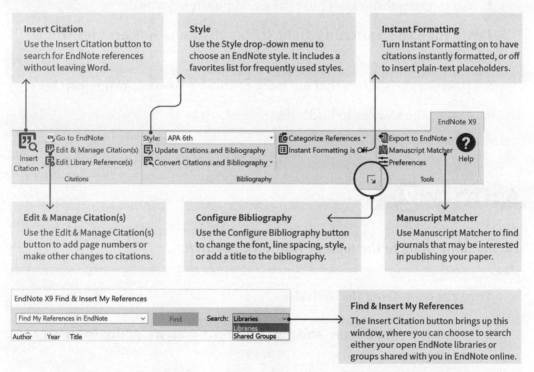

Figure 2.12   Cite Sources in Your Article (Web of Science Group, 2018)

2.3 In-Class Activities

Activity 1

Suppose you are going to do a research on the topic of "What Leads to Academic Success", how do you find the sources? How to export the source materials to EndNote?

Steps for organizing the activity:

1. Choose one of the websites that is available to you (for example: EBSCO).
2. Decide on the keywords you are going to use for searching.
3. Go to the website searching page and put in keywords.
4. Change the searching field (title, abstract, full article) when necessary.
5. Find out the sources that are most applicable to your own research.
6. Export the sources to EndNote.

Activity 2

Do the same thing to the topic of your own research.

Steps for organizing the activity:

1. Decide on your topic and the keywords you are going to use for searching.
2. Go to the website searching page of EBSCO and put in keywords.

Unit 2 **Sources**

> 3. Change the searching field (title, abstract, full article) when necessary.
>
> 4. Find out the sources that are most applicable to your own research.
>
> 5. Export the sources to EndNote for your future use.

After-Class Tasks

Task 1

Find source materials for the topic you have decided on by exploring the Internet or the library at your university. Export the sources to EndNote and organize the source materials for use in the future. Save at least 10 articles in PDF format for your research.

Task 2

Ask professors in your department to recommend 4–5 most distinguished journals in your discipline of study. Find 1–2 most typical papers in any of these journals.

(Note: *The papers can be brought to class later and used as samples for the exploration of typical features of the research papers in different disciplines of study. Students can also get themselves updated with the latest development of research in their own disciplines of study*).

Unit 3

Academic Reading

3.1 Objectives

Know how to read extensively from a large collection of papers.

Be able to locate the specific information in a research paper.

Be able to form review perspectives from extensive reading.

Learn how to take down notes while reading.

3.2 Pre-Class Learning

Watch the MOOC/SPOC videos and do the online exercises. The contents in the textbook will help you understand the lessons better.

Source: https://www.icourse163.org/

Course name: "学术英语写作与演讲" (Academic Writing and Presentation in English)

Unit 1 Topics and Sources

1.2 Academic reading

As the saying goes, excellent writing should be based on sufficient reading. This is even more often the case with academic writing where the researchers are supposed to read extensively, based on which they can be better equipped with background knowledge, find the problems of existing literature, formulate their own research questions, compare their findings with other research and support their ideas with evidence from their readings. Reading research papers helps establish a foundation for writing a research paper clearly and logically.

Reading source materials

Having searched and saved the source materials and got ready to read them, you will always find there is too much to read. When spending a couple of hours on a single article, you may well wonder when you can finish reading all of them. Don't simply grab an article and start reading it from the beginning to the end. You need to adopt the efficient reading strategies of skimming and scanning.

Collate a list of materials and read the title and abstract of each paper.

You collate a list of materials in a folder and start reading. The title usually reveals the major information of the article, such as the main topic or the major research method. But on most occasions, you also need to read the abstract to quickly find the research purpose, method, findings and conclusions so as to decide whether this article is helpful for your own research and whether it is worth the time to read the whole article.

Organize the reading list and emphasize the most important articles.

Now that you have screened all the articles, you have a shortlist of articles that you think are most important and relevant to your own research and worthy to read in detail. This can save you much time and the efficiency of reading is expected to be substantially improved.

Read the whole paper and identify the key information and take notes.

While reading the whole paper, you must form the habit of taking down notes of either general information such as the major argument, main findings and conclusions, or specific information such as the definition of an important term or the main idea of a cited research in the article. What information to be kept in your notes depends on your research topic and the content you want to incorporate into your own writing.

Start reading the related literature and note down also the source of these materials.

When you find an important point that is cited from another paper, you can check out its source in the references and read the related literature to get a more accurate understanding of the idea. This is also a good way to find related literature of the same topic.

Reading for specific information

Research papers usually share a common structure acknowledged by the research communities. A well-organized research paper shows clearly the logic of the paper. If you know the structure of the research paper, you can easily locate the specific information using a top-down strategy. Let's take the example of the research paper by Keck (2014) entitled "Copying, Paraphrasing, and Academic Writing Development: A Re-examination of L1 and L2 Summarization Practices" (See Appendix 1) and try to find the answers to the following 8 questions.

—What is the topic of the paper?

—How is the research paper organized?

—What is the purpose of the research?

—What is/are the research question(s)?

—If you want to repeat the research process, where can you find the information?

—What are the findings of the research?

—What are the analyses and explanations of the findings?

—What is the conclusion of the research?

Copying, paraphrasing, and academic writing development: A re-examination of L1 and L2 summarization practices

Casey Keck *

Linguistics Program, English Department, Boise State University, United States

Abstract

Recently, a number of scholars (e.g., Leask, 2006; Liu, 2005) have raised concerns about the discourse of plagiarism, arguing that an emphasis on cultural difference has served to reinforce stereotypes of particular L2 groups and perpetuate deficit views of L2 learners. In an effort to address these concerns, the present study revisits Keck's own (2006) comparison of L1 and L2 summarization practices and investigates (1) why both L1 and L2 writers might choose to copy or Paraphrase source text language while composing a written summary and (2) whether the strategy use of novice writers differed from that of their more experienced peers. The study found that L1 and L2 writers identified many of the same excerpts to include in their summaries, excerpts which allowed them to introduce the problem in focus and to explain the author's thesis. The study also found that the higher rate of copying observed for the L2 group as a whole could be explained by a small number of students who copied source text language extensively. In both the L1 and L2 groups, novice writers tended to rely more on source text excerpts than their more experienced peers.

Figure 3.1   Title and Abstract

By reading the **title** and the **abstract** (Figure 3.1), you can find that this article is about plagiarism, or to be more specific, rethinking plagiarism with regard to the comparison between native and second language learners' copying and paraphrasing practices.

Unit 3 **Academic Reading**

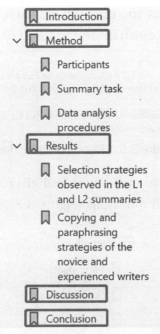

Figure 3.2 Headings of the Paper

Judging from the headings of the paper (Figure 3.2), you can find that the paper includes introduction, methods, results, discussion and conclusion, which is the structure shared by most research papers.

Abstract

Recently, a number of scholars (e.g., Leask, 2006; Liu, 2005) have raised concerns about the discourse of plagiarism, arguing that an emphasis on cultural difference has served to reinforce stereotypes of particular L2 groups and perpetuate deficit views of L2 learners. In an effort to address these concerns, the present study revisits Keck's own (2006) comparison of L1 and L2 summarization practices and investigates (1) why both L1 and L2 writers might choose to copy or Paraphrase source text language while composing a written summary and (2) whether the strategy use of novice writers differed from that of their more experienced peers. The study found that L1 and L2 writers identified many of the same excerpts to include in their summaries, excerpts which allowed them to introduce the problem in focus and to explain the author's thesis. The study also found that the higher rate of copying observed for the L2 group as a whole could be explained by a small number of students who copied source text language extensively. In both the L1 and L2 groups, novice writers tended to rely more on source text excerpts than their more experienced peers.

Figure 3.3 Purpose Shown in the Abstract

In an effort to address these concerns, the present study revisits Keck's own (2006) comparison of L1 and L2 summarization practices, moving beyond a focus on how much more L2 writers copied than their L1 counterparts to explore why both L1 and L2 writers might choose to copy or Paraphrase source text language while composing a written summary. First, the study describes the rhetorical functions that Exact Copies and Paraphrases fulfilled in the L1 and L2 summaries, as such descriptions may help us to better understand the role that textual borrowing plays in

Figure 3.4 Purpose Shown in the Introduction

The research **purpose** can be found both at the beginning of the abstract (Figure 3.3) and at the end of the introduction (Figure 3.4). Since there are some

31

problems or limitations about the previous research, there is a necessity for the researcher to do the current research.

1. Which source text excerpts did the L1 and L2 writers choose to Paraphrase in their own written summaries, and where in the summary did they choose to integrate these excerpts? To what extent did the writers within each group make similar choices?
2. To what extent did the copying and paraphrasing strategies of novice L1 and L2 writers differ from those who had more years of experience writing in a university context?

Figure 3.5　Research Questions

The research **questions** are usually raised after the research purpose. Here, the study addresses 2 research questions (Figure 3.5).

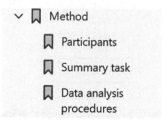

Figure 3.6　Headings for the Method Section

The **method** section in this paper shows how the research is conducted. It includes the number and the features of participants, the instruments (summary task) used to collect data, and the procedure of data collection and analysis for other researchers to repeat the process or judge the reliability (Figure 3.6).

Abstract

Recently, a number of scholars (e.g., Leask, 2006; Liu, 2005) have raised concerns about the discourse of plagiarism, arguing that an emphasis on cultural difference has served to reinforce stereotypes of particular L2 groups and perpetuate deficit views of L2 learners. In an effort to address these concerns, the present study revisits Keck's own (2006) comparison of L1 and L2 summarization practices and investigates (1) why both L1 and L2 writers might choose to copy or Paraphrase source text language while composing a written summary and (2) whether the strategy use of novice writers differed from that of their more experienced peers. The study found that L1 and L2 writers identified many of the same excerpts to include in their summaries, excerpts which allowed them to introduce the problem in focus and to explain the author's thesis. The study also found that the higher rate of copying observed for the L2 group as a whole could be explained by a small number of students who copied source text language extensively. In both the L1 and L2 groups, novice writers tended to rely more on source text excerpts than their more experienced peers.

Figure 3.7　Major Findings Reported in the Abstract

The major findings are reported in the abstract (Figure 3.7). Details of the findings are shown in the **results** section, with tables, figures and corresponding texts to describe them.

The following are some of the findings taken from the results section of the paper, with tables, figures and texts (Figure 3.8). Many people will go directly to the tables and figures to know the findings of the research because they are direct, clear, vivid, and easy to understand. They can also read the texts to understand the figures or tables better.

As Table 6 shows, for both the L1 and L2 summaries, Sequence was the most frequently observed selection strategy: 54% of the student summaries followed the original text's sequence of paragraphs when selecting excerpts for Paraphrase or copying. An additional 31% of the summaries contained Broken Sequences. Only 10 summaries (6 L1 and 4 L2) followed no apparent sequence when selecting from the source text.

Table 6
Number of L1 and L2 summaries containing each selection strategy.

	Source 1		Source 2		Source 3		Total
	L1	L2	L1	L2	L1	L2	
Sequence	20	25	18	19	24	16	122
Broken Sequence	11	9	15	12	13	10	70
No Sequence	3	1	2	0	1	3	10
One or no selections	7	6	3	2	7	0	25
Total	41	41	38	33	45	29	227

A similar pattern was observed for the L2 subgroups. Figs. 5 and 6 display the strategy use observed for L2 writers in their first year of U.S. university study and L2 writers in the U.S. for more than one year. (See Appendix A for descriptive statistics.)

As Figs. 5 and 6 show, the largest difference observed among the subgroups was in the use of Exact Copies. While the mean percentage of the summary made up of Exact Copies was 14% for L2 writers in their first year of U.S. study, it was only 3% for L2 writers in the U.S. for more than one year.

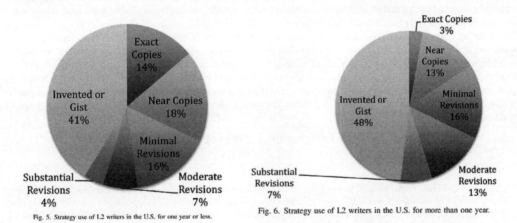

Fig. 5. Strategy use of L2 writers in the U.S. for one year or less.

Fig. 6. Strategy use of L2 writers in the U.S. for more than one year.

Figure 3.8 Sample Table, Figures and Texts in the Method Section

The **discussion** section usually gives the explanations and analyses of the findings. Here you can again find a lot of in-text citations to provide evidence from other research to support the findings, and to make comparison with other studies to show similarities and differences (Figure 3.9).

Discussion

In an effort to move beyond the question of whether L2 writers copy more than their L1 counterparts, the present study re-examined the summarization practices described in Keck (2006), with a focus on student selection strategies and variation within L1 and L2 writer groups. First, the study described which excerpts of the source text the L1 and L2 writers selected to include in their own summaries, what rhetorical functions these excerpts fulfilled, and how these excerpts were integrated into the students' own written work. Second, the study explored whether educational experience might help to explain the variation in copying and paraphrasing strategies observed within the L1 and L2 writer groups.

In its examination of L1 and L2 selection and integration strategies, the study found that, when it comes to selecting important source text excerpts to include in their summaries, L1 and L2 writers show similar preferences. Most students chose to follow the sequence of source text paragraphs when writing their summaries, which suggests that both groups felt that the order of ideas in the summary should mirror that of the original source. While a number of studies have associated this type of selection with younger, less skilled writers (e.g., Brown & Day, 1983), Sherrard (1986) observed the very same strategies in her study of English L1 university student summaries. Sherrard (1986) points out that, while many summary studies have found that older, skilled writers rely more on invented sentences, or combinations of source text sentences across paragraphs, most of these studies have focused on summaries of narrative source texts, rather than expository texts. Sherrard's findings, and the findings of this study,

Figure 3.9　Part of the Discussion Section with Citations for Comparison and Support

The **conclusion** is at the end of the paper (Figure 3.10). But you can also find a brief conclusion at the end of the abstract (Figure 3.11).

Conclusion

In both research and teaching, we are often drawn to extreme examples of student copying. This is understandable, considering the potential consequences of plagiarism, whether intentional or not. However, it is important to keep in mind that what is most noticeable is often not what is most typical—we are drawn to infrequent features of text precisely because they are different from the norm and they stand out (Biber, Conrad, & Reppen, 1998). In the case of L2 source text use, we can easily see examples of copying, but often overlook other, much more frequent, paraphrasing strategies. This not only distracts our attention from students' attempts to use source text language appropriately, but also leads to unfair stereotypes about particular student populations. While it is important to continue to investigate cases of student plagiarism, why they occur, and how they can be addressed pedagogically, equally important are efforts to describe the important role that textual borrowing plays in academic writing development and the rhetorical functions that textual borrowing strategies fulfill in a wide range of academic genres.

Figure 3.10　The Conclusion Section at the End of the Paper

Abstract

Recently, a number of scholars (e.g., Leask, 2006; Liu, 2005) have raised concerns about the discourse of plagiarism, arguing that an emphasis on cultural difference has served to reinforce stereotypes of particular L2 groups and perpetuate deficit views of L2 learners. In an effort to address these concerns, the present study revisits Keck's own (2006) comparison of L1 and L2 summarization practices and investigates (1) why both L1 and L2 writers might choose to copy or Paraphrase source text language while composing a written summary and (2) whether the strategy use of novice writers differed from that of their more experienced peers. The study found that L1 and L2 writers identified many of the same excerpts to include in their summaries, excerpts which allowed them to introduce the problem in focus and to explain the author's thesis. The study also found that the higher rate of copying observed for the L2 group as a whole could be explained by a small number of students who copied source text language extensively. In both the L1 and L2 groups, novice writers tended to rely more on source text excerpts than their more experienced peers.

Figure 3.11　The Statement of Conclusion in the Abstract

This is a typical example of how a research paper is organized. Research papers usually have similar structures to help the writer present ideas logically.

Knowing the structure of a research paper enables you to get the information you want as quickly as possible.

Note-taking

The above reading strategies can help you get the information, but they are not enough for writing your own research paper. What you need to do is to take down notes while reading. As soon as you identify the important information that is useful for your research, you will naturally take notes of it so that you can incorporate it into your own writing. Note-taking is NOT simply gathering raw material and dumping it on paper for later study. It involves reading, analyzing, thinking about, and digesting information before capturing that information for use later.

To take effective notes, you have to pay attention to the following points:

Record the bibliographic information for citations and references.

As soon as you read a book or an article, please note down all the bibliographic information such as title, author(s), year of publication, page numbers so that you can track down the source later when you need to provide citations and references.

Capture the main points and focus on the information most closely relevant to your topic.

You take down only the main points, especially those related to your research topic. They might be the definition of important terms, the classification of a concept, the major findings of a study or statements that can support your argument. When you read the article, ponder how it will be related to your writing.

Differentiate a direct quotation from a paraphrase or summary.

When you take down notes, you can paraphrase a sentence, summarize a paragraph, or directly quote from the original source. But you have to differentiate a direct quotation from a paraphrase or summary. For example, you normally put quotation marks and page number(s) for a direct quotation.

Give your own comments prompted by the readings so that you can write them in your paper later.

As is said previously, note taking involves reading, analyzing, thinking about, and digesting information. You need to keep thinking critically while reading. When you hit upon ideas, write them down immediately.

Clearly distinguish your comments from the author's writing to prevent accidental plagiarism.

Your own ideas prompted by reading can be directly put in your research paper while quotations, summaries and paraphrases contain ideas from other people and require in-text citations. If you do not distinguish them clearly, you may plagiarize unconsciously.

Reading for classifying sources

After you have read the title, the abstract or the whole article, and have taken down some notes, what you need to do is to integrate the ideas you derive from your reading into your own writing of the research background. This involves how to classify the sources and form different thematic sections for your writing.

If a certain topic is new to you, you can read other researchers' review about the topic, which will hopefully provide you with an immediate guideline of the research background. But you can't count on a single source because citing from only one article is considered plagiarism. You need to read more extensively and absorb ideas from different sources, using these ideas or contents as evidence to support or form your own ideas, to generate your review of the literature for your own research purpose.

For the purpose of finding the different guiding concepts or perspectives, you can use a matrix, or any kind of working chart, tree diagram, or table, as a useful preparatory device. A matrix helps to identify key terms in major ideas and sort studies into topical areas or perspectives, encouraging you to make clear connections between different perspectives. Here is an example to show the steps of how to classify the sources you have previously gathered and read.

- **Example**

Suppose you are doing research on automated essay scoring (AES), and have read 12 articles about this topic.

1. List reference/source materials for your literature review.

List them in alphabetic order of the first authors' last names, as is required in APA format.

Attali, Y., & Burstein, J. (2006). Automated essay scoring with e-rater? V.2. *Journal of Technology, Learning, and Assessment.* http://www.jtla.org.

Bridgeman, B., Trapani, C., & Attali, Y. (2009). *Considering fairness and validity in evaluating automated scoring.* Paper presented at the annual meeting of the National Council on Measurement in Education (NCME), San Diego, CA.

Burstein, J., Chodorow, M., & Leacock, C. (2004). Automated essay evaluation: The criterion online writing service. *AI Magazine, 25*(3), 27–36.

Chen, C., & Cheng, W. (2008). Beyond the design of automated writing evaluation: Pedagogical practices and perceived learning effectiveness in EFL writing classes. *Language Learning & Technology, 12*(2), 94–112.

Cotos, E. (2011). Potential of automated writing evaluation feedback. *CALICO Journal, 28*(2), 420–459.

Ebyary, K., & Windeatt, S. (2010). The impact of computer-based feedback on students' written work. *International Journal of English Studies, 10*(2), 121–142.

Powers, D. E., Burstein, J. C., Chodorow, M., Fowles, M. E., & Kukich, K. (2000). *Comparing the validity of automated and human essay scoring* (Research Report 00-10). Educational Testing Service.

Vantage Learning. (2005) *How intelliMetric works.* http://www.cengagesites.com/academic/assets/sites/4994/WE_2_IM_How_IntelliMetric_Works.pdf.

Weigle, S. C. (2011). *Validation of automated scores of TOEFL iBT® tasks against nontest indicators of writing ability* (Research Report 11-24). Educational Testing Service.

Wilson, J., Olinghouse N. G., & Andrada G. N. (2014). Does automated feedback improve writing quality? *Learning Disabilities: A Contemporary Journal, 12*(1), 93–118.

Yang, Y., Buckendahl, C. W., Juszkiewicz, P. J., & Bhola, D. S. (2002). A review of strategies for validating computer-automated scoring. *Applied Measurement in Education, 15*(4), 391–412.

Zhang, L. (2015). *Automated writing evaluation: Past, present and prospect.* Paper presented at TESOL international convention of TESOL Association, Toronto, Ontario, Canada.

2. Form a matrix to identify key terms in major ideas and sort studies into topical areas or perspectives (You may also manage your files in EndNote).

Read the title and abstract to fill in the matrix. For example, the following table involves information about the author(s), year of publication, thematic perspective, major ideas or findings. The author(s) and the year are easy to be located. The thematic perspective can be decided on the basis of the title, abstract and keywords. On many occasions, there may be two or more perspectives involved in an article. For example, Article 1 in Table 3.1 not only introduces the e-rater system but also focuses on its validation. Major ideas and findings can normally be found in the abstract or conclusion. When writing your own paper, you can use them as evidence to support your own ideas.

Table 3.1　A Matrix of Literatures on AES

	Author(s)	Year	Thematic perspectives	Major ideas or findings
1	Attali & Burstein	2006	System Validation	The paper describes a new version of e-rater and presents evidence on the validity and reliability of its scores.
2	Bridgeman et al.	2009	Validation	Human and e-rater scores were comparable. Essays written by students from China tend to get higher scores from e-rater than from humans.
3	Burstein et al.	2004	System Application in teaching	Criterion Online Essay Evaluation Service uses natural language processing and machine learning techniques and it is helpful for writing evaluation.
4	Chen & Cheng	2008	Application in teaching	MY Access facilitates students' early drafting and revising process, and should be followed by human feedback from both the teacher and peers.
5	Cotos	2011	System Application in teaching	IADE's (Intelligent Academic Discourse Evaluator) feedback possesses potential for facilitating language learning.
6	Ebyary & Windeatt	2010	Application in teaching	Criterion has a positive effect on the quality of writing. Students' attitudes towards its feedback are positive.
7	Power et al.	2000	System Validation	There are significant but modest correlations between the non-test indicators and between human and e-rater.
8	Vantage Learning	2005	System Validation	The paper demonstrates principles and process of how IntelliMetric™ scores essays.

(Continued)

	Author(s)	Year	Thematic perspectives	Major ideas or findings
9	Weigle	2011	Validation	Correlations between human and e-rater scores and non-test indicators were moderate but consistent. E-rater was more consistent across prompts than individual human raters on the TOEFL iBT (Internet-based test).
10	Wilson et al.	2014	Application in teaching	Writing quality improved across revisions with automated feedback, though growth decelerated over time.
11	Yang et al.	2002	Review Validation	The paper reviews the practice of validating CAS (computer-automated scoring)-system-generated scores.
12	Zhang	2015	Review System	This paper gives an overview of the principles, features and functions of some automated essay scoring systems and predicts the future development.

3. Provide a label for each thematic perspective, which will become a heading for the review.

Look at the "Thematic perspective" column, and you will find that Article 11 and Article 12 are two review articles that can provide you with a comprehensive information of a specific perspective. Article 11 is the review of research on validation and Article 12 is the review of development of systems. The rest of the articles generally cover 3 perspectives:

—development of AES systems;

—evaluation of reliability and validity;

—application in teaching.

4. Develop perspectives to explore more deeply by getting more information from the abstract and the whole article (The abstract or summary can be seen in Appendix 2).

In order to develop the perspectives into ideas of your own paper, you have to read the abstract or even the whole article to get more detailed information. You take notes while reading and put the notes into categories showing different perspectives so as to get the necessary information and form your own ideas. For example, by reading major ideas from the perspective of different AES systems, we find that there are such systems as PEG, IEA (LSA), E-rater & Criterion, IntelliMetric & MY Access in the development of AES. Ideas from the perspective of evaluation show that reliability and validity of AES are two most important aspects of evaluation, which are usually done by comparing the agreement and correlation of human and machine scoring. Pedagogical application is a necessary part of research because the purpose of doing such research is for the practice of teaching involving scoring, error detection, feedback and classroom practice, etc.

You can even generate sub-perspectives within a specific perspective whereby the topic can be explored more deeply. On the basis of the classification of articles and exploration of details, you can start writing your own review of the literature, but before that you need to think about the logic between these perspectives. For example, you can write in the order of "Introduction to Development of AES Systems", "Evaluation of the Reliability and Validity" and "Application in the Teaching of Writing" because you know the systems first, and then you judge whether the systems are reliable before applying them in teaching. The following outline of perspectives and sub-perspectives demonstrates the logical exploration of ideas within such a topic.

1. Development of AES systems
    1.1 Beginning stage
    1.2 Development stage
    1.3 Mature stage
2. Evaluation of reliability and validity
    2.1 Agreement
    2.2 Correlation
3. Application in teaching
    3.1 Scoring
    3.2 Error detection
    3.3 Feedback
    3.4 Classroom practice

Unit 3 **Academic Reading**

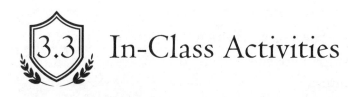

3.3 In-Class Activities

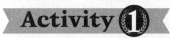

Read the paper "Connections Between Curiosity, Flow and Creativity" (See Appendix 3), and do the multiple-choices questions.

1. What is the topic of the paper?
   A. The phenomenon of flow in curiosity.
   B. The relationship between joyous exploration-related curiosity, knowledge-deprivation sensitivity, and stress tolerance.
   C. The relationship between flow, curiosity and creativity.
   D. The relationship between curiosity and creativity.

2. How is the main body of the research paper organized?
   A. Introduction→Methods and materials→Results→Discussion and conclusion
   B. Abstract→Introduction→Conclusion→References
   C. Abstract→Methods and materials→Results→Discussion and conclusion
   D. Introduction→Methods and materials→Results→Conclusion

3. What is the purpose of the research?
   A. To prove the validity of previous research.
   B. To prove flow links curiosity with creativity.
   C. To prove more curiosity leads to more creativity.
   D. To increase flow through psychology course activities.

4. Which of the following is NOT the finding of the research?
   A. Greater flow is related with higher level of creativity.
   B. There is a direct relationship between curiosity and creativity.
   C. Flow is significantly associated with joyous exploration-related

41

curiosity, knowledge-deprivation sensitivity, and stress tolerance.

D. Indirect relationships between dimensions of curiosity and creativity are significant.

5. Which of the following is NOT one of the limitations of the research?
A. Flow is a subjective concept and hard to be measured.
B. The validity of the measures is affected by the curiosity and flow measures.
C. The sample is not large enough.
D. The result is casual and not conclusive.

Steps for organizing the activity:

1. Review the contents in pre-class learning about reading for specific information and learn where you can find the information related to the questions.

2. Scan the paper to have a general picture of the organization.

3. Locate the specific part for answers to the questions.

4. Read this part and decide which of the four choices are correct.

Activity 2

Please read the article "Emotional Intelligence, Test Anxiety and Academic Stress Among University Students" (See Appendix 4) and answer the following questions.

1. What is the topic of the paper?
2. How is the research paper organized?
3. What is the purpose/objective of the research?
4. Who are the participants?
5. What instruments are used to collect data?

Unit 3 **Academic Reading**

6. What are the findings of the research?

7. Why is the level of test anxiety higher in the students of medical sciences than students of psychology?

8. What is the conclusion of the research?

Steps for organizing the activity:

1. Scan the paper to have a general picture of the organization.

2. Locate the possible parts for answers to the questions.

3. Find answers to the questions in the specific parts.

4. Check the answers in class.

Activity 3

Suppose your research topic is "Exploring the Factors for Academic Achievement at College". Take down notes from the article "Emotional Intelligence, Test Anxiety and Academic Stress Among University Students".

Steps for organizing the activity:

1. Record the bibliographic information for citations and references.

2. Focus on content most closely relevant to your topic.

3. Read and take down notes in the form of quotation, paraphrase, summary, and differentiate all these different forms in your notes.

4. Give your own comment prompted by the readings.

5. Distinguish your comments from the author's wording clearly to prevent accidental plagiarism.

Activity 4

Suppose your research topic is "Exploring the Factors Influencing Academic Achievement at College". Read the abstracts of 10 research articles (See Appendix 5) and fill in the table.

	Author(s)	Year	Perspectives	Major findings
1				
2				
3				
4				
5				
6				
7				
8				
9				

(Continued)

	Author(s)	**Year**	**Perspectives**	**Major findings**
10				

Topical areas/perspectives:

_____
_____

Subheadings and more levels

Subheading 1. _____

    1) _____

    2) _____

    …

Subheading 2. _____

    1) _____

    2) _____

    …

Steps for organizing the activity:

1. Read the abstracts of 10 research articles, focusing especially on the findings.

2. Focus on the review articles to gain some ideas for the perspectives.

3. Fill in the table with the information from the abstract. Give a summary of the findings in each research and try to figure out the perspectives.

4. Classify all the articles into topical areas according to these perspectives.

5. Form headings and sub-headings to show the logic of classification.

3.4 After-Class Tasks

Task 1

Read at least 3 articles you have searched for your research. You can use the following questions as a guide.

1. What is the topic of the paper?
2. How is the research paper organized?
3. What is the purpose of the research?
4. What are the research questions/hypotheses?
5. If you want to repeat the research process, where can you find the information?
6. What are the findings of the research?
7. Where can you find the analysis or explanation of the research?
8. What is the conclusion of the research?

Task 2

Choose one of the articles in Task 1 and take down notes while reading. Students in the same group should work on different articles.

Task 3

Working in research groups of 3 students. Share the articles you have searched for your research and read them. Try to classify them into thematic perspectives by filling in the tabe in Activity 4 in 3.3.

Unit 3 **Academic Reading**

Task 4

Prepare for a presentation to report the research based on one of the articles you consider most important for your research. Or you can present the research background on the basis of more articles.

Unit 4

Plagiarism, Paraphrase and Summary

4.1 Objectives

Develop academic honesty in research

Know how to do paraphrase

Know how to do summary

4.2 Pre-Class Learning

Watch the MOOC/SPOC videos and do the online exercises. The contents in the textbook will help you understand the lessons better.

Source: https://www.icourse163.org/

Course name: "学术英语写作与演讲" (Academic Writing and Presentation in English)

Unit 2 Plagiarism, Paraphrase and Summary

2.1 Plagiarism

2.2 Paraphrase

2.3 Summary

You have classified the sources and formed different thematic sections for your writing. Then how to integrate the ideas from what you have read into your own writing? You cannot simply copy other people's ideas without crediting the source because it is considered plagiarism, a very serious ethical issue in academic writing. What you need to do is paraphrase the sentences or summarize the paragraphs and indicate where the ideas come from by providing citations and references. In this unit, we will deal with plagiarism, paraphrase and summary. As for citations and references, they have been mentioned previously in the introduction of EndNote, and more details will be given in Unit 15.

Plagiarism

Plagiarism means copying other peoples' work. According to the Merriam-

Unit 4 Plagiarism, Paraphrase and Summary

Webster (n.d.) online dictionary, to "plagiarize" means:
- —to steal (the ideas or words of another) as one's own;
- —to use (another's production) without crediting the source;
- —to commit literary theft;
- —to present as new and original an idea or product derived from an existing source.

Plagiarism is considered to be a serious problem in the academic world and deserves severe punishment. A student who commits plagiarism will end up failing in the course. A candidate who engages in plagiarism shall be subject to disciplinary proceedings. A researcher who is accused of plagiarism will have his/her reputation ruined. Therefore, it is essential that students be educated not to plagiarize at the very beginning.

The following behaviors are considered plagiarism.
- —borrowing from the writer's own previous work without citation;
- —paraphrasing from multiple sources and fitting the information together;
- —citing some, but not all that should be cited;
- —changing keywords and phrases but copying the sentence structure of a source;
- —copying words or ideas from someone else without giving credit;
- —turning in one's own previous work;
- —relying too heavily on the original wording and/or structure;
- —containing significant parts of text from a single source;
- —including proper citation to sources without original work;
- —mixing copied materials from multiple sources;
- —including citations to non-existent or inaccurate sources;
- —submitting someone else's work as your own.

All of the above are considered plagiarism. Then how can plagiarism be avoided? You have to keep track of all the information (in Unit 2 & 3), paraphrase or summarize the original text to support your own idea (in Unit 4), and give credit by providing in-text citations and references (in Unit 2 & 15).

Paraphrase

Paraphrasing is to restate a sentence in another form to make it easier to understand. You have to restate the original sentences in your own words rather than copying too much from the source. That is, you cannot use too many original words and rely on the original sentence structure.

- **Basic steps of paraphrasing**

    1. Take short notes as you read. You can use either your own words or the keywords in the source.

    2. Close your book or put away your source materials.

    3. Write only from the notes you just took.

    4. Revise your writing and during the process you can look briefly at the source again.

- **Strategies of paraphrasing**

A better paraphrase is usually achieved by changing the part of speech, using a synonym, changing the sentence structure, changing the order, turning active voice into passive voice or vice versa, and changing from positive to negative and vice versa. Overlaps of these strategies are common to make the sentence different in form but the same in meaning.

Change the part of speech

- Example

    The developed world should contribute greatly so that human beings can survive in the future.

    Poor: The developed world should make great contributions so that human beings can survive in the future.

    Better: The advanced countries are supposed to make big contributions for human survival in the days to come.

    In the second paraphrase, "contribute" has been changed to "make contributions", and the verb "survive" has been changed to the noun "survival". Besides, "the developed world" has been changed into "the advanced countries", "should" has been replaced by "are supposed to" and "in the future" by "in the days to come". And the sentence structure is different. The adverbial clause "so that human beings can survive" is now replaced by a prepositional phrase "for human survival". The better paraphrase actually involves several strategies.

Unit 4 Plagiarism, Paraphrase and Summary

Use a synonym

- **Example**

    In the past thirty years, the country has changed greatly.

    Poor: In the past thirty years, the country has transformed greatly.

    Better: 1) The country has undergone a fundamental transformation in the past 30 years.

    2) The past 30 years have witnessed significant transformation in this country.

Here, "transform" is a synonym of "change", and "transformation" is its noun form. So it is both the use of synonyms and the change of part of speech. Besides, "in the past thirty years" is put at the end of the sentence so that the order has been reversed. In the second sentence, "the past thirty years" is placed at the beginning of the sentence as a subject and the sentence structure has been changed. The adjectives "significant" and "fundamental" are used to replace "great". Actually, quite a few other words like "substantial" or "enormous" can also be used in place of "great".

Change the sentence structure

- **Example**

    The potential of biodiesel as an alternative to regular diesel has been widely investigated.

    Poor: Many researchers have investigated the potential of biodiesel as an alternative to regular diesel.

    Better: There have been extensive investigations on the possibility of replacing regular diesel with biodiesel.

In the first paraphrase, the passive voice is turned into active voice for a change. However, it is still a close paraphrase that may be considered plagiarism. The second one is a better paraphrase that demonstrates the use of a "there be" structure, some synonymous expressions, and the change of part of speech.

Change from positive to negative and vice versa

- **Example**

    Nowadays, people try to make themselves instantly accessible to everyone at all times.

Poor: Nowadays, people try not to make themselves inaccessible to others for a moment.

Better: Nowadays, people never allow themselves the inconvenience of being temporarily unavailable.

Double negation is used here, but only minor changes are made in the first paraphrase, which looks quite similar to the original sentence. In the second paraphrase, "never allow" is negative to "try to make", "unavailable" is the opposite to "accessible". By using "allow" followed by a noun "inconvenience", the sentence structure has taken a new form.

On the whole, you have to bear in mind that a good paraphrase is based on the understanding of the original sentence and expressed with a combination of strategies to make the paraphrased sentences different in form but same in meaning.

Summary

To summarize is to restate briefly the main points of the original source in your own words. There are two essentials of summarizing. One is that a summary is a restatement in your own words, that is, you cannot use too many original words or you are plagiarizing, which is considered dishonest. But you can still keep the keywords or key academic terms in their original form. The other is brevity. A summary is much shorter than the original source and you only keep the most important information, abandoning the less important.

Summarizing is similar to paraphrasing in that they both are restatements. But it is different from paraphrasing in the following aspects: First, summarizing covers only the most important information while paraphrasing deals with almost all information. Second, a summary is much shorter than the original source while a paraphrase is almost the same in length. Finally, summarizing is done to sum up a paragraph, a passage or even the whole article while paraphrasing is done for a couple of sentences.

Here are the steps to summarize a paragraph. When the paragraph contains a topic sentence, you can

—read the paragraph and understand it thoroughly;

—find out the topic sentence and paraphrase it, which can possibly be a summary of the paragraph; and

—read the details to see whether there can be some revision to the paraphrased topic sentence.

Unit 4 Plagiarism, Paraphrase and Summary

- **Example**

A number of factors have been identified that might explain why developing writers—both students writing in their native language and students writing in a second language—copy from source texts. <u>In the case of second language (L2) writers, differences in cultural attitudes regarding the use of source texts have been cited as possible explanations for students' copying.</u> A number of discussions (e.g. Matalene, 1985; Pennycook, 1996; Shi, 2006; Sowden, 2005) have focused on non-Western, primarily East Asian, students and how cultural practices such as text memorization might help to explain the textual borrowing strategies these students employ when writing in English. Surveys of students from China, Japan, and Korea (Rinnert & Kobayashi, 2005; Shi, 2006) have also found that, when studying English in their own countries, these students receive limited exposure to writing from sources, and little, if any, instruction in summary, paraphrase, and citation. In comparison, the U.S. students interviewed in these studies reported that writing from source texts received a great deal of attention in their academic courses.

Obviously, the first sentence is not the topic sentence because the paragraph is not about different factors. The second one is the topic sentence that summarizes the whole paragraph. Of course, in order to avoid plagiarism, you need to express the meaning in your own words, using the strategies of paraphrasing. Therefore, the sentence can be revised and the possible one-sentence summary for the paragraph is as follows:

One reason for second language writers' inclination of plagiarism is their culture attitude about using the sources.

When there is not a clear topic sentence in the paragraph, you can

1) underline the keywords or take notes while reading;
2) summarize the main idea by using the keywords or notes to write a one-sentence summary of the paragraph in your own words.

- **Example**

Left to their own devices, children will not automatically select healthy foods. Their innate preference for sweet foods makes them particularly vulnerable to the highly sugared cereals, soda, and candy that are marketed to them virtually from birth. In order to develop lifelong healthy eating patterns, children need to be introduced to a variety of nutritious foods in a positive manner. Schools are potentially excellent settings for nutrition education. Virtually all children attend school every weekday and consume at least one or two meals daily on school grounds.

There might be some expressions hard to understand.

Left to their own devices	Let them make their own decisions
vulnerable to	be easily influenced or attacked by
Virtually	Actually
in a positive manner	in a positive way or positively

After getting a better understanding of the words and phrases, you should try to understand the text and underline some keywords. The most frequently repeated nouns are "children", "healthy/nutritious foods", and "school", so these might be the keywords that you can cover in the summary.

Who are you concerned for?

Children.

What is the problem?

Not having healthy/nutritious food.

How to solve the problem?

The school can help them.

Then you can use your own words to cover the information, and the one-sentence summary can be:

Schools should help children fight against eating unhealthy foods.

- **Steps for summarizing a passage (a section or several paragraphs in an article)**

  1. Underline the topic sentence of each paragraph.

  2. If there is no topic sentence, write a one-sentence summary of the main point.

  3. When you finish the passage, read all the topic sentences you have marked or written.

Unit 4 Plagiarism, Paraphrase and Summary

4. Note down the keywords and rewrite the main ideas of the topic sentences in your own words, leaving out unimportant details.

5. Use complete sentences with good transition words to write a short and concise summary of the passage.

- **Steps for summarize a research paper**

   1. State the research background and the problem in one sentence.
   2. Indicate the research aim or purpose.
   3. Clarify the method employed in the research in one or two sentences.
   4. State the major two or three findings in a brief and succinct way.
   5. Draw a conclusion or outline the implications of the research in the last sentence.

In fact, an abstract, which is going to be discussed in Unit 8, is a summary of the whole research paper that includes the most important information of different sections such as introduction, method, result and conclusion.

4.3 In-Class Activities

Activity 1

Please rearrange the order of the following plagiaristic behaviors in the sequence of seriousness.

1. using the results of your own research, e.g. from a survey, without citation;
2. paraphrasing from multiple sources and fitting the information together;
3. citing some, but not all that should be cited;

4. changing keywords and phrases but copying the sentence structure of a source;

5. copying words or ideas from someone else without giving credit;

6. turning in one's own previous work;

7. relying too heavily on the original wording and/or structure;

8. containing significant parts of text from a single source;

9. including proper citation to sources without original work;

10. mixing copied materials from multiple sources;

11. discussing an essay topic with a group of classmates and using some of their ideas in your own work;

12. submitting someone else's work as your own;

13. taking a graph from a textbook, giving the source;

14. borrowing from the writer's own previous work without citation;

15. including citations to non-existent or inaccurate sources.

Steps for organizing the activity:

1. Form groups of three students.

2. Each group gets a piece of paper with the above 15 statements printed on it.

3. Tear the paper into separate pieces to prepare for the rearrangement.

4. Discuss in groups and try to rank the statements in the order of seriousness of plagiarism.

5. Share the ideas in class and give reasons for the ranking.

Unit 4 **Plagiarism, Paraphrase and Summary**

Activity 2

Read the following "original sentence" and then practice the following techniques of paraphrasing.

Techniques of paraphrasing:

1. changing vocabulary by using synonyms;
2. changing the word class / part of speech;
3. changing word order / sentence structure.

Original sentence:

The potential of biodiesel as an alternative to regular diesel has been widely investigated.

Paraphrase 1:

_____
_____.

Paraphrase 2:

_____
_____.

Paraphrase 3:

_____
_____.

Steps for organizing the activity:

1. Read and understand the original sentence.
2. Do paraphrasing by using all of the techniques.
3. Share your paraphrase with the class, either by reading aloud to the class or typing to the WeChat group so that every student can make contributions.

学术英语写作与演讲
ACADEMIC WRITING AND PRESENTATION IN ENGLISH

Activity 3

Summarize the following passage.

> A hundred years ago news was exclusively provided by newspapers. There was no other way of supplying the latest information on politics, crime, finance or sport to the millions of people who bought and read newspapers, sometimes twice a day. Today the situation is very different. The same news is also available on television, radio and the Internet, and because of the nature of these media, can be more up-to-date than in print. For young people especially, the Internet has become the natural source of news and comment. This development means that in many countries, newspaper circulation is falling, and a loss of readers also means a fall in advertising, which is the main income for most papers. Consequently, in both Britain and the U.S. newspapers are closing every week. But when a local newspaper goes out of business an important part of the community is lost. It allows debate on local issues, as well as providing a noticeboard for events such as weddings and society meetings. All newspapers are concerned by these developments, and many have tried to find methods of increasing their sales. One approach is to focus on magazine-type articles rather than news, another is to give free gifts such as DVDs, while others have developed their own websites to provide continuous news coverage. However, as so much is now freely available online to anyone with a web browser, none of these have had a significant impact on the steady decline of paid-for newspapers.
>
> (Source: New Business Monthly, May 2010, cited from Bailey, 2011)
>
> **Steps for organizing the activity:**
>
> 1. Read the text carefully for full understanding.
> 2. Mark the key points by underlining or highlighting.
> 3. Take down notes of the key points, paraphrasing where possible.

Unit 4 **Plagiarism, Paraphrase and Summary**

4. Write only from the notes you just took, re-organizing the sentence structure.

5. Check your summary.

6. Decide on the final summary.

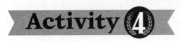

The paraphrase of the following paragraph seems close to the original version. Please try to make more changes.

Original version

Left to their own devices, children will not automatically select healthy foods. Their innate preference for sweet foods makes them particularly vulnerable to the highly sugared cereals, soda, and candy that are marketed to them virtually from birth. In order to develop lifelong healthy eating patterns, children need to be introduced to a variety of nutritious foods in a positive manner. Schools are potentially excellent settings for nutrition education. Virtually all children attend school every weekday and consume at least one or two meals daily on school grounds.

A close paraphrase (about 100 words):

If it was up to kids, they won't have the habit of selecting healthy foods. Their inborn preference for sweet-tasting food makes them susceptible to foods with lots of sugar, like cereals, canned pop, and candies that they see advertised from the day they are born. To help them learn a pattern of eating healthily, kids need to be exposed to lots of different healthy foods in a way that is positive. Schools have the potential to be a great setting to give education about nutrition. Almost all kids go to school Monday through Friday and they eat one, maybe two meals each day at school.

Paraphrase with more changes (about 80 words):
Detailed summary (about 50 words):
Summary with less details (about 30 words):
One-sentence summary (about 10 words):

Steps for organizing the activity:

1. Paraphrase the passage.
2. Summarize the passage.
3. Share answers with members in your group.
4. Give a one-sentence summary to the paragraph.
5. Compare the several versions of paraphrases and summaries and comment on them.

Unit 4 Plagiarism, Paraphrase and Summary

 After-Class Tasks

Task ①

Identify the best paraphrase among the four for each of the following two sentences.

1. The amphibia, which is the animal class to which our frogs and toads belong, were the first animals to crawl from the sea and inhabit the earth.
   A. The first animals to leave the sea and live on dry land were the amphibia, such as frogs and toads.
   B. Frogs and toads belong to the animal class amphibia.
   C. The amphibia, the animal class to which frogs and toads belong, were the first animals that moved from the sea to the earth.
   D. Frogs and toads are the amphibia that come from the sea to the earth.

2. The stages that children pass through in the development of language are very consistent. However, the exact age when they hit these milestones varies a lot.
   A. Developing children may pass through linguistic stages at different ages, although they will generally pass through each stage at some point.
   B. As children develop language skills, they usually go through the same stages, but they may reach the stages at different ages.
   C. The stages that are passed through by children in language development are very consistent. However, the exact time when they hit these milestones can be different.
   D. Language development is very different for different children, and there can be variation in the stages they go through.

Task 2

Read the following paragraph and identify the best one-sentence summary.

Kutash and Northrop (2007) studied the comfort of family members in the ICU waiting room. They found that no matter the situation, waiting rooms are stressful for the patients and their families, and it is the nursing staff's job to comfort both. From this emotional distress many family members judged the waiting room furniture as "uncomfortable" and only talked about it in a negative context. From this study we have learned that there is a direct relationship between a person's emotional state and how that person perceives the physical state he or she is in, such as sitting in a chair. Is this relationship true in reverse as well? Can the way a person perceives his or her present physical state (such as sitting in a chair) affect his or her emotional state? This is the question that the present study sought to answer.

A. Kutash and Northrup found that anxious people in intensive care waiting rooms tend to dislike the chairs in the waiting room and describe them as "uncomfortable".

B. The uncomfortable furniture in intensive care waiting rooms makes anxious people even more anxious.

C. This paragraph introduces a study that the authors conducted.

D. Basing their work on the results of a previous study, the researchers propose examining whether a person's perceived physical comfort can have an impact on their anxiety levels.

Task 3

Browse the following website, learn to recognize plagiarism and try to pass the certification test.

https://plagiarism.iu.edu/certificationTests/index.html

Unit 5

Language Improvement

5.1 Objectives

Know the academic style.

Learn how to write a good paragraph.

Know how to achieve good connection.

Learn how to use COCA to help improve word usage.

Know how to use Academic Phrasebank for sentence structures.

5.2 Pre-Class Learning

Watch the MOOC/SPOC videos and do the online exercises. The contents in the textbook will help you understand the lessons better.

Source: https://www.icourse163.org/

Course name: "学术英语写作与演讲" (Academic Writing and Presentation in English)

Unit 3 Language

3.2 Paragraph unity and completeness

3.3 Corpus–COCA

Unit 4 Connection

4.1 Old and new information principle

4.2 Keywords, pronouns and determiners

4.3 Transitions

The purpose of academic writing is to clearly convey to the readers what the writer intends to express, so the language is usually concise, accurate, objective, formal and consistent. Generally speaking, to achieve good academic writing, you have to pay attention to the following:

—Try to avoid the grammatical mistakes and write with enough accuracy.

—Pay attention to the appropriate collocations of words.

Unit 5 **Language Improvement**

—Avoid redundancy or wordiness in writing.

—Achieve variety in the choice of words and the sentence structure to avoid monotony.

—Do not write long complicated sentences at the cost of clarity.

—Achieve good connections between sentences and paragraphs.

—Show unity and completeness in a paragraph.

—Demonstrate good logic for the whole discourse.

Academic style

There are no rules for academic style applicable to all situations. In academic presentations, you are likely to hear less formal language while in academic writing you should use more formal language. That is, when you write an academic paper, you will opt to use the more formal alternatives when selecting a verb, a noun, or a word of other parts of speech. For example:

Less formal style	Academic style
Researchers *looked at* the way strain *builds up* around a fault.	Researchers *observed* the way strain *accumulates* around a fault.
A lot of investigations have been *done*.	*A considerable number* of investigations have been *conducted*.
The situation is *getter better/worse*.	The situation is *improving/deteriorating*.
There are some *good/bad* aspects about this issue.	There are some *positive/negative* aspects about this issue.
This *thing* will be *talked about* in the following chapter.	This *issue* will be *addressed* in the following chapter.

The following guidelines may help you develop a better academic style of writing.

—Use formal words such as *children, manager, for instance* instead of colloquial vocabulary such as *kids, boss, like*.

—Use accurate vocabulary. For example, distinguish the difference in usage between *rule* and *law*, or *weather* and *climate*.

—Be as precise as possible when dealing with facts or figures. For example, use *in the 1920s* rather than *about a hundred years ago*.

—Use an exact word rather than a general word. For example, *fact, topic, issue* is better than *thing, something*.

—Avoid adverbs that show your personal attitude such as *luckily, remarkably, surprisingly*.

—Use tentative expressions rather than absolute statements to draw a conclusion. For example:

Unemployment causes crime.

→Unemployment may cause crime.

—Avoid using *etc.* or *and so on*, write the general items at the end of the list. For example:

These semiconductors can be used in robots, CD players, *etc.*

→These semiconductors can be used in robots, CD players, *and other electronic devices*.

—Do not contract verb forms such as *don't, can't*, use the full form *do not, cannot* instead.

—Use the more appropriate formal negative forms. For example:

The analysis *didn't* yield *any* new results.

→The analysis yielded *no* new results.

The government *didn't* allocate *much* funding for the program.

→The government allocated *little* funding for the program.

This problem *doesn't* have *many* viable solutions.

→This problem has *few* viable solutions.

—Avoid addressing the reader as *you* (except if you are writing a textbook). For example:

You can see the results in Table 1.

→The results can be seen in Table 1.

—Limit the use of direct questions, except for your research questions. For example:

What can be done to lower costs?

→We will consider how costs may be lowered.

—Place adverbs in mid position rather than in the initial or final positions. For example:

Then the solution can be discarded.

→The solution can *then* be discarded.

The blood is withdrawn *slowly*.

→The blood is *slowly* withdrawn.

Paragraph development

Paragraphs develop the writing plan or outline. If you write each of the paragraphs well and connect them in a smooth and logical way, it will turn out to be a good research paper. To achieve this, it is essential for you to know how to write a paragraph with a clear topic sentence and strong supporting details, with unity and completeness and with appropriate coherence and cohesion.

▪ Topic sentence and supporting details

A paragraph develops a single topic with several related sentences. It is usually composed of a topic sentence and supporting details. A good topic sentence expresses the central idea of the paragraph. In other words, when a topic sentence is effective, the reader can understand what the paragraph is about without reading the supporting details. It often appears at the beginning of a paragraph because it can signal to the reader what the paragraph is about, and help prevent irrelevant material from appearing in the paragraph. Besides, it also enables readers to know what to look for in the paragraph and grasp the ideas better.

- **Example**

    Studies have also found that, over time, novice writers gradually decrease their dependence on source text language. For example, early L1 summary studies found that novice (eighth grade) writers copied or closely paraphrased individual sentences from a source text more frequently than expert (adult) writers (Winograd, 1984), that "underprepared" U.S. university students copied and paraphrased source text excerpts more frequently than "adept" (more academically prepared) U.S. university students (Johns, 1985), and that low-proficiency English L2 university students copied excerpts of the source text more frequently than high-proficiency students (Johns & Mayes, 1990). These findings have prompted both L1 and L2 researchers to argue that copying and close paraphrasing are phases through which many developing writers pass before they acquire more sophisticated ways of integrating sources into their writing (Brown & Day, 1983; Campbell, 1990; Chandrasoma et al., 2004; Howard, 1995; Hyland, 2001; Johns & Mayes, 1990; Pecorari, 2003; Shi, 2004; Sowden, 2005; Winograd, 1984).

In this paragraph, the topic sentence is placed at the beginning, supported by examples of several studies conducted by Winograd in 1984, Johns in 1985, and Johns and Mayes in 1990. The last sentence is a summary of the paragraph, which is supported by more studies listed as citations in the brackets. This is a typical example to show how the source materials can be used as supporting details of the topic sentence in your own writing.

▪ Paragraph unity

Unity of a paper means that paragraphs in the paper should stick to the topic. To observe the principle of unity, you have to follow the lead of your research purpose or thesis, which predicts the content, controls the direction, and obligates you to a single purpose. To achieve unity of a paragraph, you have to introduce only materials that are relevant to your topic, without straying from the point.

Unity of a paragraph refers to the extent to which all of the ideas contained within a given paragraph "hang together" in a way that is easy for the reader to understand. One paragraph should deal only with one main topic, and the beginning of a new paragraph signals that the writer is moving on to a new topic.

- Example

Employees' attitudes at Jonstone Electric Company should be improved. The workers do not feel that they are a working team instead of just individuals. If people felt they were a part of a team, they would not misuse the tools, or deliberately undermine the work of others. Management's attitude toward its employees should also be improved. Managers at Jonstone Electric act as though their employees are incapable of making decisions or doing their own work. Managers treat workers like objects, not human beings.

There are two main ideas presented in this paragraph. The topic sentence indicates that the paragraph will deal with the "employees' attitudes", but the paragraph changes unexpectedly to "management's attitudes", which is against the principle of unity. Therefore, to achieve unity in this paragraph, the writer should begin a new paragraph when the switch is made from employees' attitudes to managers', or use another topic sentence so that the two aspects can support the main idea and observe the principle of unity. For example:

> Both the employees and management in Jonstone Electric Company should improve their attitudes.

- **Paragraph completeness**

Paragraph completeness means a paragraph must be complete; in other words, the topic sentence must be adequately developed by facts, examples, quotations, or reasons. For example, when writing the background or literature review, you can formulate a topic sentence to state the main idea, and then use enough information that you have gained from reading, such as other researchers' findings or ideas, to support the topic sentence. While describing a figure or table, you firstly state generally what the figure or table is about, and then provide enough information to demonstrate the meaning of the figure or table. If the paragraph is too short, you need to be cautious because it may not have been fully developed and this is against paragraph completeness. A research paper with a lot of short paragraphs may suggest that there are problems in the development of topic sentences of these paragraphs and the writer need to develop or reorganize the paragraphs. The following paragraphs are taken from a student's writing:

> Wrongful convictions will bring about horrible consequences both to the people involved and to the judicial system.
>
> On the one hand, wrongful convictions will inevitably harm the lawful rights of the wronged people. In some serious cases, the wronged has even been deprived of his or her young life. Besides, wrongly-judged cases will cause great mental damage to the parents, relatives and friends of the wronged. These harms are all irreversible.
>
> On the other hand, whenever a wrongful conviction is made, the law is defied, and the judicial authority is challenged. The existence of wrongly-charged cases is the powerful evidence to show that there are defects in the judicial system.

While the second paragraph is acceptable, the first one is just a single topic sentence without development and the third one has only one more sentence besides the topic sentence. Actually, the first paragraph is just the topic sentence that guides the other two paragraphs. Therefore, you can modify by combining them into a longer paragraph as follows:

> Wrongful convictions will bring about horrible consequences both to the people involved and to the judicial system. On the one hand, wrongful convictions will inevitably harm the lawful rights of the wronged people. In some serious cases, the wronged has even been deprived of his or her young life. Besides, wrongly-judged cases will cause great mental damage to the parents, relatives and friends of the wronged. These harms are all irreversible. On the other hand, whenever a wrongful conviction is made, the law is defied, and the judicial authority is challenged. The existence of wrongly-charged cases is the powerful evidence to show that there are defects in the judicial system.

Connection: Cohesion and coherence

Connections between sentences and paragraphs are important. The connection can be referred to as cohesion and coherence, which are sometimes hard to distinguish. In fact, cohesion can be judged on the basis of how one sentence ends and the next begins. One can think of cohesion as pairs of sentences fitting together in the way two pieces of a jigsaw puzzle do. On the other hand, coherence can be decided by how all the sentences in a passage are connected. It means a train of thought smoothly presented from one sentence to the next. When a paragraph is incoherent, the sentences are discontinuous in logic, and readers may lose the thread. One can think of coherence as seeing what all the sentences in writing add up to, or the way all the pieces in a jigsaw puzzle add up to the whole picture. A writer has to make sentences in a paragraph stick together to make logical sense.

To make your writing coherent, you must think of the paragraph as expressing a single idea to which the individual sentences contribute bits of meaning. You have to balance principles that make individual sentences clear and the passage cohesive. You can use the following techniques to achieve coherence and cohesion.

- **Follow the old-new information principle**

One possible way to achieve coherence and cohesion is to put old information before new information. In other words, begin sentences with information that is familiar to your readers and end sentences with information that readers cannot anticipate. Compare the following two paragraphs:

> Some astonishing questions about the nature of the universe have been raised by scientists studying black holes in space. *The collapse of a dead star into a point perhaps no larger than a marble creates a black hole.* So much matter compressed into so little volume changes the fabric of space around it in puzzling ways.
>
> Some astonishing questions about the nature of the universe have been raised by scientists studying black holes in space. *A black hole is created by the collapse of a dead star into a point perhaps no larger than a marble.* So much matter compressed into so little volume changes the fabric of space around it in puzzling ways.

In the first paragraph, the second sentence begins with a new concept of collapsed stars and marbles, which seems to have come out of nowhere. The second paragraph is easier to follow in that the last four words of the first sentence introduce an important character—black holes in space, which is further described in the next.

- **Repeat keywords**

Repeating the keywords of the intended topic enables the readers to follow its development more easily. Without the repetition of keywords throughout your paragraph, they may lose track of the main topic. The following two examples show how the keywords are repeated to help achieve good connection.

- Example 1

    This paper describes and evaluates an academic <u>writing</u> <u>course</u> with the aid of technology for ESL learners. Such a <u>course</u> is based on a model that draws strength from the model of <u>writing</u> both as a process and as a social construct. Forty-one learners from various Asian language backgrounds attended the <u>course</u> in a large Midwestern American university. Detail of the <u>writing</u> <u>course</u> is described and evaluation is made through a questionnaire investigating the students' perceptions about the usefulness of the elements involved in the <u>writing</u> process, a paired samples t-test of pre-and post-<u>course</u>

writing, and a qualitative analysis of students' reflective ideas on how the course benefits them. The result indicates that students did improve their writing competence as a result of taking the course; and the analysis of the questionnaire shows that most students had a high opinion of the course. Therefore, it is believed that the course incorporating the integrated model has achieved the goal of helping ESL learners improve their competence and confidence in academic writing, which will enable them to cope successfully with future writing tasks in their academic disciplines.

(Source: Zhang et al., 2014. The Journal of Asia TEFL)

- **Example 2**

  Though typically, in the context of higher education, student plagiarism is associated with cheating and dishonesty; educators who work with developing writers argue that, for many students, plagiarism represents not an intention to deceive, but rather their developing competence in text-responsible writing; in these cases, most educators agree that instances of student copying should be addressed through pedagogy, rather than through disciplinary actions. Some have even questioned whether such instances of textual borrowing should be labeled as a type of "plagiarism": Students, language teachers, and university professors have all been found to disagree about what counts as textual plagiarism, and, in recent years, the idea of authorial ownership (and thus plagiarism itself) has been challenged. Nevertheless, most agree it is important to consider why students might copy from source texts when completing academic assignments, as such investigations may help us to better understand not only students' attitudes about textual borrowing, but also the role that such borrowing might play in their academic development.

- **Use pronouns**

  You can also achieve cohesion or coherence through the appropriate use of personal pronouns or relative pronouns. Personal pronouns such as "I" "you" "he" "they" "it" "one" "ones" are helpful because they allow you to write coherently and avoid making too many repetitions of the nouns they refer to. Relative pronouns such as "who" "that" and relative adverbs such as "which" "when" mark identity with a preceding noun phrase and join clauses.

Unit 5 Language Improvement

- **Example 1**

    Some people believe that capital punishment is justified for the most serious crimes such as murder and crimes against humanity. These people say that...

    Some people believe that capital punishment is justified for the most serious crimes such as murder and crimes against humanity. *They* say that...

- **Example 2**

    These buildings are being replaced for a variety of reasons. These reasons largely depend on the original purpose of the building and the needs of the community.

    These buildings are being replaced for a variety of reasons, *which* largely depend on the original purpose of the building and the needs of the community.

In the second sentence of Example 1, the pronoun "they" is used to avoid repetition and achieve coherence. In Example 2, the word "reasons" in the second sentence seems redundant and can be improved with the use of a relative pronoun "which" so that the two parts are more closely connected.

- **Use determiners**

Words such as "this" "that" "these" "those" "another" "such" "both" "all" "neither" are determiners that can better link sentences. In order to make your writing cohesive, you can use them to link the next sentence to something you have written before.

- **Example**

    We have talked about the issue of tuition for entering a community college. We must consider how to calculate credits for classes taken in a community college.

    We have talked about the issue of tuition for entering a community college. *Another* issue that we must consider is how to calculate credits for classes taken in a community college.

Obviously, the second sentence is better because the determiner "another" at the beginning of the second sentence makes the two sentences linked better and the logic between them easier to follow.

- **Use transitional markers**

Transitional markers are words or phrases used to assert the relationships between the sentences of a paragraph. Transitional markers add to the coherent and smooth development of the ideas in a paragraph. Here are some of the most common transitional markers:

Adding: furthermore, in addition, moreover, similarly, also, besides

- Example

    1) In the first place, no "burning" in the sense of combustion, as in the burning of wood, occurs in a volcano; *moreover,* volcanoes are not necessarily mountains; *furthermore,* the activity takes place not always at the summit but more commonly on the sides or flanks; and finally, the "smoke" is not smoke but condensed steam.

    2) *In addition to* examining students' choices regarding source text selection and integration, the present study *also* investigated the extent to which novice and experienced writers in the L1 and L2 groups differed in their copying and paraphrase use.

Causing: accordingly, and so, as a result, consequently, for this reason, hence, so, then, therefore, thus

- Example

    1) The study of human chromosomes is in its infancy, *and so* it has only recently become possible to study the effect of environmental factors upon them.

    2) Though the summary in Fig. 9 does not show evidence that the student is able to explain the article she read "in her own words", it does demonstrate her ability to identify the most important passages within the text. *Thus,* this type of summary writing may represent an early phase of text-responsible writing development.

Unit 5 Language Improvement

Comparing: by the same token, in like manner, in the same way, in similar fashion, likewise, similarly, in comparison

- Example

    1) Howard (1995) argues that patchwriting is an important transitional strategy in the student's progress toward membership in a discourse community. *Similarly,* Currie (1998) found that the subject of her case study used copying as a strategy for learning the language of the academic discipline she was studying.

    2) Surveys of students from China, Japan, and Korea have found that, when studying English in their own countries, these students receive limited exposure to writing from sources. *In comparison,* the U.S. students interviewed in these studies reported that writing from source texts received a great deal of attention in their academic courses.

Opposing: but, however, in contrast, though, nevertheless, on the other hand, on the contrary, unlike, still, yet

- Example

    1) It was not the first African paper, although nowadays some Tanzanians think that it was; *nevertheless,* it is the only one whose direct descendants are still in existence, and may be regarded as the first successful, viable paper edited and produced by Africans.

    2) In the case of second language (L2) writers, differences in cultural attitudes regarding the use of source texts have been cited as possible explanations for students' copying. Some have pointed out, *however,* that cultural differences are likely not the only, or even best, explanations for student textual plagiarism.

Concluding: therefore, as a result, consequently, in conclusion, to sum up, in short, in brief, in a word, in a nutshell, and so, after all, at last, finally, in closing, on the whole, to conclude, to summarize

- Example

    1) It seems to me that the successful professionals make their money not by selling their wares, but by selling their skills—by writing books, running courses, making videos, holding seminars and giving

demonstrations—*in short,* by teaching others how to do it.

2) You can change the part of speech, use a synonym, change the sentence structure. *On the whole,* a good paraphrase is a combination of these strategies to make the paraphrased sentences different in form but same in meaning.

Exemplifying: such as, for example, for instance, to illustrate, take ... as an example

- Example

  1) Each individual piece of equipment has a special contribution to make; *for example,* a tape recorder can be equally effective in stimulating discussion as a film, but films or video tapes are more effective for the demonstration of practical skills where movement is essential.

  2) You can formulate a topic sentence to state the main idea, and then use enough information that you gain from reading, *such as* other researchers' findings or ideas, to support the topic sentence.

Intensifying: in fact, indeed, actually, as a matter of fact

- Example

  1) The ideas of economists and political philosophers, both when they are right and when they are wrong, are more powerful than is commonly understood. *Indeed,* the world is ruled by little else.

  2) However, individual paragraphs differed in the number of selections they elicited. *In fact,* it was found that two or three paragraphs within each source text elicited over 30% of the paraphrases identified in the summaries of those texts.

Restating: in other words, in simpler terms, that is, to put it differently, to repeat

- Example

  1) Many people use this form of assurance as a method of financing a house purchase; *in other words,* a building society will accept the policy as a guarantee of repayment of the capital sum at the end of the term, and meanwhile you pay interest payments each month to

the building society.

2) You have to restate the original sentences in your own words rather than copying too much from the source. *That is,* you cannot use too many original words and rely on the original sentence structure.

Timing: at first, afterward, at the same time, currently, earlier, formerly, immediately, in the future, in the meantime, in the past, later, meanwhile, previously, simultaneously, subsequently, then, until, now

- **Example**

  1) *At first* a toy, *then* a mode of transportation for the rich, the automobile was designed as man's mechanical servant. *Later* it became part of the pattern of living.

  2) The figure shows that the GDP of the country rose rapidly between 2000 and 2005 and reached the peak in 2007. It *subsequently* declined steadily from 2008 to 2010 owing to the financial crisis.

Sequencing: first(ly), second(ly), third(ly), finally; in the first place, in the second place, in the third place; to begin with, next, then, after that, finally

- **Example**

  1) I like the Internet for three reasons. *Firstly,* the Internet transmits love beyond the boundaries of time and space. *Secondly,* the search for knowledge on the web revolutionized our study method. *Finally,* the Internet helps relieve people from sufferings.

  2) *First,* the study describes the rhetorical functions that exact copies and paraphrases fulfilled in the L1 and L2 summaries. *Second,* the study examines whether novice writers within each L1 and L2 group differ from their more experienced peers.

- **Use transitional sentences**

  One common way to make the transition from one paragraph to the next is to begin the second paragraph with a transitional sentence, which starts with one foot on the previous paragraph and the other on the paragraph that is just beginning. The following passage shows how transitional markers and transitional sentences are used to make it more coherent.

- **Example 1**

    Three passions, simple but overwhelmingly strong, have governed my life: the longing for love, the search for knowledge, and unbearable pity for the suffering of mankind. These passions, like great winds, have blown me hither and thither, in a wayward course over a deep ocean of anguish, reaching to the very verge of despair.

    I have sought love, *first,* because it brings ecstasy—ecstasy so great that I would often have sacrificed all the rest of my life for a few hours for this joy. I have sought it, *next,* because it relieves loneliness—that terrible loneliness in which one shivering consciousness looks over the rim of the world into the cold unfathomable lifeless abyss. I have sought it, *finally,* because in the union of love I have seen, in a mystic miniature, the prefiguring vision of the heaven that saints and poets have imagined. This is what I sought, and though it might seem too good for human life, this is what—at last—I have found.

    With equal passion I have sought knowledge. I have wished to understand the hearts of men. I have wished to know why the stars shine. And I have tried to apprehend the Pythagorean power by which number holds sway above the flux. A little of this, but not much, I have achieved.

    Love and knowledge, so far as they were possible, led upward toward the heavens. But always pity brought me back to earth. Echoes of cries of pain reverberate in my heart. Children in famine, victims tortured by oppressors, helpless old people—a hated burden to their sons, and the whole world of loneliness, poverty, and pain make a mockery of what human life should be. I long to alleviate the evil, but I cannot, and I too suffer.

    This has been my life. I have found it worth living, and would gladly live it again if the chance were offered me.

    (Source: Russell, "Three Passions I Have Lived for")

In this passage, Russell dealt with three passions, the longing for love, the search for knowledge, and the unbearable pity for the suffering of mankind. To express his passion for love, he used "first" "next" and "finally" to reveal the reasons step by step. Using a transitional sentence "with equal passion I have sought knowledge", he started to illustrate his second passion for knowledge. After finishing the discussion of the previous two passions, the writer started to relate them to the third passion "pity" with the transitional sentence "Love and knowledge, so far as they were possible, led upward toward the heavens.

But always pity brought me back to earth". By using transitional markers and sentences, Russell illustrated his ideas clearly and logically with good coherence and cohesion.

- **Example 2**

    The discourse of plagiarism constructs students from diverse cultures in particular ways: *firstly*, as culturally inferior others who must be taught how to learn other than by rote and imitation, whose learning style and strategies impede critical thinking and are likely to result in inadvertent plagiarism; or *secondly*, as desperate, embattled and inferior learners whose only means of coping in the superior world of the Western academy is to deliberately plagiarise, to take others' words and ideas as their own in various ways such as "patchwriting", in which case they are both stealing and cheating.

    As an alternative to discourse which emphasizes cultural difference, Flowerdew and Li (2007) highlight approaches which emphasize developmental and disciplinary perspectives. Because plagiarism has been the topic of discussion in not only English L2 contexts, but also in English L1 (first language) contexts, many have suggested that the demands of adjusting to a new academic discourse community play an important role in students' decisions to copy from source texts.

The first sentence in the second paragraph "As an alternative to discourse which emphasizes cultural difference, Flowerdew and Li (2007) highlight approaches which emphasize developmental and disciplinary perspectives" is a transitional sentence that smoothly links the previous paragraph about culture difference to this paragraph about disciplinary and developmental perspective of plagiarism.

COCA: Words and phrases

Corpus is a collection of naturally occurring language text. Being different from a dictionary, it provides the dynamic description of the authentic language in use. Take Corpus of Contemporary American English (COCA) for example. It contains more than one billion words from eight genres: spoken, fiction, magazines, newspapers, academic texts, TV and movies, blogs, and other web pages. Since it is free of charge, it is very popular and frequently used by teachers and learners of English in China. The major link to COCA is https://www.

english-corpora.org/coca/.

Now, we are going to demonstrate a few most frequently used functions of COCA. After you have finished registration and logged in, you can see four tabs: Search, Frequency, Context and Account (Figure 5.1).

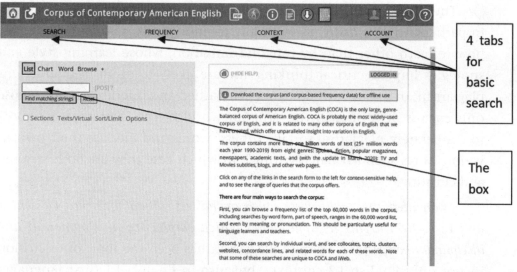

Figure 5.1　Homepage of COCA

- **Basic search**

If you are not sure whether a certain expression is appropriate in English, the easiest way is to use basic search in COCA. The "search" tab enables you to do basic searches. You only need to put the expression (a word, a phrase or a chunk, e.g. "run" "run into" "run a business") in the searching box and click "find matching strings", the computer will search for this expression in the big data of the corpus. For example, search the single word "run" by typing the word in the "box" and click "find matching strings", you can see the word frequency (Figure 5.2). Then by clicking on the word itself, you can go to lots of concordance lines, with the keyword "run" in the context (Figure 5.3). If you click the link to the context, an expanded context will be provided for more information. If you want all the word forms for "run", you only need to add the square bracket [run], then you can find all the different forms of the word "run" "running" "ran" "runs" (Figure 5.4). And again, by clicking on the word, it will give you a lot of concordance lines.

Unit 5 **Language Improvement**

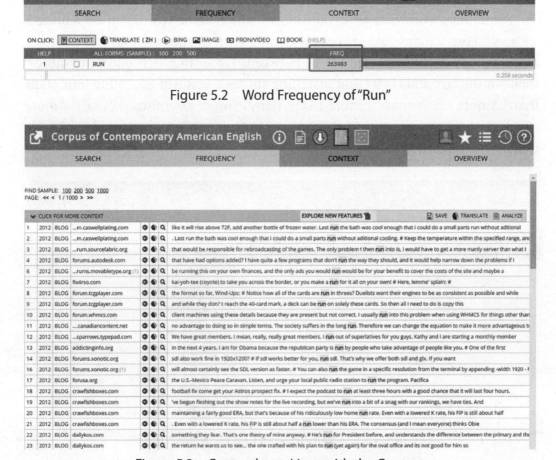

Figure 5.2　Word Frequency of "Run"

Figure 5.3　Concordance Lines with the Context

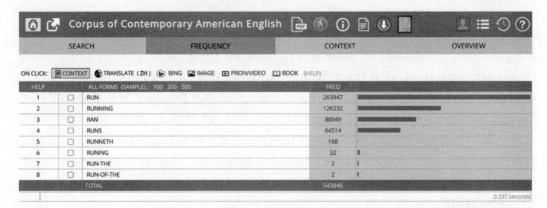

Figure 5.4　Different Forms of the Word "Run"

- **Pattern**

Sometimes, you want an expression in which some words can be replaced, such as "more... than" "as... as possible" "in... terms", you can search the pattern by using an asterisk wildcard "*" in between. For example, if you put "more * than" in the box and click "find matching strings", you will get "more important than" "more often than" "more likely than" "more complicated than" "more effective than" "more powerful than" and other expressions in order of their frequencies (Figure 5.5).

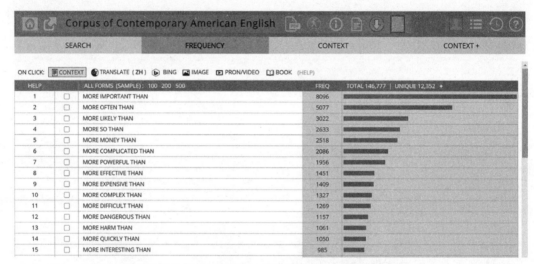

Figure 5.5   The Pattern Searched by "More * Than"

- **Phrase**

If you are not sure about which words are often used with a certain word, for example, what kind of adjectives are often used with "research" or what nouns are often used with the adjective "rough", you can search a phrase, which enables you to have accurate collocations. You can put in "ADJ research" or "rough NOUN" respectively in the box and you get "future research" "previous research" "further research" "scientific research", etc. (Figure 5.6), or "rough time" "rough day" "rough patch" "rough edges", etc. (Figure 5.7). If you don't know the abbreviations, you can choose from POS (part of speech) and obtain the same result (Figure 5.8).

Unit 5 **Language Improvement**

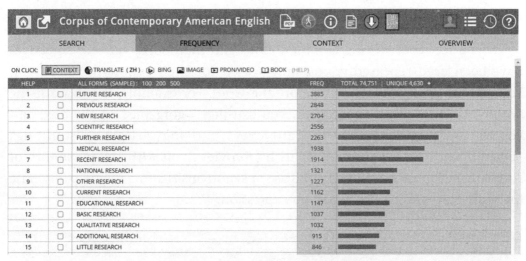

Figure 5.6   Phrase Search by "ADJ Research"

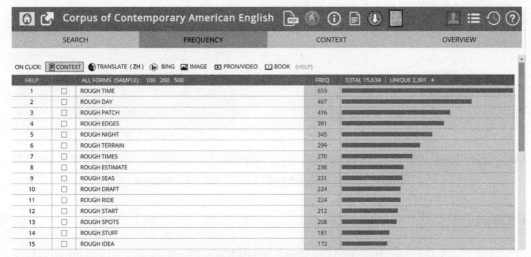

Figure 5.7   Phrase Search by "Rough NOUN"

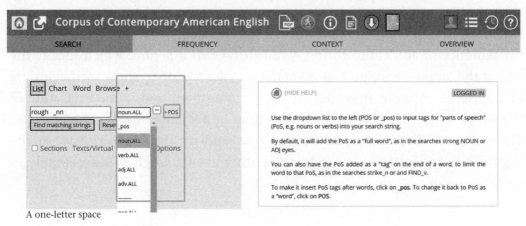

Figure 5.8   Use of POS (Part of Speech)

▪ Synonym

If you feel your writing is monotonous and the nouns, verbs or adjectives have been used repeatedly, you may search for their synonyms in COCA. You just use an equal sign "=" before the word. For example, if you want the synonyms of the word "gorgeous", you can put "=gorgeous" in the box, and you will see "beautiful" "lovely" "attractive" "striking" "elegant" "stunning" "magnificent", etc. (Figure 5.9). This list provides you with the possibility of alternative expressions. Actually, the use of synonyms is also a way to paraphrase the source text and creates variety in expression.

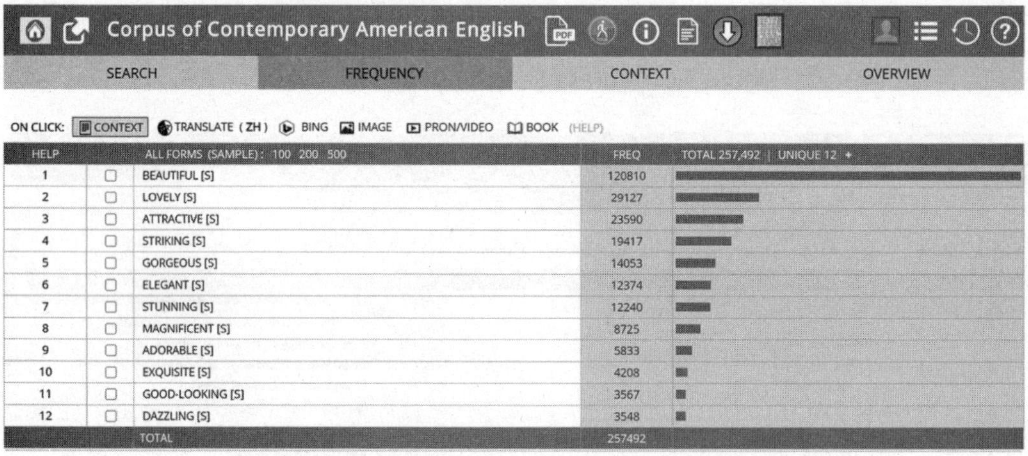

HELP		ALL FORMS (SAMPLE): 100 200 500	FREQ	TOTAL 257,492 | UNIQUE 12 +
1	☐	BEAUTIFUL [S]	120810	
2	☐	LOVELY [S]	29127	
3	☐	ATTRACTIVE [S]	23590	
4	☐	STRIKING [S]	19417	
5	☐	GORGEOUS [S]	14053	
6	☐	ELEGANT [S]	12374	
7	☐	STUNNING [S]	12240	
8	☐	MAGNIFICENT [S]	8725	
9	☐	ADORABLE [S]	5833	
10	☐	EXQUISITE [S]	4208	
11	☐	GOOD-LOOKING [S]	3567	
12	☐	DAZZLING [S]	3548	
		TOTAL	257492	

Figure 5.9 Synonyms of the Word "Gorgeous"

▪ Chart

The *chart* option shows the total frequency in each section of different registers or different years. The main function of the chart option is to help you compare the use of the words, phrases or chunks between genres or across time. For example, if you are not sure whether you can use "and" at the beginning of the sentence in academic writing, you can type in a period, which means the end of the last sentence and then capitalize A for "And" to show the beginning of a sentence. You can find that "And" is more often used at the beginning of the sentence in spoken communication than in academic register (Figure 5.10). Therefore, it is strongly recommended that students do not use "And" at the beginning of a sentence in academic writing even though it is acceptable in spoken English.

Unit 5 **Language Improvement**

SECTION	ALL	BLOG	WEB	TV/M	SPOK	FIC	MAG	NEWS	ACAD	1990-94	1995-99	2000-04	2005-09	2010-14	2015-19
FREQ	1499733	107972	95655	345563	614517	127695	100841	79463	28027	158769	203478	208376	225676	246812	252995
WORDS (M)	993	128.6	124.3	128.1	126.1	118.3	126.1	121.7	119.8	139.1	147.8	146.6	144.9	145.3	144.7
PER MIL	1,510.27	839.51	769.84	2,698.14	4,871.88	1,079.22	799.75	652.72	233.97	1,141.74	1,376.95	1,421.69	1,556.97	1,699.08	1,747.92

Figure 5.10　Comparison of the Use of AND at the Beginning of a Sentence for Spoken and Academic Register

- **Collocates**

Collocates is another way to help you search for collocations in writing. Take the previous example, what are the adjectives often used with the noun form of "research" in academic writing? You can type in "research", click on POS on the right, choose "noun.ALL" to make sure the word "research" is in its noun form. Then in the second line, you click on POS, choose "adj.ALL". In the third line, you can see some numbers in the boxes. "0" means the position of the search term, i.e. "research" in this case. The numbers 1, 2, 3, 4 means the number of words to the left or to the right of the search term. Since you want adjectives modifying "research", you need to choose the position on the left (Figure 5.11). If you choose 1, and click on "find collocates", you can have "future research" "previous research" "new research" "scientific research" "further research", etc. All of them show one adjective before the word research (Figure 5.12).

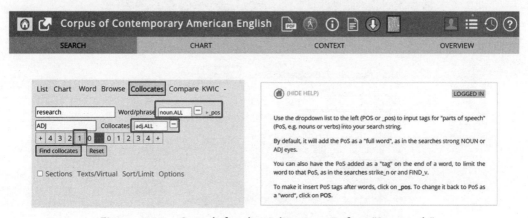

Figure 5.11　Search for the Adjectives Before "Research"

HELP			FREQ
1	☐	FUTURE	3885
2	☐	PREVIOUS	2848
3	☐	NEW	2704
4	☐	SCIENTIFIC	2556
5	☐	FURTHER	2263
6	☐	MEDICAL	1938
7	☐	RECENT	1914
8	☐	NATIONAL	1321
9	☐	OTHER	1227
10	☐	CURRENT	1162
11	☐	EDUCATIONAL	1147
12	☐	BASIC	1037
13	☐	QUALITATIVE	1032
14	☐	ADDITIONAL	916
15	☐	LITTLE	846

Figure 5.12　Searching Result of the Adjectives Before "Research" by Using Collocates

- **Compare**

You may sometimes feel confused about the difference between two synonyms. The function of *compare* will help you solve this problem (Figure 5.13). For example, "utter" and "sheer" as adjectives are similar in meaning, but what is their difference in usage? You can use the "compare" function in COCA. Put "utter_j" in the first box, "sheer_j" in the second box, and choose NOUN in the third box. The underline j means all adjectives and NOUN means this adjective is followed by a noun. Choose two words on the right. Click "compare words" and we can come to the result page (Figure 5.14).

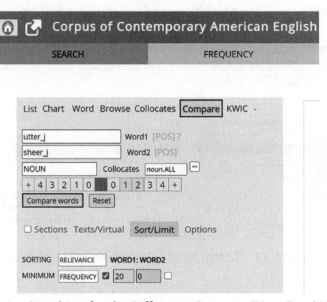

Figure 5.13　Searching for the Difference Between "Utter" and "Sheer"

Unit 5 Language Improvement

SEE CONTEXT: CLICK ON NUMBERS (WORD 1 OR 2)
SORTED BY RATIO: CHANGE TO FREQUENCY
WORD 1 (W1): **UTTER** (0.45)　　　　　　　　　　　　　　　　WORD 2 (W2): **SHEER** (2.20)

#	WORD	W1	W2	W1/W2	SCORE	#	WORD	W2	W1	W2/W1	SCORE
1	FAILURE	234	1	234.0	514.9	1	NUMBER	626	0	1,252.0	569.0
2	BULLSHIT	76	0	152.0	334.5	2	VOLUME	467	0	934.0	424.5
3	DISREGARD	74	0	148.0	325.7	3	NUMBERS	409	0	818.0	371.7
4	DARKNESS	73	0	146.0	321.3	4	FORCE	335	0	670.0	304.5
5	FOOL	37	0	74.0	162.8	5	SIZE	499	1	499.0	226.8
6	COLLAPSE	26	0	52.0	114.4	6	AMOUNT	204	0	408.0	185.4
7	DEFEAT	26	0	52.0	114.4	7	SCALE	168	0	336.0	152.7
8	GARBAGE	25	0	50.0	110.0	8	LUCK	153	0	306.0	139.1
9	DEPENDENCE	21	0	42.0	92.4	9	WEIGHT	130	0	260.0	118.2
10	MESS	20	0	40.0	88.0	10	CLIFFS	122	0	244.0	110.9
11	DESOLATION	26	1	26.0	57.2	11	MAGNITUDE	96	0	192.0	87.3
12	CRAP	50	2	25.0	55.0	12	CLIFF	88	0	176.0	80.0
13	RUIN	23	1	23.0	50.6	13	ROCK	87	0	174.0	79.1
14	HOPELESSNESS	23	1	23.0	50.6	14	QUANTITY	76	0	152.0	69.1
15	DESTRUCTION	109	5	21.8	48.0	15	WALLS	76	0	152.0	69.1
16	DISAPPOINTMENT	21	1	21.0	46.2	16	FACE	68	0	136.0	61.8
17	DISASTER	69	4	17.3	38.0	17	DROP	67	0	134.0	60.9
18	CONTEMPT	106	7	15.1	33.3	18	WALL	61	0	122.0	55.4
19	ABSENCE	30	2	15.0	33.0	19	STRENGTH	60	0	120.0	54.5
20	DESPAIR	58	4	14.5	31.9	20	FACT	53	0	106.0	48.2

Figure 5.14　Result of the Comparison of "Utter" and "Sheer"

On the left are nouns frequently used in collocation with the word "utter" while on the right are those with "sheer". Collocations of "utter", such as "failure" "bullshit" "disregard" "darkness" "fool" "collapse" "defeat" "disgrace", are usually nouns negative in meaning. In contrast, those of "sheer", such as "number" "volume" "force" "size" "amount" "scale" "luck", are neutral in meaning, or even positive such as "sheer luck". Therefore, we can use *compare* option to find out the subtle difference between the two synonyms.

The above are some basic functions of COCA, which are helpful for a writer who is not sure of a certain way of expression or needs more varieties of expressions. If you are interested and want to know more about it, you can watch the vivid demonstration in Unit 3 of our MOOC and have some practice while watching.

Academic Phrasebank: Sentence structure

On many occasions, you may have difficulty using an appropriate sentence to express your idea. Sometimes, you have to get help from a sample paper, but you must be aware of the risk of plagiarizing. Actually, you can accumulate some sentence templates and use them when appropriate. The following is the link to Academic Phrasebank, which provides you with varieties of expressions used in different parts of a research paper for different functions (Figure 5.15).

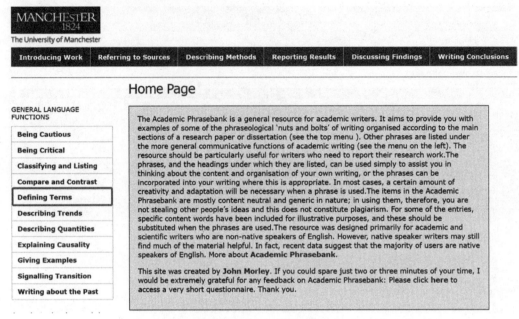

Figure 5.15　Home Page of Academic Phrasebank

For example, if you want to define a term, you click "Defining Terms" in the left column and then "Specifying terms that are used in an essay or thesis", you can find expression such as:

The term "X" is used here to refer to...

In the present study, "X" is defined as...

The term "X" will be used solely when referring to...

In this essay, the term "X" will be used in its broadest sense to refer to all...

In this paper, the term that will be used to describe this phenomenon is "X".

In this dissertation, the terms "X" and "Y" are used interchangeably to mean...

Throughout this thesis, the term "X" is used to refer to informal systems as well as...

For another example, you want to report your results, you can click on "Reporting Results" on the upper line and then "Referring to data in a table or chart", you will find such expressions:

Unit 5 Language Improvement

Table 1 Figure 1	shows compares presents provides	an overview of... the experimental data on "X". the summary statistics for... the breakdown of "X" according to... the intercorrelations among the nine measures of "X". the results obtained from the preliminary analysis of "X".

The table below illustrates The pie chart above shows The top half of the table shows The bottom half of the table shows	some of the main characteristics of the... the breakdown of...

As shown in Figure 1, As can be seen from the table (above), From the graph above we can see that It can be seen from the data in Table 1 that	the "X" group reported significantly more "Y" than the other two groups.

The results of the correlational analysis The themes identified in these responses The results obtained from the preliminary analysis of "X"	are shown are set out are presented can be compared are summarized	in Table 1. in Figure 1.

5.3 In-Class Activities

Activity 1

Read the following two paragraphs and decide which one is more academic in style? Give your reasons.

Paragraph 1. "How to make people work harder?" is a topic that lots of people have written about in the last few years. There are lots of different theories and I think some of them are OK. When we think about this we should remember the old Chinese proverb, that "you can lead a horse to water but you can't make it drink". So how do we increase production? It's quite a complex subject but I'll just talk about a couple of ideas.

Paragraph 2. Motivation has been the subject of numerous studies during recent decades, but this essay will focus on Maslow's hierarchy of needs theory (1943) and Herzberg's two-factor theory (1966). Their contemporary relevance to the need to motivate employees effectively will be examined critically, given that this can be considered crucial to a firm's survival in the current economic climate.

Steps for organizing the activity:

1. Read the two paragraphs and decide which one is more formal.

2. Underline expressions that is not academic in style in the informal paragraph and give your reasons.

3. Compare the two paragraphs and understand differences between the formal and informal styles of writing.

Unit 5 Language Improvement

Activity 2

Which of the following three expressions is the best? Give your reasons and form rules for good writing.

> 1. Car scrappage schemes have been introduced in many countries. They offer a subsidy to buyers of new cars. The buyers must scrap an old vehicle. The schemes are designed to stimulate the economy. They also increase fuel efficiency.
>
> 2. Car scrappage schemes, which offer a subsidy to buyers of new cars, who must scrap an old vehicle, have been introduced in many countries and designed to stimulate the economy and increase fuel efficiency.
>
> 3. Car scrappage schemes have been introduced in many countries. They offer a subsidy to buyers of new cars, who must scrap an old vehicle. The schemes are designed to stimulate the economy and increase fuel efficiency.
>
> *Steps for organizing the activity:*
>
> 1. Students are in groups of three, with each student having one of the expressions.
> 2. Compare the expression you have with those of other two students and find the difference.
> 3. Discuss with each other and find out which expression is the best.
> 4. Give your reasons and form rules for good writing.

Activity 3

Read the following paragraph and fill in the table.

> The rate of home ownership varies widely across the developed

world. Germany, for instance, has one of the lowest rates, at 42 percent, while in Spain it is twice as high, 85 percent. Both the U.S. and Britain have similar rates of about 69 percent. The reasons for this variation appear to be more cultural and historic than economic, since high rates are found in both rich and poorer countries. There appears to be no conclusive link between national prosperity and the number of homeowners.

Topic sentence	
Example 1	
Example 2	
Reason	
Summary	

Steps for organizing the activity:

1. Read the paragraph.
2. Fill in the table with the sentences in the paragraph.
3. Figure out how the topic sentence is supported.
4. Discuss with group members about how a paragraph can be developed with good unity, completeness and coherence by looking at this example.

Activity 4

Revise the following passage to improve the flow by putting old information first in each sentence. The underlined words are old information.

Two aims—the recovery of the American economy and the modernization of America into a military power—were in the president's mind when he assumed his office. The drop in unemployment figures and inflation, and the increase in the GNP testifies to his success in the first. But our increased involvement in international conflict without any clear set of political goals indicates less success with the second. Nevertheless, increases in the military budget and a good deal of saber rattling pleased the American voters.

Steps for organizing the activity:

1. Read the paragraph and pay attention to the underlined part.
2. Revise the order in underlined parts by using the old and new information principle.
3. Make modifications to the sentences to make them more fluent.

Activity 5

Complete the paragraph by filling in the transitional words.

This exercise will introduce you to sentence combining, _____, organizing sets of short, choppy sentences into longer, more effective ones. _____, the goal of sentence combining is not to produce longer sentences _____ to develop more effective sentences, _____ to help you become a more versatile writer.

Steps for organizing the activity:

1. Read the paragraph and try to figure out the connections between sentences.
2. Fill in the blanks with the transitional words to ensure the smooth flow of the paragraph.
3. Check the answers in class.

Activity 6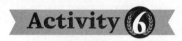

Read the paragraph and find out how the sentences are connected to ensure good coherence and cohesion.

> Sociologists have been engaged in the discussion of how mobile phones quickly change relationships between people. The article "Family Ties" attempts to characterize the effects of mobile phones on social relationships. Two main types of relationships shared between people are classified within the article. The first is the connection within "strong ties" among friends, lovers and relatives. This can be strengthened through modern technology. The author of "Family Ties" believes that although we are sometimes far away from our "strong ties" physically, we are actually closer in a psychological context through the use of mobile phones, as it allows us to call and text each other without time or location restrictions. The second relationship is classified as the "weak ties" among acquaintances. These are weakened by the wide use of modern communication tools. Nowadays, as more focus is placed on communication between close friends, we sometimes forget to say "hello" to people passing by, a simple gesture that might have been done if we were not immersed in our mobile world. In my opinion, while mobile technology indeed reinforces our "strong ties" with intimate ones it can on the other hand also reinforce "weak ties" among acquaintances. This creates a unique opportunity for people to contact each other wherever they are, regardless if they are familiar with one another or not.

Steps for organizing the activity:

1. Read the paragraph, underline the keywords and expressions intended for better connection while reading.

2. Group expressions showing the following features:
   —repeat keywords;
   —use pronouns;
   —use determiners;

Unit 5 **Language Improvement**

> —use transitional markers;
> —use a transitional sentence.
>
> **3.** Read the paragraph again to see how the paragraph is connected and understand how to write a paragraph with good connection.

Activity 7

Use COCA to find answers to the following questions.

> **1.** Is "feedback" followed by singular or plural verb form?
>
> **2.** What are the synonyms of "do"?
>
> **3.** What adjectives are used before "changes" and what verbs usually follow "findings"?
>
> **4.** What's the difference between the two adjectives "steady" and "stable"?
>
> *Steps for organizing the activity:*
>
> **1.** Log on COCA (https://www.english-corpora.org/coca/).
>
> **2.** Use different functions in COCA to find answers to the above questions.
>
> **3.** Share your answers with other students in class.

Activity 8

Please use Academic Phrasebank to find the expressions for the following items.

> **1.** Introducing works

2. Referring to sources
3. Describing methods
4. Reporting results
5. Discussing findings
6. Writing conclusions

Steps for organizing the activity:

1. Log on (Phrasebank http://www.phrasebank.manchester.ac.uk/).
2. Find the expressions for the 6 parts of the research paper.
3. Think about how to use them when writing the introduction, literature review, method, result, discussion and conclusion of your own paper.

5.4 After-Class Tasks

Task 1

Familiarize yourself with the use of COCA. Prepare yourself for using it in your writing.

Task 2

Scan the Academic Phrasebank and equip yourself with some basic expressions for writing a research paper.

Unit 6

Title and Thesis

6.1 Objectives

Know how to compose an appropriate title for the research paper.

Learn how to formulate a clear and logical thesis statement.

6.2 Pre-Class Learning

Watch the MOOC/SPOC videos and do the online exercises. The contents in the textbook will help you understand the lessons better.

Source: https://www.icourse163.org/

Course name: "学术英语写作与演讲" (Academic Writing and Presentation in English)

Unit 5 Title, Thesis and Outline

5.1 Title

5.2 Thesis

A good title is supposed to manifest the gist of the research, capture the readers' attention, and differentiate the article from papers of similar research topic. Readers always discern the value of the article at a glance of the title to judge whether it is worth reading. Therefore, it is necessary to know how to compose an appropriate title.

How to compose a title

- **Using a noun phrase**

The traditional and most popular way of composing a title is to use noun phrases, and to demonstrate the logical relationships between them.

- Example

    Large-Scale Psychological Differences Within China Explained by Rice

Unit 6 Title and Thesis

Versus Wheat Agriculture

Rapid Growth of Seed Black Holes in the Early Universe by Supra-Exponential Accretion

Greenland Temperature Response to Climate Forcing During the Last Deglaciation

The Impact of Computer-Based Feedback on Students' Written Work

- **Using a verb phrase**

Another possibility is to use an active verb instead of complex noun phrase to emphasize the process or effect.

- **Example**

    Tracking Cancer Drugs in Living Cells by Thermal Profiling of the Proteome

    Replaying Evolutionary Transitions from the Dental Fossil Record

    Considering Fairness and Validity in Evaluating Automated Scoring

    Comparing the Validity of Automated and Human Essay Scoring

- **Using a colon ":"**

When the logical relationship is complicated, or if you want to emphasize the conclusion/alternatives/methods in the title, you can use ":" to introduce a subtitle.

- **Example**

    Methodological Thinking Drills: A Novel Technique for Boosting Real-World Methodological Thinking Ability

    Unpacking Grit: Motivational Correlates of Perseverance and Passion for Long-Term Goals

    Universal Design for Learning: Scanning for Alignment in K-12 Blended and Fully Online Learning Materials

- **Using a question**

When there is no simple answer, it can be effective to put the title into a question.

- Example

  Can Automated Writing Evaluation Programs Help Students Improve Their English Writing?

  Is Artificial Intelligence a Bless or Curse for the Human Beings?

- **Using a statement**

The title can also be a statement, offering more explicit information about the result of the study. Nevertheless, this is quite rare.

- Example

  Calcium Addition Improves Salinity Tolerance of Tomato

Knowing the formats, as described above, is not enough. More important is its content. The following are some requirements for a good research paper title as far as contents are concerned.

- **Be clear, concise but include enough information**

Since the primary function of a title is to provide the precise summary of the research paper, it is necessary to keep the title clear and concise. It is recommended that active verbs be used instead of complex noun phrases, and unnecessary details be avoided. In addition, the title can neither be too short nor too long because too short a title does not convey enough information to the reader, and too lengthy a title may lose focus and distract the readers from the important information.

- Example

  Poor: Online Role-Play

  Better: Understanding the Use of Online Role-Play for Teaching Collaborative Argument

- **Demonstrate the logical relationship between noun phrases in the title**

You may tend to use the conjunction "and" to combine noun phrases because this is a comparatively easy way to formulate a title. But such a title can hardly show the logical relationship between these noun phrases. In fact, using a preposition instead of "and" can show the logic and convey more information.

- **Example**

    Poor: Selection Bias *and* the Heterosexual HIV-1 Transmission Bottleneck

    Better: Selection Bias *at* the Heterosexual HIV-1 Transmission Bottleneck

- **Avoid unfamiliar abbreviations**

Except for such well-known abbreviations as COVID, AIDS, or WTO, lesser-known or too specific abbreviations should be avoided in a title.

- **Example**

    Poor: Understanding the Reliability and Validity of AES

    Better: Understanding the Reliability and Validity of Automated Essay Evaluation

How to formulate a thesis

A thesis is a statement that summarizes the central idea of the research paper. It is usually placed at the end of the introduction. It deals with what you are writing about and what argument you support throughout your essay. In fact, a thesis is to an essay what the topic sentence is to a paragraph. A good thesis helps guide the viewpoints in the paper. It establishes a boundary around the topic, charts an orderly route for the paper and tells the reader what to expect from the rest of the paper.

A thesis is the result of a lengthy thinking process. When you formulate a thesis, you have to be very clear about what contents are to be covered in your paper, try to find and analyze possible relationships between facts, and think about the significance of these relationships. You also have to think about what conclusions you want to draw from your evidence, and what major ideas can support these conclusions. Keep asking yourself questions like "What is the main point that I want to prove/discuss?" and "How will I convince the reader that this is true?" When you refine your thesis, remember to keep your whole paper in mind all the time. You have to improve your thesis all along your writing process. At the first stage, a thesis statement is usually ill-formed or rough and can only serve as a planning tool. When you continue writing, you may find that some evidences cannot fit your "working" thesis, and that you may have deeper insights resulting from more research. So your thesis statement has to be improved to match the evidence you want to use. Sometimes your thesis needs to evolve as you have new evidence, develop fresh insights, or employ a different approach to your topic.

The wording of the thesis should be clear, comprehensible, and direct so that readers are able to predict the organization of the research paper, and find main points in the paper. Proper wording of the thesis should be based on the following principles.

- **A thesis must be expressed as a complete sentence.**

  - Example

    Poor: How life is on a farm.

    Better: Residents on a farm tend to live longer lives, have a more established sense of community, and socialize in bigger groups than do city dwellers.

The thesis must not be a fragment but a complete sentence. The first one is obviously not a complete sentence. The second one is not only complete but also shows how life on a farm is different from that in a city.

- **A thesis should be focused on a single idea.**

  - Example

    Poor: The Roman theater was inspired by the Greek theater, which it imitated and eventually the Romans produced great plays in their theaters, such as those by Plautus, who was the best Roman comic writer because of his robustness and inventiveness.

    Better: Because of his robust language and novel comic plots, Titus Maccius Plautus can be considered the best Roman comic playwright, and his plays are still successfully staged.

The first thesis has two directions and lacks focus. Students will be tempted to write on both the Roman Theater and the theatrical career of Plautus. This might result from the accumulation of two sets of notes—one on the origins of Roman theater and the other on the career of Plautus. The second is a better and more focused thesis.

Unit 6 Title and Thesis

- **A thesis should not be worded too simply.**

  - Example

  Poor: Smoking is harmful to your body.

  Better: Smoking harms the body by constricting the blood vessels, accelerating the heartbeat, paralyzing the cilia in the bronchial tubes, and activating excessive gastric secretions in the stomach.

  The first sentence is too simple to be a thesis statement because it suggests no direction, provides no structure, and proposes no specific arguments. The second thesis clarifies how smoking harms the body from four perspectives that directly shows the development in the body.

- **A thesis should not be worded as a question.**

  - Example

  Poor: What motivates a student in second language learning?

  Better: A student learning a second language can be motivated by the requirement of the course, the necessity of passing the exam, the need to study abroad, or the interest in the culture of that target language.

  A question is a good starting point for research. Indeed, most research begins with a question. But a question is not a good form of thesis statement.

- **A thesis should not be too broad or general.**

  - Example

  Poor: Children must be disciplined.

  Better: By using disciplinary techniques, parents, teachers, and police are the main agents for controlling children.

  The first thesis is too general and you may not be able to cover it adequately in a paper. The second provides three groups to discuss, which allow for the development of several main ideas and show the structure and organization of the research paper.

- **A thesis must not be expressed in muddled or incoherent language.**

  - Example

  Poor: The benefits of clarity and easy communication of a unified language compel a state to adopt codes to the effect that make bilingualism possible but preserving a single official language for transacting business and social communications.

  Better: The benefits of clarity and easy communication offered by a single official language in a state are compelling and persuasive.

  The first sentence seems long and muddled. It is much more difficult for the readers to understand than the second thesis. In fact, if your thesis is muddled, your essay tends to be muddled as well.

- **A thesis should not contain such phrases as "in my opinion" or "I think".**

  - Example

  Poor: In my opinion, smoking should be outlawed because of the adverse health effects of "passive smoking".

  Better: Smoking should be outlawed because of the adverse health effects of "passive smoking".

  Using phrases like "I think" or "in my opinion" will weaken your argument because they will make your argument seem subjective. Avoid using such phrases, and plainly state the thesis to inform your reader what you intend to prove in the article.

- **A thesis should not be worded in figurative language.**

  - Example

  Poor: The Amazons of today are trying to purge all the stag words from our language.

  Better: Today's feminists are trying to eliminate the use of sex-biased words from public documents and publications.

  Greek myths describe an all-female culture as the Amazons. But most people will be confused by the meaning of Amazon and consider it an online shopping website. Thus, Amazons, a figurative use of language to describe feminists, is too indefinite and hazy. The thesis statement should be a concise, easily understood sentence, as is shown in the second thesis.

- **A thesis must not be nonsensical.**
    - Example

    Poor: A good university education is one that is useful, fulfilling, and doesn't require study.

    Better: A good university education is one that is useful, fulfilling, and challenging.

The thesis should make sense. "A good university education doesn't require study" is nonsense. You cannot defend the indefensible or argue the unarguable. Replace "doesn't require study" with "challenging", and it will make sense.

A thesis statement is necessary for an expository or argumentative essay but may not always be indispensable for a research paper. What is more frequent in a research paper is a research question to indicate the problem that the researcher intends to solve. If it is a review article, you can write a thesis statement, which can be supported by evidences from the literature. If it is an empirical study, the thesis statement is replaced by the research objectives/aims, research questions/hypotheses that guide your whole research. Like the thesis statement, research objectives/aims or research questions/hypotheses are also put at the end of the introduction.

6.3 In-Class Activities

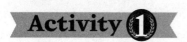

Examine the titles of the research papers you have recently read. Put them into the following groups.

> —noun phrase;
> —verb phrase;

—statement;

—question;

—colon ":".

Steps for organizing the activity:

1. Each student selects one paper that he/she has read recently. It can be a paper of his/her own discipline of study or the one that he/she is reading for the group research project.

2. Look at the title of each paper and judge which of the above-mentioned groups it belongs.

3. Figure out which of the above groups is most frequently used.

Activity 2

Answer the following questions based on the title of the paper you have selected.

—How many words does the title include?

—What are the keywords in the title?

—What is the research about according to the title?

Steps for organizing the activity:

1. Count the number of words in the title.

2. Tell what bracket the number belongs to (<=10, 11–15, 16–20, 21–25, >=26).

3. Generalize the number of words research papers mostly include.

4. Find out the keywords in the title.

5. Tell what information you get from the title and judge whether this title can arouse your interest to read the article.

Unit 6 Title and Thesis

Activity 3

Please find out the problems of the titles and try to improve them.

1. Research on Eating Patterns and Dietary Problems Among Teenagers
2. Data Analysis About Sleep Deficiency Among Undergraduates of Shanghai Jiao Tong University
3. Fast-Moving Consumer Goods
4. A Dynamic Aircraft Control System That Takes into Account Judgments from Pilots, Ground Control Center and Airborne Control System to Enhance the Safety of Aircraft
5. Applying Flipped Classroom to Academic English Teaching by Means of MOOC: A Feasibility Study Based on Course "Academic Communications in English—Writing and Presentation"

Steps for organizing the activity:

1. Divided into 5 groups, each working on one title.
2. Study the title and find out the problem.
3. Improve the title by revising it.
4. Share the revised title in class.

Activity 4

Are the following thesis statements strong or weak? Find out the problem if it is weak.

1. Pollution is bad for the environment.
2. America's anti-pollution efforts should focus on privately owned cars.

Steps for organizing the activity:

1. Do it in pairs, each one in the pair working on one thesis.
2. Study the thesis and find out the problem.
3. Improve the thesis by revising it.
4. Share the revised thesis with the partner in the pair.
5. Share the revision in class.

6.4 After-Class Tasks

Task 1

Please search for a paper of your own discipline of study. Infer what the research is about according to the title.

Task 2

Please write a title for your research paper.

Unit 7

Outline

7.1 Objectives

Know the structure of a research paper outline.

Learn how to write a well-organized outline for the paper.

Improve the logic of an outline by practicing.

 ## 7.2 Pre-Class Learning

Watch the MOOC/SPOC videos and do the online exercises. The contents in the textbook will help you understand the lessons better.

Source: https://www.icourse163.org/

Course name: "学术英语写作与演讲" (Academic Writing and Presentation in English)

Unit 5 Title, Thesis and Outline

5.3 Outline

An outline is an ordered list of the ideas covered in a research paper. Both the writer and the reader need the outline. An outline gives the writer a clear picture of the structure in mind and keeps the writer from straying away from the points. It also enables the readers to have a clear structure of the paper and get the gist of ideas easily.

Structure of an outline

The outline is usually formed like a tree branch, with each point further divided into sub-points at a subordinate level. You can number the items and subordinate items to show the relationship. The following is an example of a general outline form for writing an argumentative essay or a literature review paper:

Unit 7 Outline

1. Introduction
2. Main Point 1
   2.1 Sub-point 1
   2.2 Sub-point 2
   2.3 Sub-point 3
3. Main Point 2
   3.1 Sub-point 1
   3.2 Sub-point 2
   3.3 Sub-point 3
4. Main Point 3
   4.1 Sub-point 1
   4.2 Sub-point 2
   4.3 Sub-point 3
5. Conclusion

As for empirical studies, such as experiments or investigations using research methods, you have to follow the research paper outline which usually include the following elements:

—Introduction
—Literature review
—Methods
—Results
—Discussion
—Conclusion

Generally, these elements are involved in a research paper to demonstrate the contents logically. But there may still be some minor differences for each of the papers. For example, some research papers have no literature review but just an introduction that includes the contents of the literature review; some papers have results and discussion combined into one section; some have not a separate conclusion but include it in the discussion part; some even put the methods section at the end of the research paper. Therefore, while we learn the normal structure of a research paper, we also accept the varieties of the structures as long as our ideas can be expressed with good logic.

An outline can be either simple or detailed. A simple outline is a one-level outline. The more you read and think about your content, the more details you can add to your outline. A more detailed outline shows the depth of your research. After you have formed a one-level outline, you can use it as a guide to create a more detailed outline for your paper by moving to a two-level outline.

A two-level outline is made up of headings for the sections and their subsections of a paper. A basic two-level outline with many of the common elements in a research paper is shown below:

1. Introduction
2. Literature review
    2.1 Topic area A
    2.2 Topic area B
    2.3 Topic area C
3. Method
    3.1 Description of research design (general/optional)
    3.2 Participants/Materials
    3.2 Instruments/Measures
    3.3 Procedure (of data collection and analysis)
4. Results
    4.1 Results of the first research question
    4.2 Results of the second research question
    4.3 Results of the third research question
5. Discussion
    5.1. Discussion of results related to Question 1
    5.2. Discussion of results related to Question 2
    5.3. Discussion of results related to Question 3
6. Conclusion

- **Example 1**

The following example is the outline of the research on blended learning for teaching academic English. It also helps form a plan for the research.

Title:

Blending Online SPOC and Canvas with ZOOM Conference in Teaching Academic English

Outline:

1. Introduction

   Background

   Problem

   Purpose

2. Literature review

   2.1 Definition of blended learning

   2.2 Blended learning models

   2.3 Blended learning effects

   Limitation: None of the previous studies have ever investigated how to integrate several online platform and software to implement blended learning to academic English course against the coronavirus pandemic.

   Research questions:

   1) What is the model of online blended learning for academic English course?

   2) What are learners' perceptions of the effectiveness of the model?

3. Methods

   3.1 Participants

   3.2 Instruments

       Questionnaire

       Interview

       Students' work

   3.3 Data collection procedure

   3.4 Data analysis

4. Results

   4.1 Design of the model

   4.2 Effectiveness of the course

       Questionnaire (quantitative and qualitative)

           Pre-class

           In-class

           After-class

Interview (qualitative data)

Students' work (qualitative data)

5. Discussion

Analysis of the model

Analysis of effectiveness

6. Conclusion

Summary of major findings

Implications of the study

Limitations

Further research

- **Example 2**

This is an example of the outline written by students for their research on college students' academic performance.

Title:

The Influence of Sleep Quality and Patterns on Chinese College Students' Academic Performance and Extracurricular Activities

Outline:

1. Introduction

2. Literature review

    2.1 The significance of sleep on students' well-being

    2.2 The factors that influence sleep quality

    2.3 Limitations in previous researches

    2.4 Research purpose and questions

3. Method

    3.1 Research design

    3.2 Participants

    3.3 Instruments

        Questionnaires

        Interviews

    3.4 Data collection and analysis

4. Results

    4.1 The interaction between sleep quality and college students' academic performance

        Class performance

        Exam performance

    4.2 The interaction between sleep quality and college students' extracurricular activities

        On-campus organizations

        Off-campus hobbies

5. Discussion

    5.1 Prevalent situation of sleep patterns among college students

    5.2 Healthy sleep patterns for good academic performance

    5.3 Healthy sleep patterns for active extracurricular activities

6. Conclusion

Writing the outline helps you plan for your research. You need to read the literature on a certain topic to gain some background knowledge before you start to write the outline. You also have to think about what the research questions are, and how you do the research and design the research procedure. You even can predict the potential result in a hypothesis so that you can use the research method to testify whether the hypothesis is true or not.

After you have sketched an outline, you are supposed to read through your outline to judge whether it flows clearly and provides a good structure for a complete paper on your chosen topic. If not, modify your outline until the structure is clear and logical. A good outline serves as a useful guide for you to write a research paper.

It should be noted that subtitles in an outline show the levels of subordination, but do not fill your research paper with too many subtitles, or it will look quite strange. In most research papers, you will find that there are not so many levels of subtitles. Using a subtitle to group several paragraphs below it can help organize your content more clearly, but do not use a subtitle if there is only one paragraph in the section. A topic sentence is quite enough in this situation.

Major requirements for wording an outline

- **Parallelism**

Parallel structures are expected for an outline. The clarity and readability of an outline are improved if its entries are worded in similar grammatical forms. For the items at the same level in an outline, you must use the same structure.

- Example

1. Topic

    1.1 What topic to choose

    1.2 How to choose a topic

    1.3 How to elaborate on a topic

2. Source Materials

    2.1 Using library database

    2.2 Evaluating source materials

    2.3 Reading source materials

- **Coordination**

Coordination means topics at the same level must be equivalent in importance and derived from the same organizing principle. If they are not equal in importance, you cannot have them balanced in your writing. If you do not follow the same organizing principle, the classification will be illogical and unsystematic, making your content hard to understand. Take the example of "evaluation of writing", which covers subordinate topics such as summative or formative evaluation, and teacher, peer, self- or automated evaluation. These subordinate topics cannot be under the same superordinate topic because the organizing principles are different. Summative or formative evaluation deals with *how* to evaluate the writing while teacher, peer, self- or automated evaluation is about *who* evaluates it. Therefore, the outline can be illustrated as follows:

1. Ways of evaluation

    1.1 Summative evaluation

    1.2 Formative evaluation

2. Types of evaluators

    2.1 Teacher

    2.2 Peer

    2.3 Self

    2.4 Computer

- **Subordination**

Each sub-point should be subordinate to the superordinate point. In other words, parent headings of an outline should represent topics that are more general than sub-levels under them. And sub-levels of an outline should be more detailed than the parent heading they are under. Subordination and coordination are two necessary means to clearly display the logic of an outline. In the previous example, the first level items 1 and 2 are in coordination. The second level topics 1.1 and 1.2 are in coordination, and so are 2.1, 2.2, 2.3 and 2.4. But 1.1 and 1.2 are subordinate to 1 and 2.1, 2.2, 2.3, 2.4 to 2.

- **Division**

Division means for a point at a higher level, there are divisions of points that can make you investigate your topic more deeply and thoroughly. But be aware that if there is not much to be discussed about a topic, do not list too many subordinate items, or the paper will be filled with a lot of bare-bones headings without enough paragraphs to support your ideas.

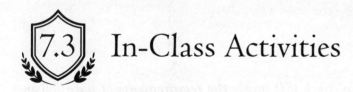 In-Class Activities

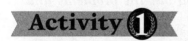

Draw figures of research paper outline and compare how similar or different the structures can be. The following is one example to show the structure of an informative or argumentative essay. Figure out the outline of a research paper.

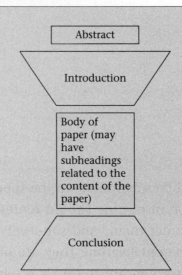

Steps for organizing the activity:

1. Work on a research paper of your discipline of study.

2. Read subtitles of the research paper.

3. Analyze the paper and draw the map showing the organization of the paper.

4. Compare the figure with those of your classmates' to see the similarities and differences.

5. Summarize the common features.

Activity 2

Read the following outline to check if it meets the requirements of parallelism, coordination, subordination and division. Try to find out the problems and then improve the outline.

Title: Confucius' Main Teaching Methods and Their Applicability to China's Education Today

Outline:

I. A brief introduction
   A. Confucius as a great philosopher and statesman
   B. A great educator

II. Confucius' two teaching methods
   A. The elicitation method
      1. Fostering the student's ability to learn by themselves
      2. In his normal day teaching, he put great emphasis on the teacher's role in giving the student guidance.
   B. The method of "teaching student in accordance with their aptitude"

III. Causes of the discontinuance of Confucius' teaching methods in modern China
   A. The May Fourth era
   B. The Cultural Revolution period is another period when Confucius' teaching principles ceased to work.

IV. The applicability of Confucius' teaching methods to China's education today
   A. Analyze problems in education today
      1. Feeding students with knowledge
      2. Teaching students in the same way without discrimination
      3. The root of problems
   B. The applicability of Confucius' teaching methods
      1. Teachers at present should learn to help students cultivate the habit of learning in an active way.
      2. Giving students opportunities to practice what they have learned
      3. It is always important to improve the ways of teaching so as to arouse students' interest.
      4. Increasing elective courses to meet students' different interests

5. More technical and vocational schools need to be set up for students given that students all have different capacities.

V. Conclusion

Steps for organizing the activity:

1. Review major requirements of an outline:
   —Parallelism
   —Coordination
   —Subordination
   —Division

2. Find out the problems in the sample outline.

3. Discuss with your group members and cooperatively find more problems.

4. Discuss in class to generalize the problems.

5. Rewrite the outline to make it more logical.

Activity 3

The following are two versions of a student's outline for a research paper entitled "Exploring the Feasibility of Applying MOOC-Based Flipped Classroom Pedagogy to Academic Writing and Presentation". Compare and tell how the second outline is improved.

Version 1

1. Introduction
2. Literature review
   2.1 Previous studies on the use of flipped classroom in higher education
   2.2 Limitations in previous studies
   2.3 Research questions

3. Research method

    3.1 Research design

    3.2 Participants

    3.3 Instruments

    3.4 Data collection and analysis

4. Results

    4.1 Whether participants are familiar with MOOC and MOOC-based flipped classroom or not

    4.2 What benefits and drawbacks flipped classrooms have

    4.3 In which aspects is a flipped approach more preferable

    4.4 To what extent should the course be "flipped"

5. Discussion

    5.1 Feasibility of applying MOOC-based flipped classroom pedagogy to this course

    5.2 Suggested MOOC course design to "flip" this course

    5.3 Suggested teaching mode to "flip" this course

6. Conclusion

Version 2

1. Introduction

    1.1 Introduction of flipped classrooms and MOOC

    1.2 Introduction of our course and indicate a gap

    1.3 Objective of our research

2. Literature review

    2.1 Previous studies on the use of flipped classroom in higher education

        —Popularity of flipped learning in recent years

        —Flipped classroom for second language teaching

        —Benefits and drawbacks of flipped classroom pedagogy

        —Method of flipping: face-to-face and online class organization

    2.2 Limitations in previous studies

2.3 Research questions

—Is it feasible to adopt the flipped classroom in academic English learning?

—If it is, how to design the course?

3. Research method

3.1 Research design

3.2 Participants

3.3 Instruments

3.3.1 Quantitative: A questionnaire

3.3.2 Qualitative: An interview

3.4 Data collection and analysis

4. Results

4.1 Familiarity with MOOC and the flipped classroom

4.2 Benefits and drawbacks of the flipped classroom

4.3 Preferred approaches for the flipped classroom

4.4 Proportion of the flipped classroom

5. Discussion

5.1 Feasibility of application (relating to 4.1, 4.2)

5.2 Course design (relating to 4.3, 4.4)

6. Conclusion

6.1 Summary of the objectives

6.2 Major findings

6.3 Important implications

6.4 Limitations and future work

Steps for organizing the activity:

1. Compare the two outlines, focusing on the differences.

2. Pinpoint where improvements have been made.

3. Discuss in groups and share your view.

7.4 After-Class Tasks

Task 1

Write a research plan. You can include the following contents.

1. Review of literature
   What have other researchers done about your research topic?
   What are the things that they haven't done?
   What is your research going to do? / What is your research purpose?
   What are your research questions/hypothesis?

2. Your method
   How are you going to design your research?
   Who are the subjects/participants or what materials will be used?
   What are the instruments you are going to employ?
   How are you going to collect and analyze the data?

3. Originality and contribution
   What is your originality and contribution?

Task 2

Write the outline for your research paper. Pay attention to the major requirements for wording an outline. Try to make a clear and logical outline for your research paper.

Task 3

Prepare for a presentation of your research plan or outline.

Unit 8

Abstract

8.1 Objectives

Explore the essentials of an abstract.

Be familiar with some sentence templates in an abstract.

Be able to write the abstract of a research paper.

8.2 Pre-Class Learning

Watch the MOOC/SPOC videos and do the online exercises. The contents in the textbook will help you understand the lessons better.

Source: https://www.icourse163.org/

Course name: "学术英语写作与演讲" (Academic Writing and Presentation in English)

Unit 6 Abstract

6.1 Essentials of an abstract

6.2 Sentence templates

6.3 Keywords

An abstract is a summary of the major ideas contained in a research paper. Many people write an abstract after they have finished the paper. But very often you are required to submit an abstract to a conference more than half a year before the conference is held. You probably have already done the research or have formed ideas about the research, but you haven't finished the research paper yet. In this case, you need to write out an abstract according to your outline beforehand and revise it later when you finish writing your research paper.

Essentials of an abstract

An abstract usually includes the following essential components:

Research background (Why is the research important? Why would a reader be interested in the research?)

Existing problem (What problem does the research attempt to solve? What is the scope of the project?)

Methods employed (Empirical studies include approaches used in the study. Other abstracts may describe the types of evidence used in the research.)

Results or findings (Empirical studies demonstrate specific findings. Other abstracts may discuss the findings generally.)

Conclusion (What can we conclude from the research? What are the implications of the work? How does this work add to the knowledge on the topic?)

Abstracts may vary in format. Some include the above five elements while some others may contain four elements of purpose, methods, findings, and conclusion. In fact, the background mingles with the problem to indicate a gap in research and imply the purpose of doing the research. Abstracts of five or four elements are both appropriate and common in research papers. These elements are clearly presented in an abstract for the author to organize ideas clearly and for the readers to get the information quickly.

An abstract of about 120–200 words is quite common, but exactly how long an abstract should depend on the requirement of the journal you submit your paper to or the requirement of the course you participate in. Let's analyze the essentials of an abstract by examining examples from published research papers.

- **Example 1**

    Abstract: 1) The prefrontal cortex (PFC) subserves reasoning in the service of adaptive behavior. **2)** Little is known, however, about the architecture of reasoning processes in the PFC. **3)** Using computational modeling and neuroimaging, **4)** we show here that the human PFC has two concurrent inferential tracks: (i) one from ventromedial to dorsomedial PFC regions that makes probabilistic inferences about the reliability of the ongoing behavioral strategy and arbitrates between adjusting this strategy versus exploring new ones from long-term memory, and (ii) another from polar to lateral PFC regions that makes probabilistic inferences about the reliability of two or three alternative strategies and arbitrates between exploring new strategies

    1. Background
    2. Problem

    3. Method
    4. Results

versus exploiting these alternative ones. 5) The two tracks interact and, along with the striatum, realize hypothesis testing for accepting versus rejecting newly created strategies.

5. Conclusion

(Source: Donoso et al., 2014. Science)

- **Example 2**

  Abstract

  Aims: To study the prevalence and correlates of psychological distress among college students in Kerala, India.

  1. Purpose

  Material and methods: 5,784 students across 58 colleges were self-administered Kessler's Psychological Distress Scale (K10) and other standardized instruments.

  2. Methods

  Results: The prevalence of psychological distress was 34.8% (Mild—17.3%; Moderate—9.2%; Severe—8.3%) with a female predominance. Students with psychological distress were more likely to report academic failures, substance use, suicidality, sexual abuse and symptoms of attention deficit hyperactivity disorder. Students with severe distress had higher morbidity.

  3. Results

  Conclusions: Psychological distress is common among college students and its association with negative correlates suggests the need for early interventions.

  4. Conclusion

  (Source: Jaisoorya et al. 2017. Asian Journal of Psychiatry)

- **Example 3**

  Abstract: 1) As computers and the Internet are increasingly employed in language teaching and learning, preparing teachers for the impending reality of online teaching is of paramount importance. 2) However, teachers are usually trained to use technology generally, without experiencing it from the perspective of students. 3) This study investigated ten in-service teachers participating in an online role-play as part of a digital education methods course

  1. Background

  2. Problem

  3. Methods

to acquire an understanding of the use of online role-play for collaborative argument. The role-play lasted for three weeks and underwent three stages: preparation, implementation and reflection. Analyses of data gathered from the questionnaire survey, the class website for role-play, the blogs and the interviews indicate that **4)** online role-play was an appropriate way for teaching collaborative argument given that the topics were well-chosen and well-prepared, and that asynchronous role-play was more helpful than the synchronous role-play given the challenge of tracking the development of ideas. Benefits and problems of online role-play through synchronous chat were analyzed and solutions were discussed. **5)** The research provides a new perspective on how teachers can be educated to integrate technology into their language instruction through their own experience of learning.

4. Results

5. Conclusion

(Source: Zhang et al., 2016. *Asia-Pacific Journal of Teacher Education*)

Typical sentence templates

To define the background and argument of the present study, you can use the following expressions, each of which presents a problem against a certain research background.

— Although (the research subject)..., (the related problem) ... is as yet *undetermined*.

— (The research subject) ..., however, (the related problem) ... remains unsolved.

— (Previous studies) have examined..., (the related problem) is that..., despite...

— (Problems in certain research area) are..., yet (the present solution) has frequently been questioned because...

— This paper describes/presents... (the argument) within... (a theoretical context)

— While (the debate on certain research subject) seems to..., (the present agreement) is still problematic.

To describe the research method and procedure, you can use the expressions below, which may involve verbs like "use" "perform" "adopt" "conduct", etc.

—Detailed information has been acquired by the authors using...

—Several sets of experiments have been performed to test the validity of...

—The technique the author adopted is referred to as...

—The experiments consisted of four steps, which are described in...

—The method/approach used in the present study is...

—The experiment/investigation in the paper is conducted by adopting...

—The procedure the present study followed can be briefly described as...

—The experiment/study consisted of the following steps: ...

—Included in the experiment were...

—Based on the idea that..., we conducted the present study, categorized..., and evaluated...

To present results, findings or a conclusion, we can use:

—The results show that...

—The results are as follows: ...

—The results of the experiment indicate/suggest that...; it is also found that...

—The investigation/experiment varied by... and the results also revealed that...

—The analysis of the samples indicates that...

—It is concluded that...; the results also imply the further study into...

—These findings of the research have led the author to the conclusion that...

"Find, reveal, show, indicate, suggest" are frequently used verbs in results and "imply, conclude, lead the author to the conclusion that" are some expressions for a conclusion. On most occasions, the conclusion is just a final statement to give a summary or indicate the implication.

Keywords

Keywords come right after the abstract. They are the words or phrases that can represent the most important ideas for a research but may not necessarily be the most frequently repeated words in your article. The function of keywords is to enable readers to quickly catch your research scope and contents. They will also make your article searchable among a vast number of articles. Usually three to five keywords are provided, mostly phrases rather than single words. The following are the keywords of the abstract in Example 3.

Keywords: Online role-play; Collaborative argument; Teacher experiencing

Now let's look at another abstract and try to find the possible key words for the research among the following list.

- **Example 4**

    Academic writing has been the subject of instruction and research for decades in most western universities. However, it is still at its embryo stage in Chinese universities. Whether and how it can be adapted to EFL learning environment in China is a question arousing controversy, which establishes the need for more research in the local background. In this study, 30 students participated in an academic writing course where a dynamic process imitating the actual research process was encouraged. We adopted the mixed methods of T-tests of students' draft/final thesis statement, draft/final outlines, One-Way ANOVA of draft/revised/final research papers, classroom observation about research process and interview about students' perceptions about the course and their progress. The results indicate that most students improve their academic writing skills, and the course imitating the dynamic research process helps EFL learners improve their competence and confidence in academic writing.

    (Source: Chen & Zhang, 2017. TESOL International Journal)

Possible keywords:

Students

Chinese universities

EFL learning

Mixed methods

Interview

Significant differences

Academic writing course

Dynamic process

Course evaluation

"Students" "Chinese universities" and "EFL learning" are too general words to describe the specific research. "Mixed methods" "Interview" and "Significant differences" are too specific without conveying the key information of this particular research. "Academic writing course" "Dynamic process" and "Course evaluation" can reflect the most important idea when an academic writing course showing dynamic process is evaluated.

8.3 In-Class Activities

Activity 1

Please rearrange the order to form an acceptable abstract and put the numbers in the following box.

1. Students themselves can be trained to seek a connection between the lecture topics, their teaching/learning experience and other subjects. Students can also come to the lecture prepared with their own personal goals and questions they would like to have addressed.

2. This paper, using a definition of interest proposed in the field of educational psychology, reports on the findings of a study conducted with a group of postgraduate students studying in an English language teacher education program at a New Zealand university.

3. "Interest" is a widely used term not only in language education but also in our everyday life.

4. The findings suggest that there are various situational and individual sources of interest that can be exploited. The topic and content of lectures seem to play a significant role in triggering student interest. Interest in the topic can be triggered not only by what the lecturer does (situational factors) but also by what the student him/herself does (individual factors).

5. However, very little attempt has been made to investigate the nature of 'interest' in language teaching and learning.

(Source: Tin, 2006. System)

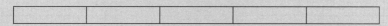

Steps for organizing the activity:

1. Read the five sentences taken from a research abstract.

2. Rearrange them according to the logic of the five essentials.

3. Fill in the boxes with the numbers before the sentences to show the logic of the abstract.

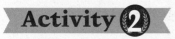

Find out the four essentials in the following abstract.

Abstract: The purpose of the present study was to investigate the relationship between optimism, social intelligence, and positive affect with students' life satisfaction. The sample included 332 students of humanities sciences (213 females and 119 males) from Payame Noor University–Tabriz branch, who were randomly selected using stratified and multiple-stage cluster sampling. Extended Life Orientation questionnaire, Tromso Social Intelligence questionnaire, Positive Affect and Life Satisfaction scales were used as data collection instruments and the data were analyzed by Pearson's correlation and hierarchical multiple regression analysis. The results of Pearson's correlation analysis indicated a positive and meaningful correlation between social information processing, social skills, optimism, positive affect, and life satisfaction. Furthermore, the results of hierarchical multiple regression analysis also indicated the direct effect of social information processing and social skills on life satisfaction that later disappeared when optimism and positive affect were introduced in the second step. In the final model, only measures of optimism and positive affect were statistically meaningful. Therefore, social intelligence and positive affect promote life satisfaction in university students.

(Source: Rezaei & Khosroshahi, 2018. European Journal of Mental Health)

Purpose	
Methods	
Results	
Conclusion	

Steps for organizing the activity:

1. Read the abstract of a research paper.
2. Find out the essentials of the abstract and fill in the table.

Activity 3

Use a slash "/" to divide the five parts of the following abstract. Also find out how to improve the keywords.

Abstract: In today's highly competitive world, students face various academic problems including exam stress, anxiety during the test, problems with homework assignments, expectations about academic success or inability to understand the subjects. Rapid changes in the education sector gave rise to stern testing procedures for evaluating students' knowledge. Thus, the main objective of this research was to investigate the possible relationship between emotional intelligence, test anxiety and academic stress among university students. The Self-Report Emotional Intelligence Test (SEIT), Test Anxiety Inventory (TAI) and Student Academic Stress Test (SAST) were administered to a sample of 200 university students (100 female and 100 male students). The results indicated that the total score of emotional intelligence correlated with the test anxiety and academic stress felt, as well as the academic success achieved, by the university students. At the same time there was a significant positive relationship between emotional intelligence, test anxiety, academic stress and gender. There was no correlation between emotional intelligence and the course of study, but there was a positive relationship between test anxiety, academic stress and the course of study. Also we found a significant positive relationship between emotional intelligence, test anxiety, academic stress and high academic performance, but a negative one between emotional intelligence, test anxiety, academic stress and low academic performance. The study conducted found that emotional intelligence, test anxiety and academic stress are significant for and predictive of the academic achievement the university students' population accomplish.

Keywords: Emotional intelligence; Test anxiety; Academic stress; Students; Management

(Source: Stankovska et al., 2018. Education in Modern Society)

Steps for organizing the activity:

1. Read the abstract of a research paper.
2. Identify the different parts of the abstract by using the "/".
3. Find out the inappropriate keywords in the abstract.
4. Improve the keywords.

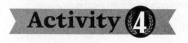

Activity 4

Find out the problems of the following abstract and compare it with the revised version.

Abstract: This article presents a model using peer assessment to evaluate students taking part in blended-learning courses (BL). In these courses, teaching activities are carried out in the form of traditional face-to-face (F2F) and learning activities are performed online via the learning management system Moodle. In the model, the topics of courses are built as a set of projects and case studies for the attending students divided into groups. The result of the implementation of projects is evaluated and ranked by all course participants and is one of the course evaluation criteria for lecturers. To assess learners more precisely, we propose a multi-phase assessment model in evaluating all groups and the group members. The result of each student in the group based on himself evaluation, evaluations of the team members, the teacher and all students in the course. There are 107 students, who participated in the course entitled Bweb application development, are divided into 20 groups conducting the course in the field of information technology is deployed in the form of blended learning through peer assessment. The results of student's feedback suggested that the usage of various peer assessment created positive learning effectiveness and more interesting learning attitude for students. The survey was conducted with the students through the questionnaire, each question with scale 5-point Likert scale that ranged from 1 (very unsatisfied) to 5 (very satisfied) to investigate the factors: Collaboration, Assessment, Technology showed that students were satisfied with our approach.

Keywords: Peer assessment; Blended learning; Many-phases assessment; Learning activities

(Source: Nguyen, 2017. Education Information Technology)

Revised abstract

Abstract: The blended learning in the form of the combination of traditional face-to-face instruction and online learning becomes more and more popular. However, how to assess learning in the blended context remains unsolved. This study aims to evaluate the effectiveness of peer assessment within multi-phase assessment model in the blended course entitled Bweb. A questionnaire was conducted to investigate the factors of collaboration, assessment and technology. The results suggested that the usage of various peer assessment created positive learning effect and more interesting learning attitude for students. Peer assessment is a satisfactory approach to evaluating learning effect in the blended learning environment.

Steps for organizing the activity:

1. Read the abstract of the research paper without reading the revised one.

2. Discuss with your group members the problems of the abstract.

3. Reorganize the contents in the abstract with regard to the structure of an abstract.

4. Compare your version with the revised abstract to see how it is improved.

8.4 After-Class Tasks

Find out what is missing in the following abstract.

Archival studies of political decision-making groups show that the public statements of policy makers in the majority are higher in integrative complexity than those of minority faction or unanimous group members. However, whether these differences reflect policymakers' private thoughts, or their public impression management strategies, cannot be inferred using only data from the public record. The experiment reported here established that in freely interacting groups composed of majorities and minorities, this pattern is obtained under private communication conditions as well as in public statements. Results suggest that cognitive flexibility in response to influence from insiders, rather than communication strategies designed to influence outsiders, underlies the differences.

(Source: Greenfield, 1998. *Journal of Experimental Social Psychology*)

Task 2

Read a paper of your own discipline of study and find out the essentials in the abstract.

Task 3

Suppose you're going to attend a conference and are required to submit an abstract but you haven't yet finished the whole paper. Write an abstract for your research paper. You may revise it after you have finished the entire paper.

Unit 9

Introduction

9.1 Objectives

Explore the three moves in an introduction.

Be familiar with some sentence templates in the introduction.

Be able to write the introduction of a research paper.

9.2 Pre-Class Learning

Watch the MOOC/SPOC videos and do the online exercises. The contents in the textbook will help you understand the lessons better.

Source: https://www.icourse163.org/

Course name: "学术英语写作与演讲" (Academic Writing and Presentation in English)

Unit 7 Introduction

7.1 Three moves in an introduction

7.2 Details about each move

7.3 Sentence templates

A Greek philosopher once remarked: "The beginning is half of the whole." Indeed, a good introduction is essential to the whole research paper, and therefore, knowing how to write the introduction is important for academic writing.

Essentials in an introduction

The "Introduction" of a research paper, whether short or long, usually has three moves you need to stick to while writing a paper. The following is the Three-Move Model for introduction by Swales (1990), with revision and adaption for classroom use.

1. Establishing a research territory (background)
    a. showing that the research is important and interesting

b. introducing the previous research

2. Establishing a niche (gap/problem)

   a. showing the controversy of the previous research

   b. or indicating the deficiency in the previous research

3. Occupying the niche (purpose, thesis, structure)

   a. stating the research purpose/asking research questions (empirical studies)

   b. or formulating the thesis (review articles)

   c. providing the structure (only for long dissertation)

In order to have a clear understanding of how to write an introduction, let's look at several examples. Examples 1–3 are taken from *Science* and *Nature*, which do not use APA format. We omit the in-text citations for convenience.

- **Example 1**

1) Heterosexual HIV-1 transmission is an inefficient process with rates reported at <1% per unprotected sexual exposure. 2) When transmission occurs, systemic infection is typically established by a single genetic variant, taken from the swarm of genetically distinct viruses circulating in the donor. 3) Whether that founder virus represents a chance event or was systematically favored is unclear. 4) Our work has tested a central hypothesis that founder virus selection is biased toward certain genetic characteristics.

The first two sentences establish a research territory by giving the definition of the key term "Heterosexual HIV-1 transmission" and the result of the transmission, thus giving the background information of the research paper.

The third sentence establishes a niche by showing a problem—"Whether... or... is unclear".

The last sentence indicates the purpose of the research. In this way, the niche is occupied.

(Source: Carlson et al., 2014. Science)

- **Example 2**

1) Over the past 20 years, psychologists have cataloged a long list of differences between East and West. 2) Western culture is more individualistic and analytic-thinking, whereas East Asian culture is more interdependent

Four sentences at the beginning of the introduction provide the background of the research paper, things scientists have done in the past 20 years, the difference between Western and Asian culture, and the meaning of analytic and holistic thoughts.

and holistic-thinking. 3) Analytic thought uses abstract categories and formal reasoning, such as logical laws of non-contradiction—if A is true, then "not A" is false. 4) Holistic thought is more intuitive and sometimes even embraces contradiction—both A and "not A" can be true. 5) Even though psychology has cataloged a long list of East-West differences, it still lacks an accepted explanation of what causes these differences. 6) Building on subsistence style theory, we offer the rice theory of culture and compare it with the modernization hypothesis and the more recent pathogen prevalence theory.

The fifth sentence "Even though..., it still lacks..." states the problem that the list does not explain the causes of the difference. Therefore, the last sentence shows what the researchers will do to fill the gap.

(Source: Talhelm et al., 2014. Science)

- **Example 3**

Blood-feeding as a behavioral adaptation is exceedingly rare in insects. Of the one million to ten million insect species on earth, only 10,000 feed on the blood of live animals. Among these, only about 100 species blood-feed preferentially on humans. When biting insects evolve to prefer humans, they can spread diseases such as malaria and dengue fever with devastating efficiency. The mosquito Aedes aegypti provides one of the best examples of specialization on humans. It originated as a wild, animal-biting species in the forested areas of sub-Saharan Africa, where the subspecies Ae. aegypti formosus is still often found living in forests and biting

This introduction is much longer than the previous two examples. It contains three paragraphs. The first paragraph establishes a research territory by showing the background information of blood-feeding insects from the behavior of blood feeding to the human-biting insects and the illness they cause. By doing this, the authors indicate that the research is important and interesting.

Unit 9 **Introduction**

non-human animals today. In contrast, the derived non-African subspecies Ae. aegypti has evolved to specialize in biting humans and thus has become the main worldwide vector of dengue and yellow fevers.

The evolutionary adaptations that help subspecies Ae. aegypti exploit humans are most clearly seen where it has been reintroduced along the coast of East Africa and is known as the "domestic" form. Researchers investigating the outbreak of an unknown illness in Tanganyika in 1952 discovered homes heavily populated by brown-pigmented "domestic" mosquitoes. Subsequent work in the Rabai region of Kenya in the 1960s and 1970s showed that domestic mosquitoes readily entered homes, preferred to lay eggs in nutrient-poor river and rain water stored in containers indoors, were resistant to starvation as larvae, and had evolved a strong preference for biting humans. Black-pigmented populations of the native African subspecies formosus, known in Rabai as the "forest" form, were found just hundreds of metres away, avoiding homes, laying their eggs in tree holes and rock pools outdoors, and preferring to bite non-human animals. These differences translated into marked divergence in capacity to spread human diseases, including chikungunya, the unknown illness from 1952, yellow fever, prevalent

The second paragraph introduces the previous research done in this area.

in Africa and South America since the sixteenth century, and dengue fever, a disease currently infecting almost 400 million people around the world each year.

Remarkably, the domestic and forest forms in Rabai remained separate in nature but were interfertile in captivity, providing a rare opportunity to investigate the genetic basis and evolution of traits that adapt mosquitoes to humans. Here we find that human host preference in domestic mosquitoes is strongly correlated with functional genetic variation in an odorant receptor, Or4, which recognizes a component of human body odor.

Words like "remained separate", "but", "providing a rare opportunity" in the first sentence of paragraph three show that there is a problem, thus indicating a gap in the previous research. The second sentence "Here we find that ... human body odor" indicates what is done in the current research to solve the problem.

(Source: McBride et al., 2014. Nature)

- **Example 4**

1) Role-play is "a social or human activity in which participants 'take on' or 'act out' specified 'roles' often within a predefined social framework or situational blueprint" (Crookwell, Oxford, & Saunders, 1987, p. 155). 2) Role-play is used as a teaching technique for a better grasp of knowledge and skills (Williams, 2012; Cakici & Bayir, 2012). 3) It is also a tool employed in the teaching and learning for the development of language abilities (Liang, 2012; Andresen, 2005) or argumentation skills (Ahlsén, 2005). 4) As computers and the Internet are increasingly employed in language

Sentence 1 establishes a research territory (Role-play).

Sentences 2, 3 & 4 show that the research is important and interesting.

teaching and learning (e.g. Andriessen, Baker, & Suthers, 2003; Beach, Anson, Kastman-Breuch, & Swiss, 2009; Thomas, Reindeers, & Warschauer, 2013), the method of role-play becomes integrated in an online environment (e.g. Wills et al., 2009; Wills, Leigh, & Ip, 2011; Beach & Doerr-Stevens, 2009). 5) However, little research has focused on teachers' own experience of using online role-play to achieve a better understanding of how the method can be used to facilitate teaching and learning. 6) This suggests the need for research on teachers' use of online role-play as part of their in-service professional development that examines the effectiveness of their own experiences as students using online role-play as well as the differences in their perceptions of the use of synchronous versus asynchronous online role-play platforms.

Sentence 5 establishes a niche (problem) by indicating a gap in the previous research.

Sentence 6 occupies the niche by stating the purpose of research and by formulating the thesis.

(Source: Zhang et al., 2016. *Asia-Pacific Journal of Teacher Education*)

The third example is a longer introduction of three paragraphs, and the three moves of the introduction can be manifested even more clearly. Whether you should provide a simple or detailed introduction depends on how long the whole paper is. You can write a short introduction for a 3000-word term paper, but a much longer one for a master thesis or a PhD dissertation.

Sentence templates

Here are some typical sentence patterns that can be used in each of the three moves in the introduction.

For the first move, establishing a research territory, you start by establishing the importance of the topic. For example:

—Recently, there has been renewed interest in...

—In recent years, there has been an increasing interest in...

—The last two decades have seen a growing trend towards...

Then you can refer to previous work to establish what is already known. For example:

—Several attempts have been made to...

—Previous research has established that...

—Recently, investigators have examined...

For the second move, establishing a niche or problem, you can identify a controversy within the field of study. For example:

—A much-debated question is whether...

—To date there has been little agreement on...

—Questions have been raised about...

Or you can explain the inadequacies of previous studies. For example:

—Previous studies have not dealt with...

—It is still not known whether...

—The nature of... remains unclear.

For the third move, occupying the niche, you can state the purpose of the current research. For example:

—The objectives of this research are to determine...

—The purpose of this investigation is to explore...

—Drawing upon..., this study attempts to...

Unit 9 **Introduction**

9.3 In-Class Activities

Activity 1

Analyze the introduction of Connections between Curiosity, Flow and Creativity (See Appendix 3).

> *Steps for organizing the activity:*
>
> **1.** Read the introduction part of the research paper.
> **2.** Try to locate the three moves in the introduction.
> **3.** Find out the problem with the introduction and try to improve it.

Activity 2

Compare and contrast the abstract and the introduction of the same paper and find out the similarities and differences.

> **Abstract:** The prefrontal cortex (PFC) subserves reasoning in the service of adaptive behavior. Little is known, however, about the architecture of reasoning processes in the PFC. Using computational modeling and neuroimaging, we show here that the human PFC has two concurrent inferential tracks: i) one from ventromedial to dorsomedial PFC regions that makes probabilistic inferences about the reliability of the ongoing behavioral strategy and arbitrates between adjusting this strategy versus exploring new ones from long-term memory, and ii) another from polar to lateral PFC regions that makes probabilistic inferences about the reliability of two or three alternative strategies and arbitrates between exploring new strategies versus exploiting these

alternative ones. The two tracks interact and, along with the striatum (纹状体), realize hypothesis testing for accepting versus rejecting newly created strategies.

Introduction

Human reasoning subserves adaptive behavior and has evolved facing the uncertainty of everyday environments. In such situations, probabilistic inferential processes (i.e., Bayesian inferences) make optimal use of available information for making decisions. Human reasoning involves Bayesian inferences accounting for human responses that often deviate from formal logic (Oaksford & Chater, 2009). Bayesian inferences also operate in the prefrontal cortex (PFC) and guide behavioral choices (Behrens et al., 2007; Boorman et al., 2009). Everyday environments, however, are changing and open-ended, so that the range of uncertain situations and associated behavioral strategies (i.e., internal maps linking stimuli, actions, and expected outcomes) becomes potentially infinite. In such environments, probabilistic inferences involve Dirichlet process mixtures (Teh et al., 2006; Doshi-Velez, 2009; Daw, 2007; Gershman & Blei, 2010) and rapidly yield intractable computations. This computational complexity problem constitutes a fundamental constraint on the evolution of higher cognitive functions and raises the issue of the actual nature of inferential processes implemented in the PFC.

(Source: Donoso et al. 2014. Science, with in-text citations adapted according to APA format.)

Steps for organizing the activity:

1. Read the abstract and the introduction of the same paper.
2. Identify the similarities and differences through analysis.
3. Discuss in groups and share your findings.
4. Summarize the similarities and differences in class.

Unit 9 **Introduction**

Activity 3

Read the introduction section of the Keck's research paper "Copying, paraphrasing, and academic writing development: A re-examination of L1 and L2 summarization practices" (See Appendix 1). Find out the three moves and write a summary.

Three moves		Topic sentence for each paragraph
First move (___-___)	Lead in (Para.1)	
	Perspective 1 (___-___)	
	Perspective 2 (___-___)	
Second move (___-___)	Problem	
Third move (___-___)	Objective and research questions	
Summary		

Steps for organizing the activity:

1. Read the introduction of the paper.
2. Find out the three moves and the details.
3. Fill them in the table.
4. Write a summary of the introduction in less than 100 words.

9.4 After-Class Tasks

Task 1

Please find out the three moves in the following two research paper introductions. The in-text citations are omitted for convenience.

Introduction 1

E-business is not just one choice available to enterprises, but every business will become an e-business. Enterprises are being pushed into global competition with the boom of information technology (IT) based on the Internet, with e-business becoming the main platform for many enterprises. The traditional business management and operation models cannot be easily fitted into the new economic environment and there are new forms of competition. Therefore, enterprises need to implement organizational changes to take full advantage of the e-business opportunities; otherwise, they will be forced out of business. Therefore, effective implementation of e-business transformation strategy is a critical factor for enterprises to gain a sustainable competitive advantage that is receiving much attention in information systems (IS) research. An IBM vice president said, "E-business transformation is not only needed by Chinese enterprises, but is also an issue of concern for all of the world's enterprises."

Most current studies are focusing on analyzing the critical factors which will affect the application and proliferation of e-business technology in organizations based on the technology adoption model (TAM), neglecting the study on how e-business impacts the organizational behavior. However, e-business applications in an organization are a series of continuous activities, so it is more valuable to explore the implementation and application of this new technology on organizational changes than only analyzing the adoption of e-business. This paper presents an e-business transformation process model based on organization transformation theory, which will help enterprise implement e-business transformation strategies more effectively.

(Source: Zeng et al., 2008. Tsinghua Science and Technology)

Unit 9 Introduction

Introduction 2

Agriculture is having increasingly strong global impacts on both the environment and human health, often driven by dietary changes. Global agriculture and food production release more than 25% of all greenhouse gases (GHGs) pollute fresh and marine waters with agrochemicals, and use as cropland or pastureland about half of the ice-free land area of Earth. Despite the intensity and impacts of global agriculture, almost a billion people still suffer from inadequate diets and insecure food supplies. Moreover, the global transition towards diets high in processed foods, refined sugars, refined fats, oils and meats has contributed to 2.1 billion people becoming overweight or obese. These dietary shifts and resulting increases in body mass indices (BMI) are associated with increased global incidences of chronic non-communicable diseases, especially type II diabetes, coronary heart disease and some cancers, which are predicted to become two-thirds of the global burden of disease if dietary trends continue. In China, for instance, as incomes increased and diets changed, the incidence of type II diabetes increased from <1% of its population in 1980 to 10% in 2008, partly because type II diabetes occurs at lower BMI levels and earlier in an individual's life in Asian than in Western populations. Moreover, diet-driven increases in global food demand and increases in population are leading to clearing of tropical forests, savannas and grasslands, which threatens species with extinction.

Because it directly links and negatively affects human and environmental health, the global dietary transition is one of the great challenges facing humanity. Meaningful solutions will not be easily achieved. Solutions will require analyses of the quantitative linkages between diets, the environment and human health, on which we focus here, and the efforts of nutritionists, agriculturists, public health professionals, educators, policy makers and food industries.

Here we compile and analyze global-level data to quantify relationships among diet, environmental sustainability and human health, evaluate potential future environmental impacts of the global dietary transition and explore some possible solutions to the diet-environment-health trilemma (Methods and Supplementary Information). To do so, we first expand on earlier food lifecycle analyses (LCAs) by searching for all published LCAs of GHG emissions of food crop, livestock, fishery and aquaculture production systems that delimited the full "cradle to farm gate" portion of the food/crop lifecycle. Next we use about 50 years of data for 100 of the world's more populous nations to analyze global dietary trends and their drivers, then use this information to forecast future diets should past trends continue. To quantify effects of alternative diets on mortality and on type II diabetes, cancer and chronic coronary heart disease, we compile and summarize results of studies encompassing ten million person-years of observations on diet and health. Finally, we combine these relationships with projected increases in global population to forecast global environmental implications of current dietary trajectories and to calculate the environmental benefits of diets associated with lower incidences of chronic non-communicable diseases.

(Source: Tilman & Clark, 2014. Nature)

Write the introduction of your own research paper.

Unit 10

Literature Review

10.1 Objectives

Know the relationship between introduction and literature review.
Know the purpose of different verb tenses in the literature review.
Know some reporting verbs and sentence templates.

10.2 Pre-Class Learning

Watch the MOOC/SPOC videos and do the online exercises. The contents in the textbook will help you understand the lessons better.

Source: https://www.icourse163.org/

Course name: "学术英语写作与演讲" (Academic Writing and Presentation in English)

Unit 3 Language

3.1 Verbs and tenses

In a research paper, the "Literature review" follows the introduction part. A separate literature review is common in most papers of social science studies that emphasize the background information, on the basis of which the researcher's own study is conducted. However, most scientific or engineering papers have only an introduction. This might be due to the fact that scientific or engineering papers emphasize researchers' own original work while papers for social science take previous research background as important foundations for the research. Generally speaking, if you want to have a detailed and thorough explanation of the background, you can choose to have a separate literature review, which, otherwise, can be included in the introduction.

Essentials of a literature review

A literature review can focus on:

—the definitions of **key terms or concepts** related to your topic;

—the prevailing **theories** that underlie the research questions;

—the description of the **studies** that support the current theories;

—the major **findings** in the area;

—the main **controversies** or **limitations** of the work in the area;

—the **rationale and purpose** of the proposed study.

If you compare the review focus with the three moves in an introduction, you can find that items 1–4 are all about the background, which is like a more detailed first move in an introduction. Item 5 is the second move-problem, and item 6 is the third move that indicates the writer's research purpose. Therefore, to some extent, a literature review is a long introduction. When writing your paper, you can choose to include the literature review in the introduction, or to separate them into two different sections. The following is the literature review of the paper entitled "Understanding the Use of Online Role-Play for Collaborative Argument Through Teacher Experiencing", you can compare it with the introduction of the same paper in Unit 9.

- **Example**

2 Literature Review

2.1 Online Role-play

The use of online role-play is based on the use of traditional face-to-face role-play, the advantages of which are combined with the potential of the online environment. The essential feature of online role-play is that the participants are able to assume a role in someone else's situation; they can do authentic tasks in an authentic context and carry out a lot of interactions such as collaboration, negotiation and debate in an online environment (Wills et al., 2009).

Explanation of the key term: "online role-play"

The use of online role-play involves collaborative learning to work together to achieve the goal of addressing and solving a problem (Alavi, 1994; Guo & Stevens, 2011). The idea of collaborative learning stems from Vygotsky's Social Learning Theory (Vygotsky, 1978)—that social interaction precedes development and that consciousness and cognition are the end product of socialization. It further assumes that knowledge can be

The prevailing theory of "collaborative learning" and "Vygotsky's Social Learning Theory"

created within a group where members actively interact by sharing experiences and taking on asymmetric roles (Mitnik et al., 2009).

Studies that support the current theories

Two typical examples of collaborative learning with the help of computers and the Internet are Computer-Supported Collaborative Learning and Collaborative Networked Learning. The former involves learners' use of technology to help support group interactions in a collaborative learning environment (Mitnik et al., 2009; Chen & Chiu, 2008). Learning in this situation is characterized by the sharing and construction of knowledge among participants who use technology to communicate; control and monitor interactions; regulate rules, tasks and roles; and mediate the acquisition of new knowledge (Mitnik et al., 2009; Stahl et al., 2006). The latter occurs through online discussions between self-directed co-learners and between learners and experts (Findley, 1988). With a common purpose, learners depend upon each other for the success of communication or finding solutions to problems. They actively communicate and interact with one another within a contextual framework facilitated by a group leader.

Researches on the use of online role-play for fostering learning have examined how participation in online role-play leads to development of certain skills and strategies. By exploring and evaluating both the content structure and behavioral patterns in learners' discussion processes, Hou (2012) found that the use of online role-play helped college students attain a deeper level of interaction and higher cognitive skills. Culley and Polyakova (2012) examined the effectiveness of synchronous role-play as a teaching strategy, finding that it enhanced students' collaborative skills and oral presentation proficiency; they highlighted the need to use real-world contexts to develop communication proficiency. These studies show that the practice of online role-play can improve

Major findings of the researches on the use of online role-play to foster learning: from the perspective of the development of skills and strategies

learners' cognitive and communicative skills, as well as their level of collaboration and interaction.

Other studies have examined issues of effective design of online role-play to foster learning. Bos and Shami (2006) researched how to adapt face-to-face role-playing situation to online environment and stated the design challenges of online role-play: sustaining engagement, promoting content-focused discussion and promoting reflection-on-action. Wishart et al. (2007) reported a study of a creative online role-play for school children and suggested recommendations for carrying out online role-play in schools, such as preparing teachers by giving step-by-step instructions, providing teachers with clear directions on how to induct their students, including more activities when students are waiting for replies of their messages, having students play a familiar role, enabling students to access previous as well as current messages, etc. Russell and Shepherd (2010) used examples of student's online role-play to develop a framework for evaluating how technologies could support role-based learning activities. The framework included two aspects: (1) learning, which involved authenticity, engagement with role, anonymity, synchronous and asynchronous communications, group and individual reflections, debriefing out of roles and resources; and (2) teaching, which contained staff and student accessibility, low set-up and running costs, activity tracking and structuring. These studies have set good examples to show how online role-play activities foster learning in terms of design challenges, implementation recommendations and technology support.

Findings from the perspective of the design of online role-play

2.2 Online role play for collaborative argument

Engaging in collaborative argument or "collaborative reasoning" (e.g. Jadallah, 2011) in online role-play requires participants to sort through, evaluate and

Introduction of the key term "collaborative argument" or "collab-

support or refute arguments to achieve some synthesis or solution (Nussbuam & Schraw (2007). Participants are operating a virtual rhetorical context based on interactions with others in ways that provide a sense of purpose and audience for their posts (Wills et al., 2009). They assume others' perspectives constituting alternative beliefs and attitudes, perspective-taking that is essential for engaging in collaborative argumentation in terms of recognizing alternative and competing arguments (Beach & Doerr-Stevens, 2009, 2011). And, through participation, they gain an understanding of the literacy practices involved in constructing a person or ethos, formulating claims with supporting evidence to convince audiences of the validity of those claims, challenging others' claims with counter arguments/evidence, and assessing and negotiating competing claims to achieve some consensus (Andriessen et al., 2003; Clark & Sampson, 2008).

orative reasoning" and related studies on online role-play for collaborative argument

A number of researches indicate the value of online role-play for fostering collaborative argumentation (Russell & Shepherd, 2010). In an online role-play environment, learners can engage themselves in collaborative arguments and negotiation through participation in online forums and debates (Andriessen, Baker & Suthers, 2003; Clark & Sampson, 2008). College students in a physical science course generated higher quality arguments as homework practice in an online asynchronous discussion than through using paper-pencil practice (Lin et al., 2012). Participants engaging in an asynchronous online role-play about Middle Eastern politics preferred the asynchronous option as providing them with time to engage in research, noting that participation in the role-play helped improve their ability to identify, evaluate and use information; to think creatively and solve problems efficiently, and to work collaboratively with others (Dracup, 2012). Beach & Doerr-Stevens (2011) examined high school students'

Findings of the researches on the value of online role-play for collaborative argumentation participation in an online role-play debate regarding the issue of their school's Internet policies on blocking access to websites. Analysis of the students' writing and interview data indicated that the students were actively engaged in generating effective arguments and demonstrates the ability to collaboratively formulate and share counterarguments.

Studies of online role-play have dealt with pros and cons of online argumentation compared with a face-to-face situation. Advantages for online role-play include assuming anonymous roles to freely voice opinions without concern for consequences, adopting and appreciating others' alternative perspectives, actively interacting with others over time and becoming engaged in the activity (Bell, 2001; Cornelius et al., 2011). Disadvantages include the fact that online role-play can be time consuming when participants are not serious about adopting roles or experience anxiety in assuming roles (Bell, 2001), as well as the propensity to adopt competitive stances in ways that foreclose the possibility of reaching consensus (Jamaludin et al., 2009). Engaging in collaborative argumentation in an online setting can also be challenging in terms of focusing the discussion, engaging in group decision-making, building trust to negotiating difference without nonverbal cues and attending to each other to build consensus (Bos & Shami, 2006).

Major findings of the studies on advantages and disadvantages of online argumentation compared with a face-to-face situation

2.3 Purpose of online role-play by teacher experiencing

However, none of the previous studies have investigated how teachers perceive online role-play for use in teaching collaborative argument, as well as how teachers may benefit from having to adopt students' roles to assess the effectiveness of an online role-play activity. Having teachers adopt the roles of being students affords them with new perspective on students' learning experience (Case et al., 2010), providing

Limitations of the work in the area and the rationale and purpose of the proposed study

them with insights that cannot be obtained simply by analyzing student learning (Sinclair, 2004). Mann (1987) even criticizes the separation of researchers and "subjects" in dominant modes of student learning research:

> Instead of rendering ourselves—as researchers and as teachers—other than and separate from the students with whom we are working, should we not reflect upon ourselves as former students and, most importantly, as past, current, and continuing learners, so that when we research into and teach students we are also researching into and teaching ourselves? (p. 182)

Adopting the positions of students, teachers may then experience some degree of empathy for their students through reflection on their own experiences as learners; they will try to avoid problems involved in the teaching process and regulate their teaching to meet students' needs. Therefore, in the present research, teachers conducted an online role-play activity by simulating a learning situation for the purpose of investigating how online role-play can be most effectively used in their future teaching practice. And, given that previous research has employed both synchronous (Culley & Polyakova, 2012; Cornelius et al., 2011) and asynchronous (Beach & Doerr-Stevens, 2011; Dracup, 2012; Lin et al., 2012) platforms, it would be useful to determine the participants' perceptions of the viability of these different platforms. The "participants" would also most likely understand the benefits and challenges of engaging in the online role-play to use it in their own classrooms through actual participation in an online role-play.

The research addressed the following questions:

1) What are teachers' understanding of using online role-plays for collaborative argument after their own experience as students?

Research questions raised on the basis of the literature review

2) What are teachers' perceptions of synchronous and asynchronous online role-plays for teaching collaborative argument?

3) What benefits and problems do teachers find out about using online role-play for collaborative argument and what are the suggested solutions to the problems?

(Source: Zhang et al., 2016. *Asia-Pacific Journal of Teacher Education*)

Tenses

Tense choice in reviewing previous research is subtle and somewhat flexible. You might see both present and past tenses in academic reading, and may feel confused about which tense to choose. Usually, tenses in the literature review depend on two main factors: the type of citation you are using and the status of the information you are providing. The following are some guidelines for the use of tenses in citations, but they are only guidelines rather than rules. Most literature reviews display a mixture of these three tenses.

- **Past tense**

Past tense is used when referring to a single study conducted in the past. It is more likely to be used for verbs related with methods, procedures, analyses and findings. Verbs commonly seen in the past tense are: *compared, examined, investigated, analyzed, found, revealed* and *studied*.

- Example

Hou (2012) *found* that the use of online role-play helped college students attain a deeper level of interaction and higher cognitive skills.

Culley and Polyakova (2012) *examined* the effectiveness of synchronous role-play as a teaching strategy.

- **Present perfect tense**

Present perfect tense refers to an area of inquiry. It is used to indicate that the research in the area is still continuing, or that the research has immediate relevance today.

- **Example**

    Researchers *have found* that peer cooperation has positive effects on writing confidence (Fox, 1980; Likkel, 2012).

    Fricke (1983) *has illustrated* that black liquor shows three rheological behaviors.

▪ Present tense

Present tense is used to suggest generally accepted knowledge of the field. Verbs related to arguments, claims, statements and suggestions often occur in the present tense. However, the past and present perfect are also possible verb forms in these situations.

- **Example**

    Beaugrande (1985) *argues* that text is a communicative event rather than a logical form.

    Smith (1995) *remarks*...

    Jones (2005) *suggests*...

    Morison (2000) *advocates*...

    Zhang (2007) *claims*...

    Burstein (2010) *maintains*...

Writers can have certain options in their choice of tenses in their literature reviews. If the writer refers to what a previous researcher did, the past tense is obligatory. However, for some verbs (e.g. *remark, suggest, claim, conclude*), the present tense can be used to refer to what the previous researchers think.

- **Example**

    Smith (2010) *concluded / has concluded / concludes* that project-based learning is very effective for engineering students to learn discipline knowledge.

The differences between the tenses are subtle. Often, shifting from the past to the present perfect and then to the present shows that the research reported is increasingly closer to writer's own opinion, or the writer's own research, or the current state of knowledge.

Unit 10 **Literature Review**

Reporting verbs

Good writers employ a variety of reporting verbs. A study by Hyland (1999) identified more than 400 different reporting verbs, nearly 50 percent of which, however, were used only once in his corpus of 80 research articles. A much smaller number of verbs tend to predominate. Table 10.1 lists the most frequently used reporting verbs from a variety of disciplines.

And furthermore, avoiding using the same word repeatedly can add variety to the paper. Synonymous verbs can usually be used to express a certain action or behavior. Here are groups of verbs that can be used alternatively in literature review:

declare, state, announce

say, remark, mention, comment, note, add

claim, maintain, assert, hold, insist, confirm, argue

express, put, suggest, propose, put forward, advance

conclude, summarize

think, consider, believe

You can also use COCA to find more synonyms of these verbs. But you cannot simply replace one with another. Be aware that they are used in the correct collocation.

Table 10.1 High Frequency Reporting Verbs for Scientific, Engineering and Social Studies

Discipline	Verbs and frequency					
	1	2	3	4	5	6
Biology	describe	find	report	show	suggest	observe
Physics	develop	report	study	find	expand	
Electrical engineering	propose	use	describe	show	publish	develop
Mechanical engineering	describe	show	report	discuss	give	develop
Medicine	show	report	demonstrate	observe	find	suggest
Marketing	suggest	argue	find	demonstrate	propose	show
Applied linguistics	suggest	argue	show	explain	find	point out
Psychology	find	show	suggest	report	demonstrate	focus

(Continued)

Discipline	Verbs and frequency					
Sociology	argue	suggest	describe	note	analyze	discuss
Education	find	suggest	note	report	demonstrate	provide
Philosophy	say	suggest	argue	claim	point out	think

(Source: Swales & Feak, 2004. Academic Writing for Graduate Students)

Sentence templates

Writers often employ a range of patterns in order to diversify the sentences in the literature review. Here are some typical sentence patterns:

- **Previous research area investigated**

    —To date, several studies have investigated...

    —A number of studies have begun to examine...

    —Researchers attempted to evaluate the impact of...

    —A great deal of previous research into X has focused on...

    —Several studies have used... to examine...

    —A number of authors have considered the effects of...

    —Numerous studies have attempted to explain...

- **Previous research established or proposed**

    —Previous research has established that...

    —Data from several studies suggest that...

    —It is now well established from a variety of studies that...

    —It has been argued that...

    —In previous studies on X, different variables have been found to be related to...

    —Many historians have argued that...

    —There is a consensus among scientists that...

    —To date / Thus far / Up to now, several studies / previous studies / a number of studies / have found/reported/shown/indicated/suggested that...

Book review

A book review is not part of a research paper. It is different from a literature review in that it is just a review of one single book while a literature review should be on the basis of many articles and books relating to a certain topic. Many researchers also like to write a book review of a recently published book they find interesting, valuable and worth recommending.

A book review is usually composed of three parts:

—a general introduction of the book, including the title, author(s)/editor(s), year of publication, publishing house, brief information about the topic and content, and the reason to recommend the book;

—a detailed summary of each chapter of the book. It is especially important to avoid repetition by using various reporting verbs and different sentence structures;

—a comment on the book focusing on its advantages and disadvantages. Tentative suggestions for improvement are given at the end of the comment.

- **Example**

    Review of The *Handbook of Automated Essay Evaluation: Current Applications and New Directions*

    Since Ellis Page (1966) published his landmark article, "The Imminence of Grading Essays by Computer", the issue of using computers to grade writing and provide feedback has been a great concern for researchers in language testing and writing instruction. Research has been done for the creation and development of systems for automated essay evaluation (AEE), or automated essay scoring (AES), which has been called the process of evaluation and scoring written prose via computer programs (Shermis & Burstein, 2003). *The Handbook of Automated Essay Evaluation* edited by Mark D. Shermis and Jill Burstein collects the most recent articles about research on AEE and provides comprehensive perspectives for addressing the following issues: AEE and writing instruction, applications of different AEE engines, validity and reliability of AEE, and discussions of aspects reflecting writing constructs in AEE. This handbook, is therefore beneficial for both researchers and writing instructors who are interested in investigating how AEE can be better applied in essay assessment and writing instruction. (A

general introduction of the book)

In the introductory chapter, Shermis, Burstein and Bursky firstly state the major concerns about AEE, namely that computers cannot evaluate essays as well as humans can. Thus they suggest a multidisciplinary approach that involves cognitive psychology and psychometric evaluations. After reviewing the early history of the application of AEE, they generalize the technology that facilities the use of AEE, such as word processing, the Internet and natural language processing (NLP), and briefly describe the evolution of commercial AEE. Finally, the authors present guidelines for how the following chapters are organized.

The next two chapters deal with AEE and the teaching of writing. Following a literature review of research on teaching and assessing writing, Elliot and Klobucar, in Chapter 2, examine models of writing constructs and report case studies conducted over a three-year period at a science and technology university. Based on previous research as well as on their own work, they conclude the chapter by pointing to directions for future developments in writing assessment.

Chapter 3 discusses AEE and writing instruction for non-native speakers. After a review of the context for assessing non-native writing and following the examination of the construct of writing intended for learners of different writing proficiencies, Weigle briefly discusses the two major functions of AEE—scoring and feedback—and gives suggestions on how to implement AEE effectively in different contexts, such as giving teachers training and support, helping students interpret feedback, and presenting the tools carefully. She states in the conclusion that failures in the implementation of educational technology do not result from problems of technology but rather from resistance from teachers and thus urges teachers to be part of the "steamroller" (p. 51) for the use of AEE.

Chapters 4 through 9 address features and functions of various AEE systems. Burstein, Tetreault and Madnani, in Chapter 4, examine how the application of e-rater fits into problem spaces in curriculum and assessment development. They begin with an introduction of features of e-rater and their relevance to writing construct. Then, they explain how NLP methods are employed to identify construct-relevant linguistic properties in text, which include the statistical and rule-based methods. Next, they describe e-rater features that use an NLP approach. They finally highlight the importance of relating e-rater development to language requirements specified in the Common Core State Standard Initiative in the United States.

Intelligent Essay Assessor (IEA) is introduced by Foltz, Streeter, Lochbaum and Landauer in Chapter 5. They describe the applications of IEA as an automatic way of assessing the content on the basis of Latent Semantic Analysis. The authors explain how IEA's scoring features are combined to score writing, and evaluate the performance of the IEA model by comparing how IEA's predicted scores match human scoring. They suggest the computation of IEA's reliability by measuring correlation, kappa, weighted kappa, and exact and adjacent agreement, and demonstrate through examples how IEA performs in evaluating the overall quality of an essay, the individual traits of writing, and the content features in short responses. They conclude that IEA provides a means to incorporate accurate scoring.

In Chapter 6, Schultz introduces the theoretical and conceptual bases for IntelliMetric modeling by examining its text features and key principles. He describes the specific process that IntelliMetric undergoes for scoring essays and displays an example of the application in scoring Chinese essays. He concludes that IntelliMetric is accurate in scoring but that the quality of the training set is of utmost importance.

In Chapter 7, Rich, Schneider and D'Brot start with a description of challenges related to a large-scale AEE implementation in West Virginia. They describe how American schools in West Virginia apply AEE technology in summative and formative assessment contexts and explain the engine on which both assessments are based. By analyzing the model of assessment that the West Virginia Education Standard Test is built upon and reporting three studies on the effect of AEE, all of which employ Writing RoadmapTM, they conclude that AEE technology could have a positive impact on student writing. They close the chapter by focusing on teacher professional development and future AEE application.

Chapter 8 presents a software tool that enables non-expert learners to use technology to assess texts related to their domains and tasks. Mayfield and Rose begin with an orientation to machine learning and continue with an explanation of models resulting from it. They then introduce the work-flow of LightSIDE and illustrate how it can be generalized to different tasks in order to help non-expert users achieve a balance between representation complexity and generality. Finally, they report three studies on essay assessment and the application of machine learning and conclude by discussing the advantages of machine learning technology, the most important of which is that it enables LightSIDE to adjust to new problems so that the users are not restricted by the basic representations available on the interface.

Brew and Leacock investigate the use of automated short answer scoring in Chapter 9. They introduce the e-rater engine by explaining how the items are developed, how the model is built, and how the scores are generated. This is followed by a description and explanation of the methods for measuring and assessing the effectiveness of automated scoring. They list some problems of using automated scoring for short answers and suggest solutions to the problems. In the conclusion, they show evidence that automated scoring can benefit short answers, but argue that it is essential that the programs offer useful and informative feedback rather than Just giving a single score.

The next five chapters are concerned with warrants and justifications of AEE. In Chapter 10, Williamson provides a framework for validity argumentation of AES. He introduces the validity theory and Toulmin's reasoning as basis for evaluating the strength of validity argument. He then elaborates the elements for argument to explain how Toulmin's model can be applied to human scoring of essays, which in turn provides a contrast for the use of this model for AES. He then considers the similarities and distinctions of human scoring and AES in construct, consistency, and interrelatedness. The chapter closes with implications of the use of AES and directions for improving its technology.

Chapter 11 is concerned with the development of a plan to support the use of AES. Attali starts with the analysis of the validity of features extracted from texts to measure the quality of an essay. Then he turns to the issue of how to combine features to determine the essay score. After that, he discusses the reliability of machine scores by examining the precision of machine scoring across prompts and the coefficients between human and machine scoring. He concludes with suggestions for combining human and machine scores and for how to measure the effects of using AES on student writing.

Chapter 12 is an overview of the methods used in scaling and norming for AES. Koskey and Shermis compare holistic and analytic rubrics and explain the scales for rating the quality of writing samples, and review the methods for forming scales in AEE, including the common standard-setting methods and differential item functioning methods. In the discussion, they raise concerns for validity issues and recommend future efforts to make meaningful scores, both in general and in AES in particular.

In Chapter 13, Bridgeman starts with a summary of the procedures for monitoring and evaluating the quality of human scoring. He explores factors that lead to problematic human scoring and ways to minimize their impact. He also discusses the criteria of the development and evaluation of machine scoring engines by focusing on how much AEE can imitate human scoring. He concludes that the relationship between human scoring and AES remains a key consideration in the future.

In Chapter 14, Lottridge, Schulz and Mitzel firstly review the literature of problems of human scoring for the purpose of presenting AES as an approach for monitoring human scoring. They then introduce an automated scoring engine named CRASE and report three studies on the identification of human rater bias, the establishment of a criterion for identifying it, and the prevention of the bias through the use of CRASE. They conclude that AES is a significant method for monitoring human rater performance.

Chapters 15 to 18 include a number of articles that analyze of relevant aspects that reflect writing constructs. Chapter 15 is concerned with grammatical error detection in AES and Gamon, Chodorow, Leacock and Tetreault explain the meaning of grammatical error by comparing error categories. Then, they contrast the grammar-based and statistically-based techniques in grammatical error detection. They also give an overview of evaluation issues that include metrics, data, and methods. They finally discuss the practice of four different AES engines (CRASE, CTB's AEE, PEG, and e-rater) and analyze how grammatical feedback affects student writing.

Chapter 16 begins with a discussion of factors that determine the coherence quality of texts. Burstein, Tetreault, Chodorow, Blanchard and Andreyev investigate how to characterize discourse coherence and how linguistic features can be modeled to build an essay evaluating system. In concluding, they emphasize the importance of including discourse coherence quality ratings in automated scoring and offering explicit feedback about discourse coherence quality in essay evaluation systems.

Another perspective for essay evaluation, sentiment analysis for evaluating argumentation, is addressed in Chapter 17. Burstein, Beigman-Klebranov, Madnani and Faulkner give an overview of the related literature on lexicon building. After describing the process of how to create a family of subjectivity lexicons, the authors develop and evaluate an automated sentiment analysis system for identifying the polarity of opinions and the intensity of polarity in students' essays. Their conclusion projects that the system will not only help identify sentiment and polarity in summarization tasks, but can also be applied to different essay modes such as product and movie reviews, and political and newspaper essays.

While most AES frameworks are modeled on human scoring, in Chapter 18 Deane explores a different approach by introducing a general cognitive framework. He gives an overview of a cognitively-based assessment framework and suggests several of its implications for AES, primarily in relation to the selection of features in AES applications and the creation of a criterion involving multiple sources of information. He concludes that the cognitive framework provides a possibility to cover a more comprehensive portion of the writing construct and a new method to support assessment and instruction through the use of AES engines.

Chapter 19 reports a study of the comparison of nine AEE engines. Shermis and Hamner evaluate the performance of these engines on the basis of a set of standard measures: distributional differences, agreement, and agreement delta. Their results show that the overall performance of AEE meets or exceeds that of human raters, but that there is some difference in the performance of each scoring engine. The authors conclude by advocating a link between public competitors and commercial vendors to provide the best product for essay assessment.

In the final chapter, Hakuta discusses the Common Core State Standards Initiative (CCSSI) and its linguistic challenges and opportunities. The author describes details of CCSSI and points out how it influences major shifts of English Language Arts, Math, and Science in the standards. The macro-level shifts inherent in CCSSI are shown in Understanding Language Initiative, which emphasizes text-based evidence for argumentation in English Language Arts, the language of reasoning for understanding mathematical practices, and the collaboration of content-area teachers to help students with complex subject-matter texts in science and technology. He concludes that CCSSI has generated new opportunities for scientists and language educators to collaborate, which is a running theme throughout the volume. (**A detailed summary of each chapter of the book**)

The Handbook of Automated Essay Evaluation gives a comprehensive illustration of major concerns in the field of AEE. It introduces the relevant theories, demonstrates the practice of AEE applications by both first and second language learners, explains the features and functions of various AEE systems, examines the writing constructs that underlie AEE systems, analyzes the reliability and validity of AEE engines, and predicts the direction for future development of AEE.

What is commendable in this book is that the editors help readers understand the issues better by co-referencing chapters for further exploration. Such an endeavor enables readers to have an overall grasp of the knowledge by relating across many different perspectives. One limitation of the book is that there is no clear division of thematic parts within the collection of articles. Classification into sections could help readers get a clearer picture of the overarching organization of the book. I, therefore, suggest that a future edition of the handbook that categorize the chapters into six parts: an introduction, AEE and the teaching of writing, AEE systems, AEE reliability and validity, aspects about writing constructs in AEE, and overall issues of AEE. Despite this limitation, it is undeniable that the book is of great benefit to those interested in the topic and will serve as a powerful driving force in the development of AEE in the future. (**A comment on the book about its advantages and disadvantages**)

(Source: Zhang, 2014. Language Learning & Technology)

10.3 In-Class Activities

Activity 1

Tick (√) the items applicable to writing a literature review.

____	1. The preparation of a literature review is a three-step process: finding the relevant literature, reading, and then writing up the review.
____	2. Your literature review should discuss problems and/or controversies within your field.
____	3. Your literature review needs to explain clearly which potential areas for inclusion have not been covered in the review and why they have been omitted.
____	4. Your literature review should focus on very recent publications because they are likely the most relevant.
____	5. Your literature review should be as long as possible in order to persuade your reader that you have read very widely.
____	6. Your literature review should help reveal gaps in the existing body of research.
____	7. In literature review you should critically evaluate each piece of the work you discuss.
____	8. An overall chronological ordering of the literature is a good approach.
____	9. Your literature review can safely ignore work not in your immediate discipline.
____	10. Literature review can help you discover conceptual traditions and frameworks that have been used to examine problems as well as help you show how your work might contribute to a cumulative scholarly or research process.

Unit 10 **Literature Review**

Steps for organizing the activity:

1. Do the activity in groups of five, each student having two statements.

2. Read the two statements and judge whether they are applicable to the writing of a literature review.

3. Explain to the whole group your judgement.

4. Find out how many of them are applicable to writing the literature review and check them.

5. Summarize the answers in class, and praise the groups of students who came up with the correct answers.

Activity 2

Compare 1) the introduction (Example 4 in Unit 9), 2) the literature review (the example in this unit), and 3) the long introduction of the paper in Appendix 1, and find out the similarities and differences.

Steps for organizing the activity:

1. Review three moves of an introduction.

2. Scan the three examples to try to locate the three moves in each of them.

3. Find out how ideas are developed to generate the research questions in the literature review.

4. Compare the similarities and differences of the introduction and the literature review of the same paper.

5. Compare the similarities and differences of the literature review and the long introduction.

6. Summarize the answers from the comparison.

10.4 After-Class Tasks

Task 1

Go over the information in the table you have previously finished in Task 3 in 3.4 of Unit 3. Make additions or revisions according to your continuous reading, and form a clear picture about the logical relationship of the literature.

No.	Author(s)	Year	Perspectives	Major findings
1				
2				
3				
4				
5				
6				

Unit 10 **Literature Review**

(Continued)

No.	Author(s)	Year	Perspectives	Major findings
7				
8				
9				
10				

Task 2

Go over the notes you have taken down for all the research papers you have read and decide on the contents you are going to involve in your writing of the literature review.

Task 3

Write a literature review for your research.

Unit 11

Methods

11.1 Objectives

Know what quantitative and qualitative methods are.

Learn how to write the methods by analyzing examples.

Be able to write the methods of a research paper.

11.2 Pre-Class Learning

Watch the MOOC/SPOC videos and do the online exercises. The contents in the textbook will help you understand the lessons better.

Source: https://www.icourse163.org/

Course name: "学术英语写作与演讲" (Academic Writing and Presentation in English)

Unit 8 Method and Result

8.1 Method: quantitative and qualitative

If your writing is not just a review of literature but involves an empirical study, such as an experiment or investigation, you have to describe the "Methods", by which you conducted your research. The methods section provides information to justify that the research is scientifically designed to obtain reliable results and draw a reasonable conclusion. Therefore, it should be presented in a clear and logical way to avoid confusion and ambiguity, and it must include sufficient information so that the experiment can be duplicated to verify that the results are reproducible. Sometimes, researchers choose to write the methods section first because it is comparatively easier for them to describe what they have done, especially when the research process is still clear in their mind.

Quantitative and qualitative methods

Research methods are designed for the purpose of answering the research questions. If the question requires the experimental method, which generates the data in the form of numbers, then a quantitative method is employed. When the research question requires non-numerical explanation, in other words, the data are in the form of words, a qualitative research method is used. On many occasions, both the methods are applied to give a thorough investigation of the research question.

Instruments for quantitative method vary from tests, questionnaire, lab experiments to a lot of others that will generate numerical data. Instruments for qualitative methods include interviews, observations, and written texts, to name only a few. Let's take two commonly used instruments: questionnaire and interview for examples to illustrate instruments for quantitative and qualitative studies.

- **Questionnaire**

If you intend to collect information from a large number of people, a questionnaire may be the best instrument. It includes quantitative data obtained by using five-point Likert scale (most agree–5, agree–4, don't know–3, disagree–2, most disagree–1) and qualitative data represented by texts to answer the open-ended questions.

If there is a well-accepted questionnaire, whose reliability has been testified, you can directly apply the questionnaire or make some modifications to serve your research purpose. Of course, you need to provide the source of the questionnaire. Otherwise, you have to design your own questionnaire. The following are some steps to follow to design a questionnaire:

—Conceptualize the aims of your study by extensive literature review and form a clear framework for the questionnaire you are going to design.

—Clarify the concepts and classifications in the questionnaire according to the framework.

—Intensify the items in each of the categories in the questionnaire.

—If necessary, test internal consistency reliability (Cronbach's α) of the items that describe similar features.

A questionnaire usually involves the following parts (See Appendix 7):

1) A title to describe what this questionnaire is about

Any questionnaire has a title for the subjects to know immediately what the questionnaire is about.

2) A beginning statement to describe the purpose of the questionnaire

A statement at the beginning of the questionnaire enables the subject to understand why the questionnaire is taken. It intends to relieve the subjects' pressure and encourage the subjects to express their true opinions by stating, for example, that the questionnaire is anonymous and the investigation is for research only.

3) Choices or blanks to get some personal information of the subjects

Personal information should be collected for two purposes. One is to demonstrate the features of the subjects and show that the subject is representative of a certain population. And the other is to divide the subjects into different groups for the researcher to do comparative study in order to know whether there are differences in the opinions between, say, male and female subjects, high proficiency and low proficiency subjects, local and international subjects, etc.

4) The main body of the questionnaire that demonstrates the items related to your purpose of investigation and options for subjects to choose from

This is the major part of the questionnaire that involves all the items you want to investigate. For example, you are going to do research on college English teaching in the international context. After reading source materials extensively, you find that most research papers about the topic deal with such aspects as the teaching objectives, teaching materials and contents, teaching methods, evaluation of teaching outcome, and technology in teaching. Each of these aspects is specified to form some statements for your subjects to make their choices.

5) One or a couple of open-ended questions for the subjects to fill in with words (optional)

If you have more to ask but find it hard to express by providing choices, you can put one or two open-ended questions at the end of the questionnaire. But don't list too many questions because people usually have no patience in answering many. If you really want to ask more, an interview will be a better solution.

Even though you write an article in English, your questionnaire can be worded in the language familiar to your subjects so that they can understand the contents better. Appendix 7 is a bilingual version of a questionnaire investigating students' opinions on college English teaching in the international context.

- **Interview**

One of the most widely used methods for gathering qualitative information is interview. An interview is a guided conversation between a researcher (interviewer) and the person from whom you wish to get information (interviewee). An interview usually follows a *semi-structured* format, which means you can develop a guide for what you plan to cover in the conversation, usually in the form of questions. However, you are also free to follow different paths of conversation over the course of the interview. In other words, you may prompt the informant to expand on certain points. Therefore, interview is a good tool for gaining detailed information when the research question is open-ended for a range of possible answers. An interview is time-consuming, and therefore not suitable for gaining information from a large number of people. You can select a limited number of subjects from the participants in the quantitative study. By conducting an interview, you can gain a deeper understanding of the complicated issues in the questionnaire or to get further information from a different perspective to explain the research question.

You can record and transcribe your interview content and quote some of them directly by using the quotation marks, or indirectly by summarizing the content. Direct quotation has the advantage of authenticity. In other words, readers can see what the interviewee has actually said. But you have to choose some representative expressions rather than writing everything down. Summarizing can help get the overall idea of the interview in a succinct way but it may not be really convincing. Therefore, qualitative research by means of interview requires sufficient quotes from interviews in addition to the authors' narrative explanations.

Elements involved

The methods section of a research paper describes how the research was conducted to answer the research questions or hypotheses. This section should be so structured as to be able to describe the participants selected or the materials used in the research, explain how the instruments were prepared or how measurements were made, and state how the data were collected and analyzed. Therefore, the methods section usually includes the following parts:

- **Study design**

The methods section typically begins with a general paragraph describing the study design and the main methodological characteristics of the study, establishing the setting for the description of participant selection and data collection. It is also acceptable that some studies do not provide the general study design but directly start with the introduction of participants or materials before other parts of the methods section, detailing the design of the study in these parts.

- **Participants/materials**

Social science studies involve human participants or subjects while most engineering or scientific studies describe materials used in the study. Participants or subjects are the sample population, the description of which includes age, gender, and other information you intend to obtain about the subjects.[1] The following are details concerning information of participants:

—the number of participants;

—the demographic characteristics, for example: gender; age; grade or major if college students are involved;

—the recruitment information such as how they are selected, and how they are assigned to groups;

—selection criteria, for example, if some participants are excluded, explain why and describe the criteria for inclusion in the study and then report the final sample size.

- **Instruments/measures**

Instruments are anything you used to get the quantitative or qualitative data in your research. Experiments, tests, questionnaires, interviews, observations and

---

[1] When working with human or animal subjects, there must be ethical considerations. Without approval from a certain organization, the research project cannot be conducted, nor can the research paper be published in a reputable, peer-reviewed science journal. For example, in the U.S., one has to get the IRB (Institutional Review Board) approval before a research is conducted.

documentary analysis are all kinds of instruments. Details have been illustrated in the previous section about instruments of questionnaire and interview for both quantitative and qualitative studies.

▪ Procedure of data collection and analysis

The next step in the methods section is to describe the data collection procedure, which is the sequence of manipulations and measurement that make up the research. Its description should follow the exact sequence of how the procedure was executed, which involves the description of basic conditions and associated measurements and the sequence of manipulations. Procedure of data analysis includes descriptive statistics and methods for statistical inference. It is closely related to the aims of the research and it describes how the data will be presented in the results section. Procedure of data analysis in the method part is different from analysis of results in the discussion part. The former is just a brief description of the procedure of how the data will be analyzed to derive the research findings while the latter is a detailed explanation of why such findings occur and how they are compared with other studies.

- Example 1

Research design

The experimental design adopted for Stage 1 involved the students in the control group learning Mandarin in a conventional classroom, while those in the experimental group learned in SL. Both groups were taught by the same instructor, learned identical material, and performed the same activities; the only difference between them was their learning environment. All of the teaching processes in both groups were recorded and analyzed to allow comparison of the differences in classroom talk during the lessons. Besides, the participating teacher was asked to write down her reflection on her teaching after each class.

Participants

The participants in Stage 1 were 20 overseas students of Chinese (mean age, 20.1 years; 13 males and 7 females), comprising 12 from Indonesia, 2 from Japan, and 6 from Vietnam. These students voluntarily enrolled in the study and were assigned to one of two groups via a random number generator: control (odd numbers) or experimental (even numbers). Each group was comprised of 10 overseas students of Chinese: six from Indonesia, one from Japan, and three from Vietnam. Table 1 lists the detailed demographics data of the participant in Stage 1.

Table 1　Participants' Demographics in Stage 1

	Experimental group (n=10)	Control group (n=10)
Age	19.1	20.8
Gender		
Male	7	6
Female	3	4
Nationality		
Indonesia	6	6
Japan	1	1
Vietnam	3	3

Instruments

In-Class Interaction Analysis Scheme

The scheme used to analyze in-class interactions was a revised form of Moskowitz's FLint System (Moskowitz, 1971), as shown in Appendix A. In the revised scheme, as in the original, there are two categories of classroom talking: teacher and student. New dialog types, however, were added to the original subcategories to incorporate the actual conversation transcripts obtained from the recorded videos.

Teaching Plans and Environments

Two teaching units were designed for Stage 1, both of which involved task-based learning. The first focused on teaching overseas Chinese students how to order meals at a restaurant, while the aim of the second was to encourage students to choose a movie that all of the group members would like to go see together. Both teaching units were taught following an identical procedure, (described in the Procedure section). In addition, the teaching environments included conventional classroom and SL scenes: in the former, practical teaching aids were used to help students understand the authentic contexts in which the conversations were happening, while in the latter, virtual scenes were created to help students to immerse themselves in an authentic context.

Unit 11 Methods

Data collection and analysis

Before the treatment (i.e., teaching phase), the experimental group received training on operating SL for two hours, such as avatar moving (including walking, running, and flying), moving objects, and wearing and removing objects. After completion of the training, the two groups worked on two units of materials for two weeks: one unit per week for one hour each. To avoid disturbing the students' regular classes, the pilot Mandarin language classes were arranged during students' availability.

Each learning unit included two parts: basic skill training and task execution. For the basic skill training, new Mandarin words and sentence patterns were introduced to the students, who were then assigned missions to execute as individuals or as a group. During the task execution, the teacher played the role of a learning supporter to provide students with real-time assistance. For example, in unit one the students first learned the dishes and food items served in a restaurant, including appetizer, main dish, and dessert. They then worked in groups, first in small groups of three or four to discuss what combinations their restaurant should serve. They then role-played as customers and restaurant owners, in turn, to practice ordering meals and providing services at a restaurant.

During the treatment, all of the teaching processes and classroom talking were recorded and analyzed. The learning processes in SL were recorded via a free screen-recording software program (Fraps). In contrast, the learning processes in the conventional classroom were recorded via two digital video cameras. All of the recorded videos were then transcribed and analyzed by two decoders who focused both on the teacher and on the student speech in class, following the in-class interaction analysis scheme.

(Source: Lan, 2014. *Language Learning & Technology*)

- **Example 2**

Participants

The participants were three elementary school teachers, three middle school teachers and four college or university teachers, all of whom took a digital education methods course for Master's program in a large Midwestern American university. They met once a week in class for attending lectures on the introduction of various digital tools. The course lasted for 15 weeks, during which they also worked individually or collaboratively online after class to explore the usage of these tools. Using online role-play for collaborative argument was a 3-week course activity including three stages: preparation, implementation and reflection. The researcher sat in the class and participated in the activity.

Instruments

This study employed case study methodology, which included a quantitative and qualitative analysis of data generated from the online role-play activity. The participants' responses to the activity were evaluated by a questionnaire using closed questions on a five-point Likert scale. The questionnaire was designed to determine participants' perceptions of the effectiveness of the online role-play and to compare asynchronous and synchronous online role-play activities. Collaborative argument contents in the form of the asynchronous forum, collaborative retrospective comments in the form of the synchronous chat, individual retrospective comments in the participants' blogs and answers to questions concerning online role-play activity from interviews were collected and analyzed.

Procedure of data collection

Preparation

Before the activity, all participants learned about online role-play through the class website created by the course instructor and a PowerPoint file of the course instructor's past experience of using online role-play for collaborative argument. They were given a link to the website for creating topics and ideas of debate, and some illustrative examples of the use of online role-play activities in various schools and universities. Requirements of the role-play activity were specified so that the participants understood the expectations for participating in the role-play.

After the participants acquired an understanding of online role-play, the topic generation process started, with reference to some examples of topic generation on the website (http://www.createdebate.com/browse/debates). Given participants interest in the issue of public versus private/charter schools, the topic chosen by the participants was "Public Schools Are Failing American Students and Therefore Should Be Dismantled," a topic about which they had prior knowledge and opinions.

Then, participants assuming different roles were divided into positions of pros and cons so that the role-play could be conducted in the form of a debate. Some adopted pro roles of local business owner, concerned conservative parent, home school founder, city council member and conservative pundit, while others took on the con roles of concerned parent, public school student, taxpayers, principal and teacher in high-poverty school. Participants adopting the same position could collaboratively work together to formulate shared arguments to achieve their goals. The course instructor participated in the activity by assuming a role or stepping out of the role to send online messages, monitoring and guiding the process.

Implementation

After the preparation stage that lasted for one week, participants employed online searches to acquire information or statistics supporting their pro or con stances. The course instructor listed some questions for participants to elicit ideas, for example:

—What does it mean when people say U.S. students are "competitive" or "not competitive" globally? Is this some sort of code for something else?

—Does school choice enhance student experiences or get in the way of delivering effective and equal education for all?

—Are standardized tests an effective evaluative tool?

—How do we realistically address the achievement gap?

Three days later, an asynchronous debate started online, with each participant being required to upload at least three postings and three replies. The asynchronous debate lasted for 7 days until all participants met online and embarked on a collaborative synchronous argument using chat room box. The course instructor participated in both the asynchronous and synchronous arguments, providing scaffolding and guidance for the implementation of the activity.

Reflection

Immediately after the asynchronous online role-play activity the group began a one-hour synchronous chat, during which the participants exchanged opinions and commented on their experience in the activity. In addition to the group reflections in the chat room, they were required to reflect in their blogs in response to questions raised by the course instructor:

—Were there differences between your personal beliefs and those of your role?

—Did your own personal beliefs on this issue change at all due to the role-play?

—How might you use an online role-play in your teaching?

When the participants met in class again, they were required to complete a questionnaire that determined their understanding of the effectiveness of using online role-play for collaborative argument, and their perceptions of synchronous versus asynchronous online role-play platforms. Participants were also interviewed, with the following questions:

—How is asynchronous role-play compared with synchronous role-play?

—What do you think of the course instructor's role in the activity?

The researchers downloaded and analyzed individual retrospective comments in participants' blogs. They also recorded the interviews, transcribing and analyzing answers generated from the questions.

Data analysis

Mean score and standard deviation of each item in the questionnaire were calculated as to participants' perceptions of online role-play. Statistical comparisons of the mean scores for items concerning synchronous and asynchronous online role-plays were not conducted given the small number of participants related to the case study. Based on the mean score of items describing participants' perceptions about details of online role-play activity, the researchers investigated what participants' general idea about online role-play would be and how they perceived synchronous and asynchronous online role-plays. The researchers categorized answers to the questions in blogs and interviews so as to find detailed information to illustrate participants' understanding about the activity. And based on the data collected from the collaborative retrospective comments through synchronous chat, the researchers categorized the types of problems occurring in synchronous online role-play, analyzed these problems and suggested some solutions.

(Source: Zhang et al., 2016. Asia-Pacific Journal of Teacher Education)

Unit 11 Methods

Sentence templates

Here are some typical sentence patterns for methods part:

- **Characteristics of the participants**

    —The participants were divided into two groups according to...

    —A random sample of... subjects was recruited from...

    —The sample was representative with respect to gender and...

    —Of all the... students, ... were female and... male.

    —The participants were divided into two groups based on their performance on...

    —Two groups of subjects were interviewed, namely X and Y. The first group were...

    —The initial sample consisted of... students, ... of whom belonged to...

- **Procedure of data collection**

    —To begin this process, ...

    —The first step in this process was to...

    —Prior to data collection, the participants received an explanation of the project.

    —When inviting the participants, the purpose of the research was clearly explained.

    —After training, the participants were told that...

    —On completion of X, the process of parameter estimation was carried out.

    —Once the samples were extracted, it was...

    —Following analysis of X, it was necessary to...

    —The subjects were then shown... and were asked to...

    —Finally, questions were asked as to the role of...

    —The final stage of the study comprised a semi-structured interview with participants who...

- **Procedure of data analysis**

  —Changes in X and Y were compared using...
  —Regression analysis was used to predict the...
  —The correlation between X and Y was tested using...
  —T-tests were used to analyze the relationship between...
  —In order to assess Z, repeated-measures ANOVAs were used.

11.3 In-Class Activities

Activity 1

Study the two examples in this unit and find out the different parts involved in the method. Try to understand how the research is conducted.

> *Steps for organizing the activity:*
>
> 1. Scan the two examples of method part in this unit. Carry out the activity in pairs, each student working on one of the examples.
> 2. Find out the different sections of the method part in the examples.
> 3. Go over the details in each section.
> 4. Underline the words to show the procedure of doing the research.
> 5. Draw a flow chart to show the procedure of the study.
> 6. Share the information with each other through discussion.
> 7. Summarize the major points in the method part of a research paper.

Unit 11 **Methods**

Activity 2

The following flowchart illustrates the production of colored plastic paper clips in a small factory. Write a report describing the production process.

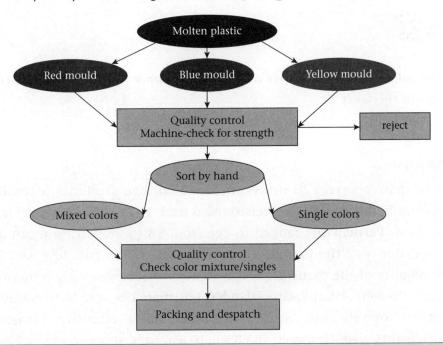

Steps for organizing the activity:

1. Study and understand the flowchart.
2. Give a general account of what it is about.
3. Give detailed description of the steps.
4. Share your description of the figure with your group members.
5. Give an oral report in class.

11.4 After-Class Tasks

Task 1

Read the following method part of a research paper and compare it with the examples in this unit.

Methods

Participants

Participants were 120 undergraduate college students attending a medium-sized Southeastern university who were given course credit for their participation. Participants ranged in age from 18 to 26, with a mean age of 18.94. A majority of the participants were female (70%) and 30% were male. Also, a majority of the participants was Caucasian (85.8%), 9.2% were African-American, 1% were Asian/Pacific Islander, less than 1% were Native-American, less than 1% were Hispanic, and 2.5% reported "other" ethnicity. A majority of the participants were freshmen (85.8%), 10.8% were sophomores, 1.7% were juniors, and 1.7% were seniors. The average GPA reported was 3.16 with a range of 2.30. A majority of the participants were single (92.5%), 3.3% were married, 2.5% were divorced, 1.7% were engaged.

Measures

A measure of fearful animal attitudes was obtained using Aspelmeier's (2002) Radford Avoidant Beast Interaction Test (RABIT) which assesses the degree of participant's negative attitudes regarding small fury animals and their perceived likelihood of avoiding interactions with small fury animals. Participants rated 12 items on a seven point numerical rating scale as to how descriptive they were of them (1 = very undescriptive of me, 7 = very descriptive of me). For items one through six, ratings were scored and summed such that a higher score indicated more negative attitudes toward small fury animals (NATSFA), with M = 4.55, SD = 2.12, and range = 6.99. Cronbach's Alpha (an estimate of internal consistency) was .89. Examples of the NATSFA scale items are: 1) "The Easter Bunny makes me sweat" and 2) "I often feel that vicious rabbits are lurking in the shadows." For items 7 through 12, ratings were scored and summed such that a higher score indicated a greater perceived likelihood that one would avoid interactions with small fury animals (AISFA), with M = 3.89, SD = 2.57, and range = 6.85. Cronbachs Alpha was .88. Examples of the AISFA scale items are: 1) "I would probably never go to a park that did not implement squirrel control techniques" and 2) "I would never wear a baby seal fur coat for fear of being attacked by it."

Procedures

Participants initially agreed to spend two consecutive nights in the Radford Animal Avoidance Research-Center (RAAR), After receiving informed consent, a catheter was surgically inserted into the participant's gallbladder. Over the first night of testing, hepatic secretions were measured. The average rate of bile production was recorded in milliliters per hour, M = 3.2, SD = 1.8, range = 13.5. After the first night, the catheter was removed and participants were allowed to continue with their daily routine until 9:30 pm at which time they returned to the lab for further testing. During the second night of testing, pancreatic secretions were measured. Participants' blood sugar levels were measured every hour, in order to establish each individual's rate of insulin production measured in micrograms per hour, M = 12.5, SD = 7.2, range = 50. After the second night of testing, participants were given both the RABIT and the Pit Sweat measures of small fury animal phobia. After completing the measures participants were thanked for their participation and asked if they had any questions or concerns. It should be noted that during the second night of testing, it was discovered that several participants (33) were not secreting insulin do to diabetes. It was decided not to exclude these participants in that it would be useful to compare these participants with non-diabetic participants with respect to small fury animal phobia.

(Source: http://writing2.richmond.edu/writing/wweb/psychology/proposalmethods.pdf)

Write the method section for your research paper.

Unit 12

Results

12.1 Objectives

Learn how to demonstrate your results.

Learn how to present and describe tables and figures.

Be able to write the results of a research paper.

12.2 Pre-Class Learning

Watch the MOOC/SPOC videos and do the online exercises. The contents in the textbook will help you understand the lessons better.

Source: https://www.icourse163.org/

Course name: "学术英语写作与演讲" (Academic Writing and Presentation in English)

Unit 8 Method and Result

8.2 Tables and figures

8.3 Analysis of examples

The "Results" of a research paper is to present the major findings of your research. The results should be presented in an orderly sequence of the research questions. Tables and figures are essential means for displaying the results. Clear and brief descriptions of the corresponding tables and figures are also necessary in this section.

Demonstration of results

In order for the research paper to be systematic, the results section can be organized in relation to the research question(s) and the research methods. For example:

- **There is only one research question**

What are learners' perceptions of the effectiveness of blended learning?

The instruments in the methods are:

—questionnaire;

—interview.

The results can be presented with subtitles to show the two instruments:

—quantitative results from the questionnaire;

—qualitative results from the interview.

- **There are more than one research questions**

    —What is the model of online blended learning for academic English course?

    —What are learners' perceptions of the effectiveness of the model?

    The instruments in the methods are:

    —case study (for the first research question);

    —questionnaire, interview, case study of students' work (for the second research question).

The results section can include two parts, with subtitles showing the relationship to the research questions and the methods. For example:

—design of the model (relating to the first research question), such as tables, figures and text descriptions;

—effectiveness of the model (relating to the second research question):

   a. questionnaire

      tables, figures and descriptions

   b. interview

      quotations from the interview

   c. case study

      analysis of samples taken from students' work

In general, the content of your results should include the following elements:

—the context for understanding the results by restating the research questions;

—major findings in the logical sequence of the methods section;

—non-textual elements, such as figures, tables, etc;

—a systematic description of the results, highlighting points relevant to the research questions.

Which results to present depends on the research question(s). Therefore, the results section does not need to include every result you get from research. If some of your results fail to support your hypothesis, do not ignore them. Report them in the results section and state in your discussion section why the negative result emerges from your study. As a matter of fact, the negative result offers the possibility to write a more engaging discussion section.

Description of tables and figures

Tables and figures help to summarize a large amount of data that is essential for the reader to know but too difficult to include in the narrative format. Both tables and figures can help the reader visualize the important results more easily. Tables present numbers or text in columns, with each column under a label. Figures are visual presentations of results, including graphs, diagrams, photos, drawings, schematics, maps, etc. The word "Figure" can be abbreviated as "Fig." while "Table" is never abbreviated. Each table or figure must have a title and be numbered consecutively, for example, Table 1, Table 2, Table 3..., or Figure 1, Figure 2, Figure 3..., or Fig. 1, Fig. 2, Fig. 3...

Every figure or table in the paper must be referred to in the text, by either directly stating it as part of the sentence or putting it in the brackets. For example:

—The population consuming dairy products in the year 2014 is much larger than that in 1990, as can been seen in Figure 2.

—Students have a high preference for the use of different types of communication strategies in their daily communication (See Table 5).

When you interpret the table or figure, you have to give a general statement to indicate what the table or figure is about. For example:

—Figure 4 illustrates the difference between A and B.

When you describe the details of the table or figure, you don't usually describe everything in it. The basic rule is to choose the most important information, such as:

—information relating to your research questions;

—information showing significance (e.g. $p<0.05$);

—information with maximum or minimum score;

—information showing turning points; and

—information demonstrating similarities and differences.

Here are two examples to show how a table or figure is described.

- **Example 1**

    Table 1   Means of PC Virus Infection in U.S. Businesses

Source	Percentage
Disks from home	43%
Electronic bulletin board	7%
Sales demonstration disk	6%
Repair or service disk	6%
Company, client, or consultant disk	4%
Shrink-wrapped application	3%
Other download	2%
Disk from school	1%
Local area network supervisor disk	1%
Purposely planted	1%
Came with PC	1%
Undetermined	29%

    Source: Academic Writing for Graduate Students (Swales & Feak, 1994)

Table 1 shows the most common modes of infection for U.S. businesses. As can be seen, in the majority of cases, the source of the virus infection can be detected, with disks being brought to the workplace from home being by far the most significant (43%). However, it is alarming to note that the source of nearly 30% of viruses cannot be determined. While it may be possible to eliminate home-to-workplace infection by requiring computer users to run antiviral software on diskettes brought from home, businesses are still vulnerable to major data loss, especially from unidentifiable sources of infection.

- **Example 2**

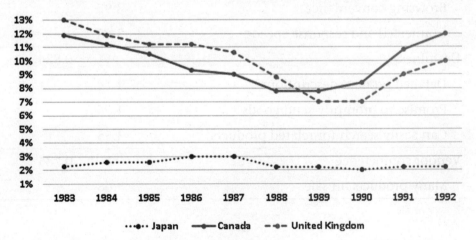

Figure 2   Unemployment Rates of Three Countries from 1983 to 1992

Figure 2 shows/exhibits/demonstrates/illustrates the unemployment rates of United Kingdom, Canada and Japan from 1983 to 1992. As can be seen in the figure, UK and Canada share the tendency of a V-shaped decrease and increase in the unemployment rate ranging from 7% to 13%, with the turning point in the year of 1989. On the other hand, Japan seemed to be more stable in the unemployment rate, with a marginal fluctuation within 2 to 3 percent. In short, Japan enjoyed a much lower unemployment rate than the other two countries by at least 4 percent. This might result from the economic policy adopted in Japan.

The following is a complete results section from a research paper, with a table, a figure and the text to describe them.

- **Example**

   Results

   Regarding the reliability, the survey had strong internal consistency with all multiple-item constructs achieving Cronbach's α (which is a measure of internal consistency) of 0.705 or higher (See Table 1) in SPSS14.0, so they were deemed acceptable. The results indicate that all the constructs are valid and reliable.

Table 1　List of Construct Indicators and Reliability

Construct	**Mean**	**Cronbach's α**
Perceived ease of use		0.849
Aesthetic feeling of webpages	3.71	
Browsing convenience	3.97	
Connected and response speeds	3.65	
Usefulness		0.834
Detailed product descriptions	4.19	
Promise to promptly send goods	4.06	
Can easily search for related products	3.55	
Vendor competence		0.786
Many products on sale	3.68	

(Continued)

Construct	Mean	Cronbach's a
High scores on C2C platform	4.10	
Good comments on previous transactions	4.08	
Introductions and recommendations by third parties		0.705
Recommendations of friends	3.77	
Links from the C2C portal	3.57	
Number of successful transactions	3.24	
Vendor's attitudes as perceived by consumers		0.901
Patiently answering buyers' questions	3.99	
Promised good after-sales service	4.05	
Cordiality with buyers	4.18	
Consumer purchase intention		0.915
Would like to purchase something in the C2C	2.78	
Expect to purchase in the C2C within six months	2.76	

Figure 2 presents the significant structural relationships among the research variables and the standardized path coefficients. Most of the hypotheses were strongly supported except for H3. For H1, the result indicated that perceived ease of use has a significant effect on the perceived usefulness ($\beta=0.95$, $p<0.01$), and thus, the perceived ease of use is an important determinant of perceived usefulness. The data also shows that perceived usefulness has a significant direct influence on the behavioral intention to purchase (H2: $\beta=0.46$, $p<0.01$). The vendor competence was found to be insignificant (H3). This implies that compatibility has an indirect effect both on the behavioral intention to use through the perceived usefulness and on the actual use through the behavioral intention to use. The results further confirm that the recommendation of a third party positively and directly influences the intention to purchase (H4: $\beta=0.18$, $p<0.01$). For H5, the vendor's attitude has a significant positive effect on the behavioral intention to purchase in C2C ($\beta=0.31$, $p<0.05$).

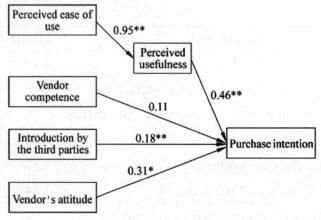

Figure 2　Empirical Results (*, p<0.05; **, p<0.01)

(Source: He et al., 2008. Tsinghua Science and Technology)

Sentence templates

Here are typical sentence patterns for reporting the research findings:

- **Referring back to the research aims or procedures**

—The first question aimed to...

—The next question asked the informants...

—Items on the questionnaire measured the extent to which...

—To distinguish between these two possibilities, ...

—The first set of analyses examined the impact of...

- **Referring to data in a table or chart**

—Table 1 / Figure 1 shows/compares/presents/provides/illustrates an overview of... / some of the main characteristics of...

—As can be seen from Figure 1, ...

—As (is) shown in Figure 1, ...

—From Table 1, we can see that...

—It can be seen in Table 1 that...

—The results obtained from the analysis of X are shown in Table 1.

Unit 12 **Results**

- **Surveys and interviews: Reporting participants' views**

    —All the participants demonstrated...

    —Some felt/argued that..., while others considered that...

    —This view was echoed by another subject who...

    —Whilst a minority mentioned that..., all agreed that...

    —Only a small number of respondents indicated that...

    —A small number of those interviewed suggested that....

    —The majority of participants agreed with the statement that...

    —When asked about X, the participants were unanimous in the view that...

- **Quoting from the interview data**

    —As one interviewee said/commented/ put it: "..."

    —For example, one interviewee reported: "..." Another interviewee said: "..."

    —Other responses to this question included: "..."

    —One individual stated that "..." And another commented "..."

- **Describing trends, high and low points**

    —Figure 2 shows/reveals that there has been a slight/steep/sharp/steady/ gradual/marked rise/increase/fall/drop/decline/decrease in the number of...

    —Production of X peaked in March.

    —The number of X reached a peak/a low point during...

    —The rate fell to a low point of...

- **Introducing differences and similarities**

    —X is different from Y in a number of aspects: first, ... second, ...

    —X differs from Y in a number of ways: ...

    —There are some important differences between X and Y: ...

    —Both X and Y share some key features such as...

    —There are several similarities between X and Y: ...

    —The effects of X on human health are similar to those of Y.

    —Studies found that X and Y are essentially identical.

205

—This interpretation differs from / contrasts with / is different from that of X who argue(s) that...

—In contrast to / Compared with X, it is...

—By contrast / In contrast / On the other hand, ...

—Similarly / Likewise / In the same way, ...

12.3 In-Class Activities

Activity 1

Read the results of the following two research papers and find out the problems.

1. "Emotional Intelligence, Test Anxiety and Academic Stress Among University Students" (See Appendix 4)

2. "Optimism, Happiness and Self-Esteem Among University Students" (See Appendix 6)

Steps for organizing the activity:

1. Do it in pairs, each reading one of the papers.
2. Scan the results part of the paper.
3. Find out the problems concerning the tables, figures and texts.
4. Read more carefully and find out other possible problems.
5. Discuss with each other to exchange your ideas about the problems.
6. Share your findings of the problems in class.

Unit 12 **Results**

Activity 2

Study the figure below and fill in the blanks with the words or phrases from the table.

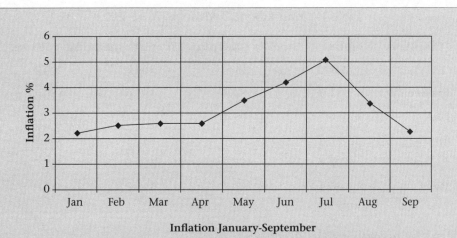

Inflation January-September

Verb ↗	Adverb	Verb ↘	Adjective + noun
grow (grew)	slightly	drop (dropped)	a slight drop
rise (rose)	gradually	fall (fell)	a gradual fall
increase (increased)	steadily	decrease (decreased)	a sharp decrease
climb (climbed)	sharply	decline (declined)	a steady decline
also: a peak, to peak, a plateau, to level off, a trough			

(Source: Bailey, 2011. *Academic Writing: A Handbook for International Students*)

The graph shows that inflation (A) _____ slightly between January and February and then (B) _____ until April. It subsequently climbed (C) _____ to July, when it (D) _____ at just over 5 percent. From July to September inflation (E) _____ steeply.

Steps for organizing the activity:

1. Look at the table, learn the words in the table that can be used to describe the figure above.

2. Study the figure to perceive the tendency of development.

3. Use the words to fill in the blanks.

Activity 3

Describe the following table.

Table 1　International Tourism in 2012–2013

Country	Number of tourists (million)		Tourists spending (billion)	
	2012	2013	2012	2013
France	83.0	84.7	$53.6	$56.1
USA	66.7	69.8	$126.2	$139.6
Spain	57.5	60.7	$56.3	$60.4
China	57.7	55.7	$50.5	$51.7
Italy	46.4	47.7	$41.2	$43.9

Steps for organizing the activity:

1. Study and understand the table.
2. Tell what it is about by giving a general description.
3. Focus on the important information and give a detailed description.
4. Share your description of the table with your group members.
5. Give an oral report of the table in class.

Unit 12 **Results**

Activity 4

What are the problems in the following writing to report the two figures?

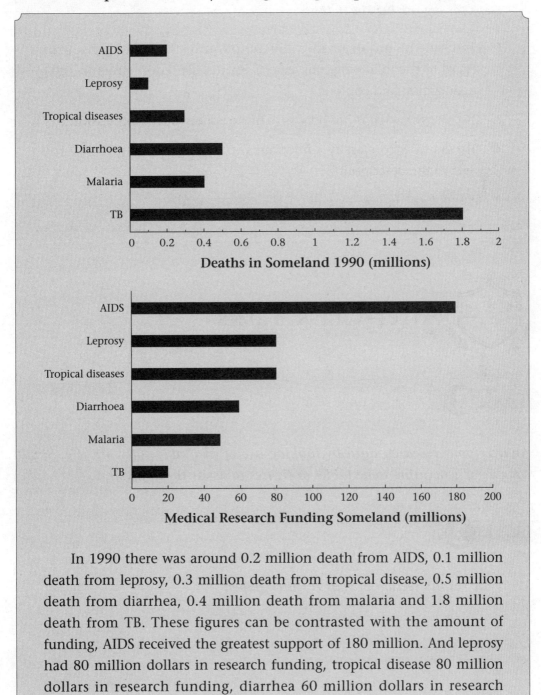

In 1990 there was around 0.2 million death from AIDS, 0.1 million death from leprosy, 0.3 million death from tropical disease, 0.5 million death from diarrhea, 0.4 million death from malaria and 1.8 million death from TB. These figures can be contrasted with the amount of funding, AIDS received the greatest support of 180 million. And leprosy had 80 million dollars in research funding, tropical disease 80 million dollars in research funding, diarrhea 60 million dollars in research

funding, malaria 50 million dollars in research funding and TB 20 million dollars in research funding.

Steps for organizing the activity:

1. Find out the problems in the description of the two figures with regard to the following four aspects: words, sentences structure, text organization and content.

2. Discuss with each other how to achieve variety in the expressions.

3. Discuss how to classify some items in the figures to improve the logic in the description.

4. Describe the figures by making the comparison.

12.4 After-Class Tasks

Analyze your research data by making use of available software (e.g. SPSS) capable of generating some tables or figures to assist the analysis.

Task 2

Write the results section of your research paper.

Unit 13

Discussion

13.1 Objectives

Know the rules and functions of a discussion.

Learn to analyze findings in the discussion.

Be able to write the discussion of a research paper.

13.2 Pre-Class Learning

Watch the MOOC/SPOC videos and do the online exercises. The contents in the textbook will help you understand the lessons better.

Source: https://www.icourse163.org/

Course name: "学术英语写作与演讲" (Academic Writing and Presentation in English)

Unit 9 Discussion, Conclusion, Citations and References

9.1 Discussion

The purpose of the "Discussion" in a research paper is to interpret the significance of your research results according to what was already known about the research problem being investigated, and to give explanation to new understandings or insights about the problem. The discussion should be closely related to the research questions or hypotheses you posed and the literature you reviewed, but mere repetition must be prevented. It should explain how your research will deepen the reader's understanding of the research problem. It is an important part to state your interpretation of the research results, explain the implications of your findings, and compare the similarities and differences between the results of your research and those of other studies.

Functions of a discussion

The discussion usually serves the following functions:

- **Explaining the results**

    —Judge whether the results are expected and give explanations of each set of results.

    —Give detailed explanation of the findings that are unexpected or especially profound.

    —If necessary, indicate unusual or unanticipated patterns or trends emerging from your results and explain them.

- **Showing the originality or significance**

    —Relate your results to the findings from other studies and make comparison.

    —Revisit key sources already cited in your literature review and add new sources for a thorough interpretation and a deeper understanding.

    —Demonstrate how your findings are similar to other studies to support your findings, or how they are different from other studies to show the originality of your research.

- **Deducing**

    —State how the results can be applied more generally in order to manifest the significance of your research.

- **Proving/Disproving hypothesis**

    —Give possible conclusion arising from the results.

Contents in a discussion

You can use subheadings or topic sentences to lead the discussion so that interpretations of the findings are grouped into themes related to the research hypotheses or questions. With such classification, the discussion can be more systematic and logical. For example, the research questions are:

—Is it feasible to adopt flipped classroom in academic English course?

—If it is, how to design the course?

The findings are shown in the following thematic groups related to the research questions.

—familiarity with MOOC and the flipped classroom (relating to Question 1);

—benefits and drawbacks of the flipped classroom (relating to Question 1);

—preferred approaches for the flipped classroom (relating to Question 2);

—proportion of the flipped classroom (relating to Question 2).

Contents in the discussion are also classified into thematic groups that are related with the research questions and results:

—feasibility of application (relating to Question 1 or Results 1 & 2);

—course design (relating to Question 2 or Results 3 & 4).

The discussion normally involves the following contents:

- **Basic contents**

    —brief statement of each of the major findings;

    —explanations of the causes of expected or unexpected findings; and

    —comparison with similar studies.

- **Contents of higher level**

    —alternative explanations;

    —analysis of unexpected findings;

    —inference from the findings; and

    —possible conclusion arising from the results.

- **Contents in the conclusion**

    —implications of the study;

    —acknowledgement of the study's limitations; and

    —recommendation for further research.

The first group of contents are basic and indispensable for the discussion. What you usually do when writing the discussion is to start by restating briefly each of the major findings and analyze them one by one. These analyses should include the explanation of the causes and the comparison with others studies, which are the most essential contents of the discussion. In the analysis, you have to cite a lot of sources to support your explanations or to relate the sources to your own research by comparison.

The second group of contents show a more advanced requirement of writer's knowledge and experience. Alternative explanations are encouraged, which will make your discussion more thorough and comprehensive. Unexpected findings are very common in research. You can begin with a description of unexpected findings, and interpret its possible significance in relation to the overall study. Making inference from the study requires a strong foundation of the research background and relevant theory, capable of provoking deep thoughts about the study. Drawing conclusion from the research is a logical thinking process based on reliable evidence. It is therefore necessary for you to establish a solid foundation of the knowledge about your research area through extensive reading of the relevant source materials and years of accumulation of research experience in the field.

The third group of contents are usually in the conclusion of a research paper. But owing to the fact that different research papers have different structures, some of them do not have a separate conclusion part. In this situation, the implications, limitations and recommendation for further study can be included in the discussion section.

The following are some examples to demonstrate how the writers discuss the findings.

- **Example**

   Discussion

   (1) After investigating independent and combined associations between Screen time (ST) and Physical activity (PA) and perceived stress among college students, our findings indicated that, among female students, those reporting HST and LMPA were more likely to experience stress. Moreover, our results showed that the combined effects of PA and ST were significantly associated with perceived stress among females, but not males.   *(1) Findings in general*

   (2) The present study found that students with low to moderate PA were more likely to experience stress. (3) Regular PA has many beneficial effects for health, such as promoting cardiorespiratory fitness (Aires et al., 2010) and reducing the risk of ischemic heart disease (Batty, 2002), stroke (Batty & Lee, 2002), diabetes (Jeon et al., 2007), and cognitive disorders   *(2) Research finding 1*

   (3) Explanations of the causes

(Larson et al., 2006). (4) Several studies have also showed that PA was associated with stress. Indeed, Vankim and Nelson (2013) found that students who met vigorous PA recommendations were less likely to report poor perceived stress, while Gerber et al. (2014) associated vigorous PA with lower stress among young adults. Another study also showed that regular exercise could protect against the negative emotional consequences of stress (Childs & de Wit, 2014). (5) Possible explanations for PA's effects on stress could include its beneficial effects on brain neurotransmitters, as well as on increasing levels of motivation and positive emotions, reducing stress and pain (Ekeland et al., 2004; Paluska & Schwenk, 2000). (6) Meanwhile, one survey observed a clear negative correlation between stress and sleep quality (Almojali et al., 2017). (7) This association could be mediated by PA, given that exercise regulates temperature and improves sleep onset through vasodilation for peripheral heat dissipation (Driver & Taylor, 2000). (8) Thus, PA can decrease stress and improve behavioral and emotional regulations by positively affecting sleep quality.

(9) The present study also revealed that participants with high ST were more likely to experience stress. (10) The American Academy of Pediatrics Committee on Public Education (2001) recommend that the ST of children and teenagers is not>2 h per day, but the median value for ST of college students was 6 h per day in our study, which was much higher than the recommendation for children and teenagers. (11) Indeed, studies have shown that high ST was associated with poor health attributes, such as overweight and obesity (Lane, et al. 2014), depression risk (Liu, Wu, & Yao, 2015), and low self-esteem (Russ et al., 2009). Moreover, several studies had already indicated that increased self-reported use of

(4) Comparison with other research

(5) Alternative explanation

(6) Comparison with other research

(7) Alternative explanation

(8) Possible conclusion

(9) Research finding 2

(10) Explanations of the causes

(11) Comparison with other research

electronic media was related to stress among young adults (Thomée et al., 2011) or females (Thomée et al., 2007). (12) One study also found that increased use of information and communication technology was associated with stress among young adults (Thomée et al., 2010), possibly because ST contributes to a sedentary lifestyle, which was highly correlated with stress. Accordingly, An et al. (2015) found that prolonged sedentary time was associated with risk for stress symptoms, and reducing sedentary behaviors could be one approach toward reducing perceived stress. (13) Moreover, Trinh, et al. (2015) showed that high ST was associated with poor mental health, while Opoku-Acheampong et al. (2017) found that stress levels were negatively correlated with self-reported mental health. (14) Furthermore, ST may consume time that could have otherwise been used for other activities. As such, spending more time on screen-based activities could lead to less time spent on sleep. (15) Despite the aforementioned potential mechanisms explaining the association between ST and perceived stress, some uncertainty exists regarding the causal relationship between electronic media use and stress. Indeed, Caplan (2010) found that students with high levels of perceived stress might be more inclined to show increased media use as a form of avoidant coping. (16) Therefore, further research is needed to determine whether ST and stress are interrelated or whether both factors accompany each other.

(17) The present study also investigated the association between the combined effects of PA and ST and perceived stress among college students. (18) Accordingly, our results showed that students reporting both HST and LMPA, both HST and VIPA, and both LST and LMPA were more likely to experience stress. (19) One possible underlying reason could be a potential threshold where sufficient

(12) Explanations of the causes

(13) Comparison with other research

(14) Explanations of the causes

(15) Inference from the findings

(16) Possible conclusion

(17) Reference to the research objective

(18) Research finding 3

(19) Explanations of the causes

time spent on high PA compensates for high ST. One study also negatively correlated high ST with vigorous PA among females (Melkevik et al., 2010). (20) Several studies had already confirmed that the combination of ST and PA had an impact on physical and psychological health. Accordingly, one study showed that Japanese adults with insufficient PA and high ST were significantly more likely to become overweight (Liao et al., 2011). Moreover, Feng et al. (2014) found that high PA and low ST could reduce the prevalence of depressive problems, while Wu et al. (2015) revealed that low PA and high ST could increase the risks of mental health problems and poor sleep quality. Similarly, the present study also confirmed that the combined effects of ST and PA influenced health. (21) Thus, increasing PA among individuals with prolonged exposure to electronic media might be a suitable approach toward reducing the risk of perceived stress. (22) The present study found the interactions between gender and the two exposures (ST and PA) in their association with perceived stress were not significant ($P = 0.143$ for PA × Gender and $P = 0.440$ for ST × Gender, data not shown in results), and the three way interaction (ST × PA × Gender) was also not significant ($P = 0.787$, data not shown in results). (23) This implies that gender does not affect the associations of ST and PA with perceived stress. However, significant gender differences in the effects of PA and ST on perceived stress were still observed, with complex underlying reasons. (24) One study indicated that significant interpersonal sensitivity was more frequently observed among female than male students (Nyström et al., 2018). Moreover, Troisi (2001) found that females were more likely to feel the stressful effects of negative interpersonal events, while Van Wijk and Kolk (1997) showed that females

(20) Comparison with other studies

(21) Possible conclusion

(22) Research finding 4

(23) Unexpected finding

(24) Comparison with other studies

might selectively pay attention to bodily cues and were more likely to report the symptoms they perceive to others. Another study found that males were more likely to use active and instrumental coping behaviors, while females were more likely to use passive and emotionally focused behaviors (Ptacek et al, 1992). Matud (2004) also found that, compared to males, females believed their life events were more negative and less controllable, and that their coping style was more emotionally focused. (25) These differences in stress perception and coping style between males and females may promote increased vulnerability of females to stress despite similar PA and electronic media exposure.

(25) Explanations of the causes

(26) Some study limitations should be considered. First, considering the cross-sectional design employed herein, we could not establish causal inferences from the associations between ST and PA and perceived stress. Second, samples from only one university, located in Shenyang, Northeast China, were included. Thus, our results cannot be generalized to all college students. Third, some variables, such as ST and PA, were assessed using a self-reported questionnaire, which might influence actual associations due to common method bias (Podsakoff et al., 2003). Indeed, studies have shown that self-reported variables (Montag et al., 2015), as well as self-report assessments of technology use, such as ST (Araujo et al., 2017; Junco, 2013), are typically biased. (27) Therefore, objective measurements, such as those obtained by tracking via applications, are needed in future studies. (28) Finally, although we controlled for some confounding factors, we could not adjust for all possible related variables, such as psychological symptoms, health complaints and so on. Mood (2010) reported that logistic regression estimates are affected by omitted variables, even when these variables

(26) Limitations of the study

(27) Recommendation for further study

(28) Limitation of the study

are unrelated to the independent variables in the model. (29) Therefore, future studies should involve a more comprehensive set of covariates and make it as a strategy to obtain a clearer understanding of the effects of PA and ST on stress.

(29) Recommendation for further study

(Source: Ge et al., 2020. Addictive Behavior)

Sentence templates

The following are some typical sentence patterns for the discussion:

- **Stating the major findings of the study**

    —It is found that...

    —The present study tested the hypothesis that...

- **Explaining the causes of the findings**

    —A possible explanation for these results may be...

    —The result may be explained by the fact that...

    —The reason for the result might be that...

    —This inconsistency may be due to...

    —The increase could be attributed to...

    —There are two likely causes for the differences...

- **Relating the findings to those of similar studies**

    To show the similarity

    —The results are the same as those reported in Wang (2018) who suggested that...

    —Results are consistent with Bos and Shami (2006) who found that...

    —Results are similar to those described in Zhang (2010)...

    —The result is in line with findings by Allen and Sirmans (2013) who...

    —This study supports evidence from previous observations (e.g. Smith, 2006; Jones et al., 2011).

    To show the differences

    —Results are different from those obtained by Goyal (2017)...

    —This outcome is contrary to that of Smith et al. (2001) who found...

—These results disagree with some researchers (e.g. Chen, 2010; Bachman & Smith, 2005)...

- **Analyzing unexpected findings**

    —One unanticipated finding was that...

    —A possible explanation is that..., which suggests that...

    —What is surprising is that...

    —This might be due to the fact that...

    —However, little support was obtained for the hypothesis that...

    —This unexpected result can be interpreted in several ways...

- **Suggesting the implications in theory or practice**

    —An implication of this is the possibility that...

    —These findings may help us to understand...

    —This finding, while preliminary, suggests that...

    —This finding has important implications for developing...

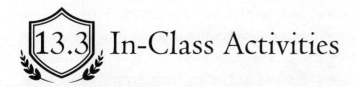 In-Class Activities

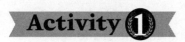

Read the following discussion to identify the sentences indicating the findings, explanation of findings, comparison with other research, or possible conclusion from the findings. Fill in the blanks with the numbers ahead of the relevant sentences.

Discussion

(1) The results showed that the total score of emotional intelligence correlated with test anxiety, academic stress and academic achievement

among university students. (2) The obtained results are similar with the results obtained by other researchers (Heather & April, 2009) that test anxiety affects students in the field of assessment and evaluation of their abilities and achievements. (3) Some researchers found that test anxiety is associated with some negative and positive evaluations and accompanying emotions (Rain, 2010). (4) Some other studies revealed that academic stress was strongly associated with several dimensions of emotional intelligence (Credo, 2015). (5) Concerning the causal ordering of the test anxiety—emotional intelligence relationship, there are reasons to hypothesize that test anxiety predicts changes in students' emotional intelligence. (6) College students are faced with a unique set of stressors that may be overwhelming, thus altering the abilities to cope with a situation. Strategies to reduce stress have been associated with emotional intelligence in university students (Curvet et al., 2006). (7) Based on this, we can conclude that emotional intelligence may influence test anxiety and academic stress components.

(8) In our study we found that female students have higher level of emotional intelligence, test anxiety and academic stress than male students. (9) Existing literature reveals the same information about these parameters in female students (Sanchez-Nunez et al., 2008). (10) One of the reasons behind the increasing levels of emotional intelligence of female students may be due to the biological and psychological differences between males and females. (11) Also, females tend to stay with the emotions expressed by others as emotional empathy, but males tend to focus on activities that need to be done in order to come out of those emotions. (12) Another reason may be that female students have more tension, anxiety, stress and physical rigidity when they face exams.

(13) At the same time, we found that there were no differences in the level of emotional intelligence and academic stress among students who studied medical sciences and psychology, but the level of test anxiety was higher in the students of medical sciences. (14) These differences may be due to the pedagogical practices where allied medical sciences involve more satisfying academic tasks, i.e. consulting with patients. (15) Also, results indicated that emotional intelligence, test anxiety and academic stress are the common cause for the students' poor academic performance during examination. (16) The results with

regard to academic stress are also in line with those obtained from other studies (Keenan & Pearisburg, 2003). (17) All have reached the conclusion that students with better academic achievement had a higher level of emotional intelligence, test anxiety and academic stress.

(Source: Stankovska et al., 2018. Education in Modern Society)

Paragraph 1

Findings _____

Explanations of the causes _____

Comparison with other research _____

Possible conclusion from the findings _____

Paragraph 2

Findings _____

Explanations of the causes _____

Comparison with other research _____

Possible conclusion from the findings _____

Paragraph 3

Findings _____

Explanations of the causes _____

Comparison with other research _____

Possible conclusion from the findings _____

Steps for organizing the activity:

1. Scan the text and underline the words that signal a finding, explanation, comparison with other research, or possible conclusion from the findings.

2. Read the sentences more carefully and fill in the blanks with the numbers ahead of the identified sentences.

3. Compare your answer to that of your group members.

4. Discuss with your classmates to give reasons for your answers.

5. Check answers in class.

Activity 2

Find out the problem(s) with the following discussion written by a student. Give comments on how to improve it.

Discussion

According to the table above (Table 3), we get the overall correlation between various sleeping indices and academic performance. The prime sleeping index is Pittsburgh Sleep Quality Index (PSQI). The students of top 20 percent academic performances have negative sign on PSQI while the students with average academic performances have positive sign. It means that a higher PSQI score, a better sleeping quality cannot help the good students achieve top scores on the exams but it helps other general students keep their own academic performance on the average level.

However, on the second row of Table 3, we find that sleeping before exams has a positive influence on top students' academic performances. So students who have enough sleep before exams may have more possibility to get the high score during the exam. And students without enough sleep right before the exam tend to get the lowest grades.

The third row and the fourth row are showing the correlations between studying at late night and studying in the early morning and students' academic performances. From the information given by the table, staying up late to study holds back students to become the top 20% while it helps students to reach the average academic performance level. And getting up early to study indeed helps students get scores. It is simple and obvious to understand the difference between late night and early morning because early morning is always the best time to learn the new things while the late night should be used to rest instead of studying and working. Therefore, staying up to study is not a good deal because it usually reduces the students' energy on the next day, which also has a bad influence on the studying efficiency.

What is interesting is correlation between sleep efficiency and the academic performance. From the table, the positive sign of sleep efficiency appears on column "80%~100%" and the negative sign appears on column "0~20%", which means the higher sleep efficiency the students have during the night, the more possible they get the poor scores during the exams. The result from the last row completely exceeds our previous expectations. The reason can be attributed to the method of data acquisition and processing we use. All data are collected from the questionnaire spreading on the social media like WeChat and QQ, which limits the total amount and restrict the variety of students surveyed. If we collect data from a larger number of questionnaires, the more precise result of correlations between sleep efficiency and academic performance can be concluded.

Steps for organizing the activity:

1. Scan the text and try to find out whether the discussion includes the basic contents required.

2. Read more carefully to figure out the problems, if any.

3. Discuss with your group members and share your opinions.

4. Share your suggestions for revision in class.

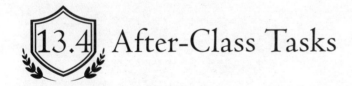# 13.4 After-Class Tasks

Task 1

Think about the causes of your research findings and try to use some sources to support your explanations.

Task 2

Compare your research findings with the related studies to find out the similarities and differences.

Task 3

Please write the discussion part of your own paper.

Unit 14

Conclusion

14.1 Objectives

Know elements involved in a conclusion.

Be able to write the conclusion of your own paper.

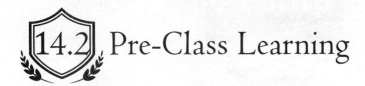
14.2 Pre-Class Learning

Watch the MOOC/SPOC videos and do the online exercises. The contents in the textbook will help you understand the lessons better.

Source: https://www.icourse163.org/

Course name: "学术英语写作与演讲" (Academic Writing and Presentation in English)

Unit 9 Discussion, Conclusion, Citations and References

9.2 Conclusion

A "Conclusion" is like the final chord in a symphony. It gives the audience a sense of completeness. In academic writing, a well-written "Conclusion" can add to the value of your research. The conclusion allows you to finally clarify the issue in your paper, summarize your thoughts, demonstrate the importance of your ideas, and present your reader with a new view of the topic.

Approaches to a conclusion

In the conclusion, you can briefly restate the arguments or purposes of your research, and explain why they are important. Then, you summarize your major research findings rather than just exhibit a list of points. Besides, you explain the implications of your findings, such as the theoretical contribution or practical application of your research. Finally, you have to acknowledge that there is more to be explored and describe briefly the issues for further research. The following are some major elements usually involved in the conclusion of a research paper, followed by some examples with explanations.

Unit 14 Conclusion

—restatement of major arguments or purposes;

—summary of major research findings;

—implications of the findings;

—limitations of the research; and

—suggestions for future research.

- **Example 1**

(1) The research shows that it is possible for the incorporation of the model that draws strength from both writing as a process and as a social interaction, with technology as an aid in an academic writing course. (2) The elements involved in the model are manifested in the course and appreciated by the students. Most students were satisfied with the activities, tasks and assignments and favored the idea of using computers and the Internet as an aid to writing. They also employed different kinds of strategies for completing the tasks and activities smoothly and successfully and did a lot of cooperative work during the writing process. (3) The evaluation of the course suggests that the course has achieved the goal of helping learners improve their academic writing competence and confidence, which will enable them to cope successfully with future writing tasks. (4) The limitation of the study is that the number of subjects is not big, and it was conducted over a relatively short period of time. (5) A longitudinal study with more subjects could yield more useful and convincing results.

(1) Main arguments

(2) Major findings

(3) Implication

(4) Limitation

(5) Further research

(Source: Zhang et al., 2014. The Journal of Asia TEFL)

- **Example 2**

(1) This research investigated how teachers experience the use of online role-play for collaborative argument so that they could have a better knowledge

(1) Main arguments

229

of how technology enhances learning and doing.

(2) The results indicate that while online role-play can provide an effective process of learning, successful implementation of the activity depends on topic choice, level of participation, and quality of collaboration. It is also found that asynchronous can be more effective than the synchronous online role-play given differences in the time to respond and formulate arguments. While there are benefits of using online role-play for collaborative argument, challenges exist, especially in a synchronous environment, suggesting the necessity to find solutions.

(2) Major findings

(3) This research provides some pedagogical implications for teaching argumentation by using online role-plays. First, it is important to select appropriate topics about which students have substantial prior knowledge as well as topics in which they have interest so that they can formulate informed arguments about that topic. Second, an asynchronous online role-play may be a preferable option over synchronous online role-play for developing students' thinking and communication ability. Third, preparation time should be ensured to conduct background research and to envision and define roles. Fourth, instructions on how to collaboratively build alliances with peers are necessary so that they can coordinate formulation of arguments supporting other allied roles. Fifth, the number of participants for the activity can be 6–10 to ensure enough roles on each side, but not so many as to cause difficulty in tracking the development of ideas. A large class can be divided into several groups to ensure the smooth implementation of the activity. Finally, reflection on the role-play activity is essential to identify what has been learned about an issue and how to improve the future use of online role-plays.

(3) Pedagogical implications

(4) The study yields some implications for how to conduct a teaching methodology research. Instead of separating researchers, teachers and students in dominant modes of student learning research, the researcher and teachers in this study reflected upon themselves as learners. As Case et al. (2010) put: Having teachers participate in the online role-play activity helps them acquire the perspective of their own students so that they gain different insights into the experience of learning to reflect on the multifaceted and complex issues of learning.

(4) Methodological implications

(5) The study also demonstrates a new perspective of teacher education that teachers acquire their knowledge of a particular teaching method by experiencing and imitating the actual learning process of their students. Teachers' perceptions of online role-play after their own practice can shed light on how online role-play can be more effectively employed in their own classrooms. Besides, the study added to the knowledge of teacher education by demonstrating how a teacher education purpose can be realized through the teacher educator's personal involvement in the learning activity instead of merely giving instructions on general concepts and skills. The study also sets an example of how teachers are trained both on-and offline to familiarize themselves with a new approach for computer-aided teaching and learning.

(5) Implications for teacher education

(6) One limitation of this study is that the quantitative aspect to the study could only yield some tentative results given the small sample size, suggesting the need for further research involving larger number of participants. Another limitation is that the research did not clarify how the role-play activity was assessed, suggesting the necessary research on how to assess the activity when it is implemented on students, and what extent to

(6) Limitations and further research

which the assessment can motivate students to put in more efforts required for extending and lifting their thinking. Further research is also needed to determine how the teachers' experience as students would have an impact on their teaching when their students actually participate in online role-plays, as well as how to develop teachers' ability to give certain instruction to help influence the quality of arguments in online role-play as well as to transfer participation in online role-play to improving critical thinking ability, communicative ability, and writing proficiency.

(Source: Zhang et al., 2016. Asia-Pacific Journal of Teacher Education)

Sentence templates

Here are some sentence templates for the conclusion of a research paper.

- **Restatement of major arguments or purposes**

    —This paper has argued that...

    —The aim of the present research was to examine...

    —The purpose of the current study was to determine...

    —The main goal of the current study was to determine...

    —This project was undertaken to design... and evaluate...

    —The present study was designed to determine the effect of...

- **Summary of main research findings**

    —This research has shown that...

    —The major finding was that...

    —The experiments confirmed that...

    —This study has found that generally...

    —The most obvious finding to emerge from this study is that...

    —One of the more significant findings to emerge from this study is that...

Unit 14 Conclusion

- **Implications of the findings**

    —The results of this study indicate that...

    —These findings suggest that in general...

    —The findings of this study suggest that...

    —An implication of this is the possibility that...

    —The current data highlight the importance of...

    —The findings of this research provide insights for...

    —The principal theoretical implication of this study is that...

    —These findings have significant implications for the understanding of how...

- **Limitations of the research**

    —A limitation of this study is that...

    —It is unfortunate that the study did not include...

    —The scope of this study was limited in terms of...

    —The study is limited by the lack of information on...

    —The most important limitation lies in the fact that...

    —The main weakness of this study was...

    —An issue that was not addressed in this study was whether...

- **Suggestions for future research**

    —This would be a fruitful area for further work.

    —More broadly, research is also needed to determine...

    —Considerably, more work will need to be done to determine...

    —These findings provide the following insights for future research: ...

    —This research has thrown up many questions in need of further investigation.

    —Further research should be carried out to establish/determine...

    —Further studies need to be conducted in order to explore...

14.3 In-Class Activities

Activity 1

Read the following two conclusions and fill in the table below.

Conclusion 1

The network efficiency model is used to define the structural vulnerability of road network in this paper. The framework of the road network structural vulnerability measurement and improvement model is proposed. The actual network vulnerability analysis is carried out on Shanghai freeway network. It can effectively identify the critical components of road network. According to graph theory, two kinds of structural design optimization for road network are proposed to improve the road network robustness. This study only considers the structure of road network attributes (connectivity), regardless of the dynamic flow in road network. How to combine this model with the dynamic flow in road network is an interesting future research direction.

(Source: Yin & Xu, 2010. Shanghai Jiao Tong Univ. (Sci.))

Conclusion 2

This paper has raised a number of issues regarding the teaching of listening comprehension. It has argued that gaining insights into the beliefs about L2 listening held by learners is an important first step for teachers who wish to help their students address the problems they experience. Further research is needed to discover the extent to which a combined approach of addressing maladaptive beliefs about listening as a skill in which improvement is difficult to achieve, and instruction in strategy use and skill application, can have lasting benefits for listening achievement.

(Source: Graham, 2006. System)

Unit 14 **Conclusion**

Elements	Conclusion 1	Conclusion 2
Thesis or summary of arguments		
Major findings		
Implication of findings		
Limitations		
Further research		

Steps for organizing the activity:

1. Do the activity in pairs, each of the students working on one of the conclusions.

2. Read the conclusion, find out the relevant elements in the conclusions, and put them in the table.

3. Discuss in pairs and tell each other the reasons for your answers.

4. Share the answers in class.

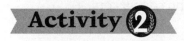

Please read the conclusion of an SJTU student's paper and give comments.

Conclusion

The study is about researching and analyzing the relationship between sleeping quality and academic performance in China. We all know that sleeping plays a major role in our memory, our physical and our mental state. For the college students, they constantly receive new knowledge and information daily and consume much energy to fulfill their daily schedule. Obviously, sleeping is the basis and foundation of the college life. For the college students, getting a high score during the exam and achieving a good academic performance are always their main goals. They need to find a way to balance the studying and the sleeping.

From the study above, we know that enough sleep at night is necessity for the college students. Every college student should keep 7 to 9 hours of sleep time every day. What's more, the sleeping before the exam is of the greatest importance which has a great impact on the students' performances during the exam. Though students are willing to spend much time to prepare an exam, it's not recommended to stay up late at night because the night is the time for sleeping but not studying. Staying up only gets half the result with duplication the efforts. Instead, early to bed and early to rise is the key to high studying efficiency. In general, each part of time has its own use. A good balance of sleeping time and studying time definitely helps college students get better academic performances.

Steps for organizing the activity:

1. Read the conclusion.

2. Try to find out the summary of arguments and major findings, implication for findings, limitations, or further research.

3. Figure out what is lacking and how to improve the conclusion.

14.4 After-Class Tasks

Task 1

Figure out the limitation(s) of your research and think about what else can be done to improve your research.

Task 2

Write the conclusion of your research paper.

Unit 15

Citations and References

15.1 Objectives

Be able to provide correct in-text citations.

Be able to list accurate references.

15.2 Pre-Class Learning

Watch the MOOC/SPOC videos and do the online exercises. The contents in the textbook will help you understand the lessons better.

Source: https://www.icourse163.org/

Course name: "学术英语写作与演讲" (Academic Writing and Presentation in English)

Unit 9 Discussion, Conclusion, Citations and References

9.3 Citations

9.4 References

Citations and references are indispensable in a research paper. You need to provide the in-text citation to any idea you get from other researchers and, at the end of your paper, a reference list of the articles, books or other sources you have referred to in your writing. The items in your references should be an exact match with those in your in-text citations. That is to say, you can neither list in your references an item that is not cited in your text nor include a citation of the source in the text without listing it in your references.

Different journals may require different formats of citations and references. The APA (American Psychology Association) format is generally adopted by journals of social, psychological and behavioral sciences. The AMA (American Medical Association) format is used in the journals published by the AMA, as well as in hundreds of other scientific journals. The IEEE (Institute of Electrical and Electronics Engineers) format is commonly accepted in technical fields, particularly in computer science.

Unit 15 Citations and References

You can download software such as EndNote, Zotera or Mendeley to help you manage citations and references. The advantage of using the software is that you can instantly switch to a different format when the need arises. It is nevertheless necessary for you to check the format carefully since citations and references automatically derived from the software may go wrong in format due to the possible inaccuracy in some of the sources. Here, we take the example of the APA 7th edition (American Psychological Association, 2020).

In-text citations

- **One author**

    The name of the author is part of the sentence.

    Oxford (1998) investigated...

    The name of the author is not part of the sentence.

    ... (Oxford, 1998).

- **Two authors**

    When the work is done by two authors, name both authors in the signal phrase or in the parentheses each time you cite the work. Use the word "and" between the authors' names within the text and "&" in the parentheses.

    Research by Benson and Chik (2021) showed...

    ... (Benson & Chik, 2021)

- **Three or more than three authors**

    When citing a source with three or more authors, use the first author's surname followed by "**et al.**".

    Harris et al. (2020) argued...

    ... (Harris et al., 2020)

- **Multiple sources for the same citation**

    If there are multiple sources that can support the same idea, place all the sources in alphabetical order and separate them with a semicolon.

    ... (Ellis, 2020; Johnson, 2015; Nakamura et al., 2018).

- **Several works by the same author**

If you cite two or more sources by the same author, arrange them by the year of publication in chronological order, with the surname appearing only once.

>Bloom (2018, 2019, 2021) claimed that...

If the works are published in the same year, use a, b, c after the year to differentiate.

>Green (2018a, 2018b, 2018c) illustrated that...

- **Web document**

If you cite a web document, use the author-date format. If no author is identified, use the first few words of the title in place of the author. If no date is provided, use "n.d." in place of the date.

>Degelman (2020) summarizes...
>
>... (Gender and Society, n.d.).

Quotations

When a direct quotation is used, always include the author, year, and page number. A quotation of fewer than 40 words should be enclosed in double quotation marks and incorporated into the formal structure of the sentence. For example:

>Patients receiving prayer had "less congestive heart failure, required less diuretic and antibiotic therapy, had fewer episodes of pneumonia, had fewer cardiac arrests, and were less frequently intubated and ventilated" (Byrd, 1988, p. 829).
>
>As pointed out by Thorne et al. (2009): "Digital vernaculars remain largely unaddressed within instructed L2 curricula or, worse, are trivialized or vilified as stigmatized varieties" (p. 815).

A lengthier quotation of 40 or more words should appear (without quotation marks) apart from the surrounding text, in block format, with each line indented from the left margin. For example:

>Mann (1987) even criticizes the separation of researchers and "subjects" in dominant modes of student learning research:
>
>>Instead of rendering ourselves—as researchers and as teachers—other than and separate from the students with whom we are working, should

we not reflect upon ourselves as former students and, most importantly, as past, current, and continuing learners, so that when we research into and teach students we are also researching into and teaching ourselves? (p. 182)

References

- **Journal article**

    Author, A. A. (Year). Title of article. *Title of Periodical, volume number* (issue number), pp–pp.
    - Example

    Park, J. (2020). Benefits of freewriting in an EFL academic writing classroom. *ELT Journal, 74*(3), 318–326.

- **Book**

    Author, A. A. (Year). *Title of work: Capital letter also for subtitle*. Publisher.
    - Example

    Baddeley, A. D. (1986). *Working memory*. Oxford University Press.

- **Edited book**

    Editor, A. A., & Editor, B. B. (Eds.). (year). *Title of work: Subtitle*. Publisher.
    - Example

    Boekaerts, M., Pintrich, P. R., & Zeidner, M. (Eds.). (2000). *Handbook of self-regulation*. Academic Press.

- **Article in an edited book**

    Author, A. A., & Author, B. B. (Year). Title of article. In A. Editor & B. Editor (Eds.), *Title of book* (pages of chapter). Publisher.
    - Example

    DeKeyser, R. (2007). Skill acquisition theory. In B. VanPatten & J. Williams (Eds.), *Theories in second language acquisition: An introduction* (pp. 97–113). Lawrence Erlbaum.

- **Report**

    Author, A. (year). *Title of report* (Research Report No. xx). http://www.ngo.

xxxxxx.pdf

- Example

Attali, Y., & Powers, D. (2008). *A developmental writing scale* (Research Report No.08-19). http://www.ets.org/Media/Research/pdf/RR-08-19.pdf

▪ Newspaper article

Author, A. A. (Year, Month Date). Title of work: Capital letter also for subtitle. *Newspaper*, page number.

- Example

Schultz, S. (2005, December 28). Calls made to strengthen state energy policies. *The Country Today*, pp. 1A, 2A.

▪ Thesis

Author, A. M. (year). *Title of dissertation* (Doctoral dissertation). http://www.university/etd/

- Example

Wang, H. (2005). *Investigating the collocational behavior of Chinese EFL learners* (Doctoral dissertation). http://thesis.lib.sjtu.edu.cn/sub2.asp?paperid=8713

▪ Conference paper, poster session

Author, A. (Year, Month). *Title of paper*. Paper presented at the meeting of the Society, City, State.

- Example

Zhang, L. (2021, May). *Blended learning for academic English against the COVID-19 pandemic*. Paper presented at the annual meeting of the CEAPA-BALEAP International Conference, Suzhou, China.

▪ Internet Source

Author, A. (Year). *Webpage name*. http://web address

- Example

Driscoll, D., & Brizee, A. (2016). *Commas: Quick rules*. https://owl.english.purdue.edu/owl/ owlprint/607/

Unit 15 **Citations and References**

15.3 In-Class Activities

Activity 1

Use EndNote to insert in-text citations and references to your paper.

Steps for organizing the activity:

1. Prepare a paragraph taken from your own writing.
2. Put the cursor to the place you want to insert a citation.
3. Click on EndNote X9 in the Word Toolbar.
4. Make sure the instant formatting is "On".
5. Click on "Insert citation" and find the source you want to cite.
6. Click on the source and the "Insert" icon.
7. After inserting all the sources in the paragraph, convert them to plain text.

Activity 2

Find out the errors with the in-text citations and the references according to APA 7th Edition.

Critical thinking is a complex concept that has been defined in a number of ways as metacognition (Richard Paul, 2005), logical argument analysis (Watson, G., & Glaser, E. M., 2006), and careful weighing of the evidence to support a claim (1998, Bensley). While most educators agree that it is vital to teach critical thinking (Flores et al 2012; Wyer 2009), we do not always agree on the definition or specific skills we are hoping to instill in students (CHENAULT & DUCLOS, 2008). With this challenge in mind, we set out to create classroom modules that promote critical, empirically based thinking skills. We based the modules on Bernstein's (2007) five steps for critical thinking. He proposed that students needed to think about the claim "what am I being asked to believe?", evaluate the evidence, consider alternative interpretations of the evidence, and, finally, draw conclusions. These steps are similar to the subtests in the Watson-Glaser critical thinking test (Watson & Glaser, 2006.) In addition to these constructs, we sought to address potential barriers to critical thinking, such as biases, emotional reasoning, overuse of personal experience or small case studies, and reliance on authority, which are suggested by Myers in 2009. We therefore created the following seven steps to critical thinking as the foundation around which we then designed our classroom teaching modules.

References

Richard Paul. (2005). The state of critical thinking today. *New Directions of Community Colleges*, *2005*(130), 27–38.

Watson, G., & Glaser, E. M. (2006). *Watson-Glaser Critical Thinking Appraisal: Short Form Manual*. Pearson.

Flores, K. L., Matkin, G. S., Burbach, M. E., Quinn, C. E., & Harding, H. (2012). Deficient critical thinking skills among college graduates: Implications for leadership. Educational Philosophy and Theory, 44(2), 212–230.

Wyer, K. (2009). *U.S. faculty: Civic engagement, diversity important goals for undergraduate education.*

Chenault, T. G., & Duclos, E. (2008). An act of translation: The need to understand students' understanding of critical thinking in the undergraduate classroom. *The Journal of Effective Teaching, 8.*

Bernstein, D. A. (2007). Promoting critical thinking and active learning in psychology courses. Keynote presentation given at the Mountain States Conference on the Teaching of Psychology. Durango, CO (October 6–7).

Myers, D. G. (2009). *Psychology*: *Ninth Edition.*

(Source: Kraus et al., 2013. *The Journal of Effective Teaching*, with modification)

Steps for organizing the activity:

1. Read the paragraph and pay attention to the in-text citations while reading.

2. Check whether there are mistakes by referring to the APA format in the textbook.

3. Revise the mistakes with in-text citations.

4. Check whether there are mistakes in the references and revise them.

5. Check the format of the references, for example, whether they are in alphabetic order, and whether the second and subsequent lines of each entry are indented.

6. Check whether the in-text citations match the items in the references.

15.4 After-Class Tasks

Task 1

Use EndNote to insert in-text citations and references for your own paper in the APA format, and check them carefully to make sure they are in the correct format.

Task 2

Go over your paper to make sure that citations are provided to whatever idea that is not your own.

Peer-Review and Revision

16.1 Objectives

Know how to do peer-review and revision.

Be able to give peer-review comments to each other.

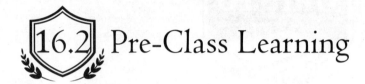

16.2 Pre-Class Learning

Peer-review

Peer-review is the evaluation of a paper by one or more people of similar competence. Peer-review is not to help you feel better, but to help you understand the problems and improve the quality of the research paper. In other words, it is not a reviewer's job just to say nice things, but to test arguments and identify problems. Therefore, both encouragement and suggestions are expected.

The benefit of peer-review is to make you write with a real audience in mind, which can motivate you to compose an acceptable draft. Moreover, in the peer-review discussion, you will have to explain and defend your ideas, which helps clarify and develop the ideas. Finally, and most importantly, you will be more sensitive to the strengths and weaknesses of your own paper after you have critically reviewed other people's work.

In order to have an effective peer review, you can refer to a checklist to make sure everything meets the requirements. The following is a checklist for the peer-review of a research paper.

—Does the total number of words meet the requirement?

—Is the language clear and succinct, with no grammatical mistakes?

—Does the layout of the paper look nice and clear?

—Does the title clearly identify the topic of the research?

—Does the abstract include objectives (background, problem), method, result, and conclusion?

—Are there three moves (background, problem/gap, purpose/thesis/filing the gap) in the introduction?

—Does the literature review have good logic and lead to your research question?

—Does the method include participants/materials, instruments/measures, data collection and analysis?

—Are there titles for the figures and tables? Are the tables and figures placed appropriately? Are they referred to and described in the text?

—Does the discussion have citations of sources? Are the findings explained and analyzed with good reasons, and compared with other research in the discussion?

—Does the conclusion involve the summary of arguments, findings, implications, limitations and further studies?

—Does the paper have a logical outline, which meets the requirements of parallelism, coordination, subordination and division?

—Are unnecessary subtitles avoided?

—Does each paragraph deal with one topic?

—Are all the paragraphs thoroughly developed?

—Are the transitions good to show the coherence and cohesion?

—Is each part of the paper logically related to the others?

—Are all the borrowed ideas provided with citations and reference? Are the citations and reference in the required format?

To do peer-review, you can directly add, delete or transpose parts of the text by means of the "edit" function in "review". You'd better choose "all notes" so that your peer can track the changes you have made, and you can also use "add notes" to give comments (Figure16.1).

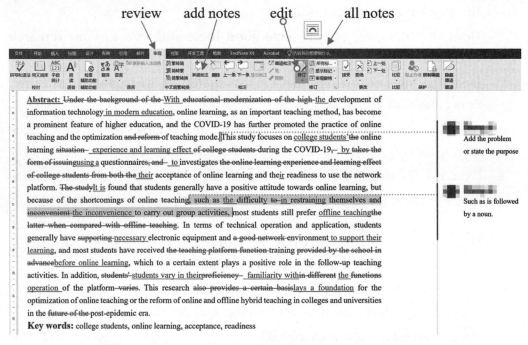

Figure 16.1   Functions in Word Toolbar for Peer-Review

Revision

Revision is both a psychological and mechanical process. It is psychological because you have to adapt the language to fit a particular audience. For example, in academic writing, the audience of the research paper may be your advisor, your colleagues or your classmates who share the same research interest or discipline of knowledge. Therefore, you have to revise your writing to make it more formal and academic. Revision is also mechanical in that the draft may be filled with misuse of language, misstatements of opinions or errors of facts. When you revise your writing, you will find a lot of mistakes in grammar, the language used, and the ideas expressed. You will find some paragraphs are tedious and overstuffed with details while some others are too simple and require more information. Therefore, you need to keep revising and polishing your writing. The following are some typical problems in students' writing, with suggested revisions and comments.

- **Too many subtitles**

Many students tend to include too many subtitles because they think subtitles help to show the main ideas and logic clearly. However, there being

Unit 16 Peer-Review and Revision

too many subtitles in a research paper is inappropriate because this may leave people the impression of a list of contents that are not well-developed. Actually, a subtitle is used to group several paragraphs to help readers understand the section better. So you can delete some subtitles that are not necessary or replace them with the topic sentences that can also show the main ideas clearly. Look at the example of the results part of a student's research paper.

- **Example**

    3. Results

    3.1 Statistics for people's lifestyle habits and perception of cancer

    3.1.1 Lifestyle habits

    3.1.1.1 Water

    For Question 1, 62 (55.36%) people drink water before breakfast, while the rest do not pay much attention on water after getting up. People who do not drink water account for almost 50%. This should be improved since water is important for our health and can remove waste from our body.

    3.1.1.2 Diet

    When it came to the second and third questions, 73.21% of the participants have breakfast every day and 82.14% eat vegetables and fruit daily. Only a small number of them have unhealthy eating habits. So our participants showed good lifestyle.

    3.1.1.3 Exercise

    However, the answers to Questions 4 and 5 were not as positive as the previous ones. 62 (55.36%) people do not have the habit of exercising every day, which account for more than half of our participants. What's more, only 16 (14.28%) people can do sports for more than 30 minutes while others cannot and even do not exercise at all. This phenomenon was sobering, and we should take action to change it.

The problem here is that there are 4 layers of subtitles, with only one or no paragraph under each. Therefore, "3.1 Statistics for people's lifestyle habits and perception of cancer" can be deleted, and "3.1.1.1 Water", "3.1.1.2 Diet" and "3.1.1.3 Exercise" can be changed into topic sentences of the paragraphs. The following is the revised version.

3. Results

3.1 Lifestyle habits

For Question 1 concerning drinking water, 62 (55.36%) people drink water before breakfast, while the rest do not pay much attention on water after getting up. People who do not drink water account for almost 50%. This should be improved since water is important for our health and can remove waste from our body.

When it came to the second and third questions about diet, 73.21% of the participants have breakfast every day and 82.14% eat vegetables and fruit daily. Only a small number of them have unhealthy eating habits. So our participants showed good lifestyle.

As far as exercise is concerned, the answers to Questions 4 and 5 were not as positive as the previous ones. 62 (55.36%) people do not have the habit of exercising every day, which account for more than half of our participants. What's more, only 16 (14.28%) people can do sports for more than 30 minutes while others cannot and even do not exercise at all. This phenomenon was sobering, and we should take action to change it.

- **Lack of paragraph completeness**

A paragraph should meet the requirement of unity and completeness. If two topics are involved in a paragraph, you have to divide the paragraph into two, with each focusing on one topic. You also need to add information to paragraphs that seem hollow and inadequate in content. You can read more source materials and find information that can be added to these paragraphs. You'd better delete irrelevant information and add relevant supporting details to fully develop these paragraphs. Here are examples taken from students' writings:

- Example

Original: Jet propulsion is a practical application of Sir Isaac Newton's third law of motion stated as "for every force acting on a body there is an opposite and equal reaction".

Revised: Jet propulsion is a practical application of Sir Isaac Newton's third law of motion stated as "for every force acting on a body there is an opposite and equal reaction". For aircraft propulsion, the "body" is atmospheric air that is caused to accelerate as it passes through the engine. The force required to give this acceleration has an equal effect in the opposite direction to act on the apparatus producing the acceleration.

Obviously, the original paragraph is not a complete one because it lacks supporting details. This phenomenon occurs very often in many students' writings. The paragraph contains only one sentence, with no more information to support it. The revised paragraph is complete with more information elaborated in the two sentences that follow and support the topic sentence.

- **No appropriate transitions**

When revising your draft, you also have to check whether sentences and paragraphs are well-connected. In other words, you need to pay special attention to the transitions within and between paragraphs. You can achieve the linkage by using transitional markers or transitional sentences to make sure that the sentences and paragraphs are logically linked together.

- Example

Original: Wrongful convictions will bring about horrible consequences both to the people involved and to the judicial system. Wrongful convictions will inevitably harm the lawful rights of the wronged people. The wronged has even been deprived of his or her young life. Wrongly-judged cases will cause great mental damage to the parents, relatives and friends of the wronged. These harms are all irreversible. Whenever a wrongful conviction is made, the law is defied, and the judicial authority is challenged. The existence of wrongly-charged cases is the powerful evidence to show that there are defects in the judicial system.

Revised: Wrongful convictions will bring about horrible consequences both to the people involved and to the judicial system. On the one hand, wrongful convictions will inevitably harm the lawful rights of the wronged people. In some serious cases, the wronged has even been deprived of his or her young life. Besides, wrongly-judged cases will cause great mental damage to the parents, relatives and friends of the wronged. These harms are all irreversible. On the other hand, whenever a wrongful conviction is made, the law is defied, and the judicial authority is challenged. The existence of wrongly-charged cases is the powerful evidence to show that there are defects in the judicial system.

Transitional markers, as shown by the underlined words in the revised version, make the writing smoother and the logical relationship clearer.

- **Lack of clarity**

Students tend to have a wrong idea that writing academically means writing lengthy sentences, including many clauses in them. But the fact is that long sentences are difficult to compose and, if not properly written, are possible to be misunderstood. Sometimes, they are not clear in structure, leading to ambiguity in meaning. Actually, it makes no sense to produce long sentences at the cost of the clarity of meaning. Let's look at the example from a student's writing. Can you make sense of the following sentence?

- **Example 1**

    Original: The event that AlphaGo defeated Lee Sedol declares a new period when AI can do much better than human beings in a particular field after some training that won't take much time even if humans have been familiar with this field and have practiced a lot, let alone those fields that spring up recently and that neither humans or AI is familiar with.

    Revised: The event that AlphaGo defeated Lee Sedol declares a new period when AI can do much better than human beings in a particular field after some training. Even if humans can be an expert in this field by practicing a lot, new fields are springing up at so remarkable a speed that it is almost impossible for a human being to be familiar with it in a short period of time.

- **Example 2**

    Original: This paper discusses the factor of success on the viewpoints of cultural brand and selling methods from the culture of the bud to use design to make the culture brand specific, and finally to the establishment of consumer society groups such a process which shows that the use of cultural brand of this business can be a good way to establish consumer purchasing habits and makes Apple Corp successful.

    Revised: This paper discusses the factor of success in the viewpoints of cultural brand and selling methods. Starting from the culture of the bud, to the design of the culture brand, and finally to the establishment of consumer society groups, the process shows that the use of cultural brand of this business can be a good way to develop consumer purchasing habits and make Apple Corp successful.

In the above two examples, the revised sentences are clearer and easier to understand, with long sentences divided into shorter ones and some modifications made.

- **Inaccuracy**

Accuracy of language is important for writing. Students tend to make a number of grammatical errors in their drafts. Therefore, proofreading your paper for accuracy is quite essential. The following are some of the typical mistakes most frequently made by Chinese students in their writing:

- Example

1. The verb does not agree with the subject in number.

  a. In China, the tradition of "xiao", which ask the children to keep a good relationship with their families and follow their parents' order, are taught at a very early age. (asks, is)

  b. When the number of stores become larger, the company will assume that the demand for the clothes are higher as well. (becomes, is)

2. The logical subject of "v+ing" does not agree with that of the main clause.

  a. The method used in this study is the SEIR model, which is often adopted when predicting the future trend of a certain virus. (we predict)

  b. However, when taking action to control the epidemic, there are problems about how to make the strategy more efficient, whether we can predict the further development of the virus so that we can plan for the next step. (we have to solve problems)

3. The verb is not in the correct form.

  a. Therefore, theme music should show the unique styles and features of different cultures according to their own characteristics and adapts to the tone of the movie. (adapt)

  b. The method requires the firm to make good use of the figures they have collected online, that is, analyzing the figures, make accurate guess of consumers' shopping habits and predict their behavior when buying the clothes. (making, predicting)

4. The pronoun disagrees with the noun or another pronoun it refers to.

    a. Another point is that <u>cameramen</u> need to risk <u>his</u> life while working in severe and dangerous places. (their lives)

    b. They know that they will be tided out if <u>they</u> don't make changes <u>itself</u>. (themselves)

5. The word order is inverted in a clause, as if in a question (i.e. the verb comes before the subject).

    a. It is still not known what factors will influence the quality of online learning for undergraduates and how <u>can we</u> cope with these factors. (we can)

    b. There have been numerous studies on people's behavior when playing video games, which intend to explain what affect people's consuming process and why <u>do people</u> spend money on virtual products from online sales. (people)

6. The sentence is not complete.

    a. Because it is unable to carry heavy cameras, which limits the qualities and the functions of its production. (There is no main clause.)

    b. A more sophisticated model in which interest develops through four continuous stages. (There is no predicate.)

7. The collocation is inappropriate.

    a. But with the public awareness <u>arising</u>, the virus gradually stands no chance to spread in a large scale. (rising)

    b. However, very few methods have been <u>executed</u> so as to adapt to the tendency of the popularization of international law. (employed/used/adopted)

8. The part of speech is wrong.

    a. And some of them may even <u>threat</u> people's lives. (threaten)

    b. As a result, they have to leave their children at home, which makes them hard to be under <u>protect</u>. (protection)

▪ Redundancy

Redundant expressions are unnecessary words used to repeat what has already been stated. If you have redundant expressions in your draft, try to delete them to avoid wordiness and make your writing more concise.

- **Example**
    a. They are constantly working on <u>new innovations</u> in space exploration.
    b. The conference will start at 9 am on the <u>following dates below</u>.
    c. <u>The reason for this is because</u> the unemployment rate is too high.

As "innovation" means the introduction of new things, ideas or ways of doing something, there is no need to add the word "new" before it. "Following" has already carried the meaning of "below" and there is no use repeating it. The word "reason" should not be used together with "because". We either use "the reason for this is that…" or "this is because…"

▪ Shift in person

It can also be found that students shift between the first person "I" / "we", the second person "you", and the third person "she/he" / "they" frequently in their papers. In fact, you'd better use persons consistently.

- **Example**

Poor: Many students feel that they can hardly improve their English proficiency after they have reached a certain level. We call this phenomenon fossilization. But this does not mean you cannot improve your English at all. As a matter of fact, if we are given enough input at this stage, we can still make much progress.

Better: Many students feel that they can hardly improve their English proficiency after they have reached a certain level. This phenomenon is called fossilization. But this does not mean they cannot improve their English at all. As a matter of fact, if they are given enough input at this stage, they can still make much progress.

Above are some typical problems from students' writing. Try to use the peer-review checklist to make sure that your paper meets the requirements before it is submitted.

16.3 In-Class Activities

Activity 1

Take turns to have a discussion of the research paper with the teacher. The following is a sample schedule for the discussion.[1]

Groups	Students' names	Scheduled time
1	Student 1 Student 2 Student 3	10:00–10:20
2	Student 1 Student 2 Student 3	10:20–10:40
3	Student 1 Student 2 Student 3	10:40–11:00
4	Student 1 Student 2 Student 3	11:00–11:20
5	Student 1 Student 2 Student 3	11:20–11:40

Steps for organizing the activity:

1. Do after-class Task 1 of this unit first. Each student reviews two other students' work (first draft) in your group and gets 2 reviewers' comments from the peers.

2. Read your peers' comments, on which you may agree or disagree.

3. Discuss with your peers to come up with a better version.

4. Do after-class Task 2. Submit your revised version (second draft) for teacher comments.

5. Read the teacher's written feedback before class and prepare questions to ask.

6. Understand the teacher comments through discussing with your teacher face to face or via online platform (e.g. Tencent conference).

7. Do after-class Task 3. Revise your writing and submit your final version.

---

1 This activity is done in groups of 3 students who cooperate in doing research and writing the paper all through the semester. The in-class activity will be done alternatively with after-class tasks.

16.4 After-Class Tasks

Task 1

Review your peer's research paper according to the guidelines. You can use "edit" or "add notes" so that your peer is able to track your revision comments. Explain your comments when necessary.

Task 2

Revise the first draft of your research paper and submit the second draft.

Task 3

Revise the second draft according to the teacher's written and oral feedback and submit the final version.

Unit 17

Presentation Content

17.1 Objectives

Know how to turn a research paper into a presentation.

Learn what elements are involved to start and end a speech.

Know how to make the content clear, logical and well-organized.

17.2 Pre-Class Learning

Watch the MOOC/SPOC videos and do the online exercises. The contents in the textbook will help you understand the lessons better.

Source: https://www.icourse163.org/

Course name: "学术英语写作与演讲" (Academic Writing and Presentation in English)

Unit 10 Presentation

10.1 Speech content

After you have finished your writing, you may need to present your academic work in a class or at a conference. In this case, you should condense a much longer paper into a presentation, the length of which is determined by the requirement of the conference. Learning to present your work is important because it allows you to share your research with a wider audience and invites critical comments about your work, which help you to improve your research. Remember to make your ideas clear, logical, well-organized and to the point so that your audience will have no trouble following you.

Introduction

Well begun is half done. First impression is important, especially in a presentation, and academic presentation is no exception. A good introduction arouses the listeners' interest in your presentation. And it also boosts the presenter's confidence when the speaker sees the interest, attention and pleasure on the audience's faces.

The four major objectives of an introduction are to gain attention and interest of the audience, reveal the purpose and topic of the speech, establish credibility and good will of the speaker, and preview the body of the speech. The following are some essentials in an introduction:

—**Greetings** (Greet the audience and give a brief self-introduction.)

—**Attention getter** (Attract the audience immediately and absorb them in your research topic.)

—**Topic** or **thesis** (State the topic or thesis clearly, and reveal the theme of the presentation.)

—**Purpose** (State why it is important to do your research and to give the presentation.)

—**Credibility** (State your qualification, emphasize your experience, knowledge or perspective briefly, and show that your research is credible.)

—**Outline** (Preview the outline and give a roadmap to guide your presentation.)

▪ Greetings

Greeting the audience is relatively easy, such expressions as "Good morning, everyone", or "Mr. President, ladies and gentlemen, good afternoon!" will do. After greeting the audience, you can give a brief introduction of your name and institution. Actually, on many occasions, the host of the conference may help introduce you to the audience. You can also display the information of the research topic, name and institution of the speaker on the first page of your PowerPoint slide.

▪ Attention getter

Whether your speech can immediately attract the audience and arouse their interest depends mostly on the attention getter in your introduction. Even in an academic presentation, the use of an attention-getter can be a big plus to your speech. Here, we are going to introduce some effective attention getters, such as a surprising statistic, an interesting story, a question, a humorous statement or an interaction with the audience. They can be used either individually or in combination.

1. Giving amazing information and statistics

Your research may involve some numbers or statistics. Even though they usually appear in the body of your research paper rather than in the introduction, you can use some of the statistics that you think are most surprising as an attention getter of a presentation. The unexpected statistics can be very impressive and easily capture the attention of the audience. For example, research has been done on the killing effect of a certain kind of deer, Bambi. The researcher can start his presentation by providing numbers, which will make the audience feel quite surprised and eager to hear the explanations.

- Example

Bambi vs. Jaws. No contest on which is deadlier, right? It's... Bambi. A deer is 20 times more likely to kill you than a shark. Every year in the United States, deer-car collisions kill more than 200 people.

Amazing Information, especially if accompanied by a visual aid, can jolt your audience to attention. Once you have attracted their attention, it's much easier to keep them absorbed in your presentation.

2. Presenting a quotation or a proverb

Another good way to arouse the audience's interest is to start with a famous quotation. You may choose a quotation from a famous person, a song, a poem, or a movie or you may use a proverb. Here is how a speaker uses a proverb to add flavor to the introduction of a speech about the Great Wall.

- Example

In China there is a saying—"You won't be considered a great person if you haven't been to the Great Wall." I visited the Great Wall last year when I was in China. I don't know if it made me a great person, but I do know that the wall is indeed great.

A quotation in your introduction may appeal to your audience. However, the quotation should be familiar to the audience and it shouldn't be too lengthy or the audience may feel bored with it.

3. Telling a story

Another method of catching your audience's attention is sharing a story, which gives the presentation a more personal feel. The story can be your personal experience or a historical anecdote. People enjoy listening to stories, especially amusing, dramatic or suspenseful ones. Even in the academic presentation, a story about the presenter or his research experience may bring the presenter closer to the audience. However, you have to make sure that the story is related with your topic and naturally leads your audience to be engrossed by your speech. Let's take the example of "8 Secrets of Success".

- **Example**

    The professor has done research on what leads to success. In his presentation, he started by telling a story that he once met a girl from a poor family, who asked him a question about the way to success. He struggled for the answer but felt bad for not being able to give a good answer. This motivated him to conduct a long-term research on a large number of successful people and he found the answers in the end. This story leads naturally to the main part of his speech—research findings.

4. Asking a question

Possibly the easiest opening is one that presents one or more questions to be answered in the presentation. This is effective because questions may well coincide with those the audience have in their mind when they see your topic. A research paper usually has one or more questions that lead the whole paper. In order to find the answers to the questions, the researcher will conduct a series of studies. For example, in the speech of "How He Found the True Face of Leonardo", the presenter began with a question.

- **Example**

    At the beginning of his presentation, the speaker demonstrated a picture on the screen and asked his audience a question: "Is this the face of Leonardo da Vinci or isn't it?" Then he answered the question by displaying the process of how he conducted the research and came to the findings. The question at the beginning of the presentation immediately attracts the audience to the rest of the presentation.

5. Showing sense of humor

A sense of humor can make people laugh. Laughing signifies the audience's happiness and interest in what you are saying. You can tell jokes but you need to be careful with this method. Make sure it is appropriate, and actually provokes laughter. The following example shows how Ellis, a professor of applied linguistics, started his presentation about second language teaching and learning.

- **Example**

    After looking around the lecture hall and finding the audience were mostly female English teachers, Ellis said, "Oh, I think applied linguistics in China is female linguistics."

Laughter came from the audience because there were actually few male English teachers sitting in the hall. The listeners were immediately attracted by the speaker's sense of humor, which shortened the distance between the speaker and the listeners. In fact, not only in the beginning, if a speaker is humorous all through the presentation, the speech will better appeal to the audience.

6. Involving your audience

Interacting with your audience at the beginning of your presentation is a quick way to motivate them and get them involved. You may ask them to tell you their answers to a certain question. You can take a vote to see how many of them are for or against an idea. You can even ask them to do something together with you. Look at the example of "How to Make Stress Your Friend".

- **Example**

    A professor gave a presentation about her studies on stress. She firstly asked whether they had experienced little, moderate or much stress in the past year. Then she made her own confession by saying that her former idea of treating stress as something negative was wrong and naturally led to her study about how stress could be helpful to people. The audience got involved and started to think about the presentation topic and how it was related with their own experiences. This involvement could easily attract the audience to the presentation and they would eagerly expect the answer from the presentation.

- **Topic or theme**

As a statement of the topic or theme is essential in the introduction of a research paper, you need to state the topic or introduce the theme of your speech in a presentation as well. It sets the direction for the rest of the presentation and gives your audience a reason to listen. Let's look at the following two examples:

- **Example 1**

    Today I would like to share with you some of the wonders of the Great Wall.

- **Example 2**

    I'm going to talk to you this afternoon about academic presentations and how to give academic presentations.

In Example 1 about the Great Wall, after the attention-getter in the form of a quotation: "You won't be considered a great person until you've been to the Great Wall", the speaker went on by introducing the topic of the wonders of the Great Wall. Example 2 shows that the professor was giving a lecture on how to give academic presentations, and he also had a clear theme. In both examples, the audience are able to know what to expect from the presentation and whether they are interested in the theme and content. Once you have illustrated a thesis, make sure it is clear and consistent throughout the presentation.

▪ Purpose

In order to let your audience know why your speech is worth listening to, you can also relate your topic to your audience by talking about the things that may affect them directly. In the following example, after introducing the topic of his speech about how to give an academic presentation, the professor tried to relate it to students' university life so that they will realize the importance of his lecture and listen more attentively.

- **Example**

    That's a very important thing for students to know as you have a lot of accessed oral presentations on your courses here in the university. It's a very important part of your student life.

In a research paper, the purpose of the research is usually clarified in the introduction as well. It explains why the research is worth doing. Likewise, you can state your research purpose in a presentation but it is suggested that it be related to your audience, showing that your research is important and worth listening to.

Credibility

Credibility is important, especially for a research presentation. Your audience need to trust you and believe what your will tell them. Therefore, you can establish the credibility for your presentation by showing why your research is reliable and giving your audience a good reason to listen to your speech. Let's look at Richard John's presentation of "8 Secrets of Success".

- Example

The speaker told the audience: "So here we are, *seven years, 500 interviews* later, and I'm gonna tell you what really leads to success and makes TEDsters tick." The audience might have listened to other people talking about what led to success but this presentation could be more valuable because it was not the presenter's personal thoughts or the conclusion drawn from experiences of a few successful people. It was a 7-year research based on more than 500 people, which was a big plus to the credibility gained through investment of so much time and involvement of so many people.

Outline

An outline shows the audience the structure of the presentation. Without a clear outline in the introduction, many people may not be able to sort out the presenter's ideas. Therefore, the presenter can help the audience by including an outline in the presentation. Another purpose an outline can serve is that it provides a smooth lead-in to the body of your speech because it signals that the body of the speech is about to begin. Take the previous two examples about wonders of the Great Wall and academic presentation, the presenters provided the outline at the end of the introduction.

- Example 1

I'll focus on the three major stages of its construction, moving from the first phase during the Qin Dynasty, to the second phase during the Han Dynasty, and concluding with the third phase during the Ming Dynasty.

- Example 2

Firstly, I'm going to tell the structure of a presentation. The second part is going to be more detailed about the elements of that structure. Thirdly, I'm going to talk about something of signposting, that is, how to make the

Unit 17 **Presentation Content**

audience follow your direction. And the fourth part, how to make what you say easy to understand or how to make yourself clear to your audience. Fifth, I'm going to talk about the importance of conclusions. And the last part is about questions, how to ask and deal with questions from your audience.

In these two examples, the speakers introduced the outline of their presentations so that the listeners could easily get the gist of the contents. If the time for the presentation is limited, you needn't utter the details of the outline word by word. Briefly mention it and list the outline on your PowerPoint slide.

The above are the six essentials in an introduction. Whether you have to cover them all depends on the length of time allotted to your presentation. If it is short, the introduction should not be too long, approximately 10 percent of allowed time of your presentation is appropriate. Even if you want to cut the introduction short, the greeting, the attention getter, and the theme are all necessary.

Body

In the body of your presentation, you start to deliver the major content with regard to the subject you are studying or the specific topic. The various logical orders, as detailed below, can help render the presentation easy to follow.

- **Problem-solution order**

The problem-solution order explores how to solve a problem or propose a particular solution. A research paper usually states the problem in the introduction and the rest of the paper is in fact the solution to the problem. Research questions are usually raised to approach the problem and the researcher will try to answer the questions by doing research and analyzing the research findings. Therefore, the whole research is actually presented in problem-solution pattern, from the raise of a problem on the basis of the research background, to the method used to solve the problem, and to the result, discussion, and conclusion as a solution to the problem. Generally, most researchers give presentations at an academic conference following the same order as the research paper, such as background, problem, objectives, research questions, methods, results, discussion, and conclusion. In this way, the speakers reveal their research findings gradually to reflect the logical thinking process. And this strong sense of logic will attract the audience to the speech.

- **Topical order**

Topical order is one in which contents are organized by sub-topics, equal in importance. It is usually applied when your research is based on the review of other researches or when you introduce the background of your empirical study. You summarize what others have done from different perspectives and try to lead to some new findings from the review of literature. You can quote from other people, give examples or statistics, and explain and analyze some phenomena.

- **Chronological order**

Chronological order is the order of time, which is usually used to report the development of something or the procedure of doing something. To be more specific, the development of a theory, a product or a technology and the procedure of doing research or conducting an experiment are likely to be introduced and presented in chronological order. This order is also usually applied to the description of the procedure of data collection and analysis in the methods of a research.

- **Cause-effect order**

The cause-effect order is usually appropriate when you present the results and discussion of your research. Using the cause-effect order, you can demonstrate the research findings one by one, as shown in your research paper, and give explanations of the causes to these findings respectively. You can also compare your findings with other studies to show why your research is original or significant.

Conclusion

The conclusion is the final chord that impresses your audience in a presentation. The purpose is to leave the audience with a positive impression, a sense of completeness, and the inclination to think about the topic. It is the last opportunity to get your point across and convince the audience that they have learned something from your presentation. Here are essentials to conclude or close your presentation.

Unit 17 Presentation Content

- **Repeating the topic, purpose or thesis**

    This strategy enables you to echo the introduction by referring back to the topic, purpose or thesis. If you begin by describing a scenario, you can end with the same scenario as proof that your speech is helpful in creating a new understanding. You may also refer to the introductory remarks by using keywords or parallel concepts and images that you have also used in the introduction.

    - Example 1
        In conclusion, the Great Wall of China enjoys a rich history.

    - Example 2
        That's all about how to make a good academic presentation.

- **Summarizing the main points**

    It is advisable to include a brief summary of the main points in the conclusion of your presentation. Don't worry about repeating yourself because this is expected in an academic presentation. Summarizing the main points will reinforce them and make your ideas fit together.

    - Example 1
        Built over the course of more than 2,500 years during the Qin, Han and Ming Dynasties, the Great Wall is a magnificent feat of human engineering.

    - Example 2
        In summary, our lecture covers the contents of the structure, the transitions, the delivery of a presentation, and the questioning after a presentation.

- **Extending your topic**

    In the conclusion of your presentation, you can also extend your topic by suggesting the implications of your research and proposing the areas for further research. This will render your presentation informative and thought-provoking.

    - Example 1
        While the wall no longer continues to fend China from the invaders,

it does continue to play a central role in Chinese culture and international identity. Now that you know a little more about the wall, I hope you have a fuller appreciation of why it is regarded as great, not just in China, but throughout the world.

- **Example 2**

There are several limitations of our study that should be mentioned. First, the limited distribution of questionnaires makes the study less persuasive and representative as our sample size is a potential source of bias. Second, we relied on self-reported symptoms of sleep disturbances and sleep patterns which may not be reliable. Finally, a lot of our conclusions are drawn upon empiricism instead of biological experiments. So in the future, we may work with students from biology major to find the scientific proofs for the impact of sleep on students' overall performance.

Transitions

A presentation can be divided into the introduction, the body, and the conclusion. And the body may include further sections. In order to help your audience follow you from one section to the next, you can use "signposting language" or transitional language as clear signals. Once you finish your introduction, you have to indicate that you are moving to the first section of the body of your presentation. You can do the same when moving between the sections of the body and when coming to the conclusion of your speech. Transitions relate the previous points to the upcoming points, showing how they relate to one another and support the thesis and enabling the audience to understand the major points better. Examples of transitions are:

—OK, that was the introduction, let's start with the first part.

—Let me move on to my point about...

—I'll move to my next point, which is...

—Now, let's turn to...

—Let's now look at...

—Before I conclude, let me...

—Now I'm about to conclude my presentation...

—Let me sum up the main points again...

—Before I close my speech, I would say...

—Let me wrap up the points...

Unit 17 **Presentation Content**

17.3 In-Class Activities

Activity 1

Watch the video clips. Figure out what kind of attention getters are used in the presentations and fill in the table.

Presentation title	Attention getter
8 Secrets of Success	
How He Found the True Face of Leonardo	
The Great Wall	
How to Make Stress Your Friend	
Love No Matter What	

Activity 2

Watch the video clips. Find out the logical orders of the presentations and fill in the table.

Presentation title	Logical order
8 Secrets of Success	
The Technology of Storytelling	
How He Found the True Face of Leonardo	
Keep Your Goals to Yourself	

Activity 3

Watch the presentation "The Shape Shifting Future of the Mobile Phone", and note down the transitional sentences in the following blanks.

Transition in the Introduction:
_____

Transitions in the body:
1. _____
2. _____
3. _____

Transition in the conclusion:
_____
_____

17.4 After-Class Tasks

Task 1

Watch the presentation and analyze how the elements we discussed in this unit are realized.

Script

In China there's a saying, you won't be considered a great person until you've been to the Great Wall. I visited the wall last year when I was in China. I don't know if it made me a great person, but I do know the wall is indeed great.

As you can see from this photograph the wall is great in beauty, with its long arms resting on rolling hills, and its towers peering across the valleys.

Unit 17 Presentation Content

Today I would like to share with you some of the wonders of the Great Wall. I'll focus on the three major stages of its construction, moving from the first phase during the Qin Dynasty, to the second phase during the Han Dynasty, and concluding with the third phase during the Ming Dynasty.

Let's start more than 2,000 years ago when the first parts of the wall were built. The beginning of the Great Wall as we know it, dates to 221 B.C. when Emperor Qin Shihuang ordered its top general to lead 300,000 soldiers in rebuilding and connecting separate old walls that have been built by princes of Warring States. In just 12 years, Qin had a 3,000-mile-wall, using primarily wood frames filled with stones and compacted earth. While the wall proved effective in keeping out the tribes and to invade China from the north, it created a descent within China. According to Arthur Wardroom the Great Wall of China from history to myth, ditches on the roadside were filled with corpses of men who have been forced into construction of the Great Wall. Compelled in the hard labor and burdened by heavy taxes to finance the project, the people grew unhappy. And a year after Qin's death, the peasants revolted. While the war stood, the empire collapsed.

The second major period of the construction of the Great Wall occurred during the Han Dynasty, which lasted from 206 B.C. to 220 A.D. Emperor Wu Di ordered expansion of the existing wall to protect land won when his army defeated the northern tribes. Workers added 300 miles to existing wall. They built wooden frames which they filled with willow reeds and mixture of fine gravel and water. As you can see from this picture of the ruins of the Han Wall, it was very different in construction and appearance from the Great Wall as it exists today.

The third major building period of the Great Wall occurred 1,100 years later during the Ming Dynasty. In 1368 during the first year of the Ming Dynasty, Emperor Zhu Yuanzhang ordered more expansion of the wall. Subsequent Ming emperors strengthened and extended the wall further until it reached its current length. Builders of the Ming wall made three important architectural advancements which resulted in the distinct features of the wall as it exists today. You can see those features especially well in this photograph. First, rather than using earth and stone, they used kiln-fired bricks to create a stronger wall. Second, they erected more than 3,000 beacon towers to watch the mountain path for potential invaders. These towers arise from the wall like mighty outposts and one of the most striking aspects of the wall when you see them in person. Third, the Ming builders made the wall so large that it would be almost

impossible to break through. In fact, the wall is so wide that soldiers could ride several horses abreast along the top of the wall.

In conclusion, the Great Wall of China enjoys a rich history. Builder of the course more than 2,500 years during the Qin, Han and Ming Dynasties, it is a magnificent feat of human engineering. While the wall no longer continues to fend China from the invaders, it does continue to play a central role in Chinese culture and international identity. Now that you know a little more about the wall, I hope you have a fuller appreciation of why it is regarded as great, not just in China, but throughout the world.

Prepare for your speech, design a good attention-getter and check whether your introduction meets the following requirements.

Yes	No	Requirements for the Introduction
		Do I gain the attention and interest of my audience by using one or more attention-getters?
		Have I established my credibility?
		Have I related the speech to my audience?
		Do I have a thesis statement or an outline of the main points to be covered in the speech?
		Is the introduction limited to 10–15 percent of the allowed time of my speech?
		Have I been creative in devising my introduction?
		Have I polished the language of my introduction?
		Have I practiced the delivery of my introduction so I can present it fluently, confidently, and with sustained eye contact?

Unit 17 **Presentation Content**

Task 3

Prepare for the presentation of your research paper. Try to employ each essential element you have learned in this unit.

Unit 18

Speech Delivery

18.1 Objectives

Learn how to deliver speech effectively.

Know how to reduce speech anxiety and improve confidence.

Learn how to use visual aids appropriately.

18.2 Pre-Class Learning

Watch the MOOC/SPOC videos and do the online exercises. The contents in the textbook will help you understand the lessons better.

Source: https://www.icourse163.org/

Course name: "学术英语写作与演讲" (Academic Writing and Presentation in English)

Unit 10 Presentation

10.2 Speech delivery

10.3 Questions and answers

Imagine that you are among the audience for a presentation, what might draw your attention, stimulate your imagination, inspire your motivation, and promote your understanding? In fact, besides the content, the way you deliver a speech is a crucial determinant of success in speech. An audience not only listens to your ideas, but also responds to the way you use your voice and your body. Therefore, you have to deliver your speech in a lively, flexible and interesting way.

Essentials for delivering a good speech

In order to make an effective delivery of your speech, you need to be:

Confident. Confidence is especially important when you are giving a presentation. You will not be so confident in public speaking if you lack experience or if you are not so sure about the content you deliver. Therefore, you had better create chances to speak in public so as to gain experience. You also need to practice as much as possible beforehand to be familiar with what you are going to talk about. Confidence contributes to the effectiveness of the delivery and the audience prefer a presentation given by a confident speaker.

Natural. Being natural is also very important to the good delivery of a presentation. Some people feel very nervous and behave awkwardly while giving a presentation. Some other people design gestures or speak in a pretentious way. Your delivery should be natural, and your facial expressions, gestures, and movements should all appear natural and spontaneous.

Enthusiastic. Enthusiasm or passion is essential for presentation. The audience will get motivated, attracted or persuaded by a passionate speaker, whether the content is about a general or academic topic. Presenting academic contents does not mean you have to be very formal, or even dull, without showing your passion. If you show enthusiasm in your presentation, people will feel your passion and interest in your research, and they will tend to listen to your presentation with more interest as well.

Direct. An effective delivery is direct in that it requires the speaker to connect personally with listeners by building a good relationship. You'd better maintain eye contact with your audience, use a friendly tone of voice, use positive facial expressions such as smiling, and position yourself so that you are physically close to the audience. You can even have interactions with the audience to create a good atmosphere and be emotionally close to your audience.

Aspects of good delivery

Now we are going to explain how to make an effective delivery of a speech from the aspects of how to use language, manipulate your voice and your body, practice your speech, and reduce anxiety.

▪ Using effective language

The language of a presentation is different from that of a research paper. When giving a presentation, you should not use exactly the same words and sentences from your research paper by reading them out. You need to present it in a way that sounds good to the ears of your audience. The spoken language is different from the written language, so you have to make the language meant for the ear rather than for the eye and be plain rather than complicated.

Making effective use of your voice

How to manipulate your voice well while delivering a speech is essential for an effective presentation. People's voices vary. A good voice is an asset for a public speaker but it is not a necessity. You can make your speech just as attractive by maintaining good control of the following aspects of your voice:

—volume,

—rate,

—tone,

—pauses,

—pronunciation, and

—articulation.

Volume is the loudness of your voice. Be considerate to everyone in the room and adjust your voice to an appropriate volume, making sure that they all can hear you. Your voice in a presentation should always be louder than in a daily conversation.

Rate is the speed at which you utter words. Some people have the wrong idea that speaking fast means fluency and try to speak as fast as they can. As a matter of fact, speaking too fast will make it hard for your audience to follow you. Very often, you may find it hard to understand a speaker who reads very fast from his paper. Therefore, speak neither too fast nor too slowly.

Tone is a vocal sound with reference to its pitch, quality, and strength. Normally, a rising tone is used in a question and a falling tone in a statement. Different tones show different emotions, happy or sad, angry or satisfied, sincere or sarcastic. Even the same words uttered with different tones can indicate different meanings or emotions. The variety of tones will make your voice sound vivid rather than dull and flat.

Pauses in a speech do not mean you are not fluent or unable to continue. Mark Twain once said: "The right word may be effective, but no word was ever as effective as a rightly timed pause." A pause can signal the end of a thought unit and lend dramatic impact to a statement. Use pauses to modulate your rate and rhythm. But when you pause, make sure that you do so at the end of the thought unit.

Pronunciation has a great influence on your speech although it may not be decisive. Native speakers are more tolerant of pronunciation errors but people usually expect a higher degree of accuracy in formal speeches. An academic presentation does not require perfect pronunciation but your pronunciation should not hinder people's understanding. Therefore, try to make sure the keywords are pronounced correctly. You also need to pay attention to the words that are difficult for you to pronounce and practice until you can utter them correctly.

Articulation is the clarity of your voice. Make your speech sound clear and precise rather than indistinct and sloppy. On most occasions, poor articulation results from failing to manipulate the lips, tongue, jaw and soft palate. When making a speech, try your best to utter words clearly so that your audience can follow your presentation more easily.

- **Making effective use of your body**

Your body language, rather essential in a presentation, sometimes speaks louder than your words. So while you are speaking, please pay attention to:
—personal appearance—dress appropriately;
—stance—stand appropriately;
—eye contact—keep frequent eye contact with your audience;
—facial expressions—smile to build confidence and connection;
—gesture—use a variety of gestures naturally; and
—body movement—move your body at a comfortable pace.

Personal appearance contributes to the success of a speech. People see you before they hear you, so you should dress and groom appropriately to make a favorable first impression. Remember, good personal appearance will not only leave good impression to your audience but also boost your own confidence.

Stance means the way you stand. You can decide to stand or sit depending on the type of presentation, the size of the audience and the room where you are presenting. If it is a presentation involving more emotions, standing is better than sitting because that will make the presentation more effective. But you cannot stand still, always resting your hands at side, in the front or at the back, which makes you look quite nervous and awkward. Stand with your back straight, and you will look energetic rather than sloppy.

You have to keep **eye contact** with your audience. This is essential in a presentation because looking at your audience can build trust between you and your audience. What do you feel when someone is looking down or aside while talking to you? Do you feel the person is impolite, nervous, or dishonest? Many people read from their paper while making a speech, which kills eye-contact. And such monotonous reading may well result in loss of attention from your audience. However, it is impossible to look at everyone in the room at the same time. What you can do is to look at someone and talk for a while as you do in a one-to-one conversation, then you look at another one, and keep talking.

You also need to have an appropriate **facial expression**. Whether you are confident or not can be judged by your facial expression. You usually smile to build confidence and connection with your audience. As a matter of fact, your facial expression is affected by your emotion. When you have passion and confidence, your face radiates. But when you feel nervous, your face is either stiff or twisted. So you have to overcome nervousness to have a natural and confident facial expression.

Gesture is how you move part of the body, especially the hands or the head, to convey an idea or meaning. Appropriate gestures will add to the effect of a speech. Accomplished presenters gesture frequently while nervous speakers hardly do. Some novice presenters design gestures for a speech, but if not natural, they will cause distraction, reduce the effect and make the speaker look pretentious. In fact, experienced and confident speakers don't design gestures, the gestures just come about naturally when they speak. Therefore, a speaker should learn to be natural and confident and let the gestures take care of themselves.

You need to pay attention to the **movement of your body** while giving a speech. Novice speakers are often not sure what to do with their body. Some stand still behind the podium, others pace back and forth across the podium, and still others repeatedly shift their body from side to side. In fact, when you rise to speak, try to look calm by striding confidently to the podium. When you reach the podium, give yourself some time to get set, establish eye contact with your audience and then start to talk. During the speech, you needn't stick to the podium, you can get close to your audience, or you can move your steps while speaking. Take steps that are slow and deliberate. Stop and center yourself after every three or four steps. When you reach the end of the speech, you can maintain eye contact after you stop talking to make sure your speech sinks in.

- ### Reducing speech anxiety

Speech anxiety is the sense of fear or panic that overtakes a person when he or she is called upon to speak in public. Speech anxiety is extremely common for people. The following factors may lead to the anxiety of public speaking:

—lack of preparation;

—lack of public speaking experience;

—feeling inadequate;

—being too self-conscious; and

—lack of credibility.

When you feel inadequate, unprepared or inexperienced, you will get nervous and anxious in the presentation. Therefore, you have to do something to overcome anxiety, such as:

—being familiar with your material;

—practicing your speech;

—imagining yourself to be successful;

—knowing your topic is worthwhile and believing your audience will enjoy it;

—warming up your voice;

—not rushing to a start;

—not apologizing for being nervous;

—turning nervousness into positive energy;

—acting confidently and feeling confident;

—concentrating on your message;

—using visual aids; and

—gaining experience.

The more you prepare for your presentation, the less anxious you will be. After you have done your research and rehearsed your speech, the task will not be so difficult as it seems at the beginning. However, even if you are quite prepared, you may still feel nervous when it is time to start your presentation. As a matter of fact, even experienced speakers sometimes get nervous. Remember that feeling nervous can actually help you if you turn anxiety into positive energy. You may have butterflies in your stomach before the speech, but when you start speaking, you will calm down gradually and feel yourself filled with energy and confidence.

Practicing delivery

Practice makes perfect. Before presentation, it is necessary for you to make full preparation for the speech. Nobody can give a good presentation without rehearsal. Even the most experienced public speaker like Steve Jobs practices thoroughly before a speech. The more you practice, the more confident you will be, and the better you will perform in the presentation. The following are some guidelines for you to practice speaking and rehearse your presentation:

—start your practice early;

—prepare your speaking outline;

—go through your outline aloud to check how it can be translated into a whole speech;

—practice your speech silently for several times, using only the outline and visual aids;

—practice delivery in a loud voice;

—polish and refine your delivery;

—time yourself;

—practice in front of a full-length mirror;

—audio-record your delivery when practicing;

—videotape yourself if possible; and

—arrange for an audience to listen to you and invite comments and suggestions.

Visual aids

Visual aids are quite useful in the presentation. They can remind you of the speech contents, help combat stage fright and make you feel less nervous. They enable the listeners to understand you better and remember the speech more easily. They can promote the audience's interest and motivation, making them more attracted and engrossed. They even help build credibility and make you sound more professional.

Some typical types of visual aids are real objects and models, pictures, graphs and charts, tables, and audio and video clips. In a university, there are blackboards or white boards, flipcharts, overhead projectors, handouts and PowerPoint in which the pictures, graphs and videos can be included.

Objects and models are three dimensional aids that you bring to the stage or class to help you demonstrate something or explain a process.

Pictures include the photographs, drawings and maps. You can use your own high-quality photographs taken with your digital camera, or use the high-quality images available online. However, be cautious of copyright issues if you use pictures online.

Graphs and charts can help you illustrate a point better. There are pie charts, bar charts, line charts, and flow charts. A pie chart is used to show percentages while a line chart can demonstrate trends. A bar chart is to show changes in quantity over time or to compare quantities, and a flow chart is most appropriate for presenting the steps of a process.

- **Examples**

Pie chart

Bar chart

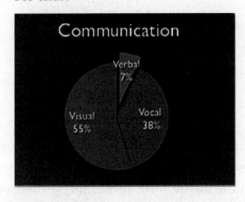
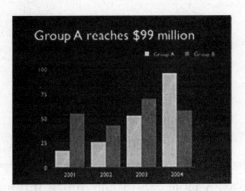

Line chart

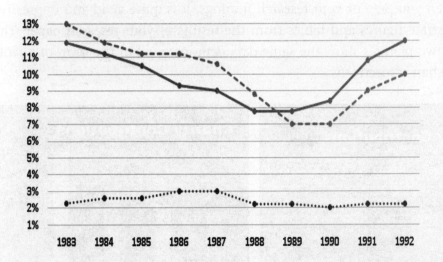

Flow chart

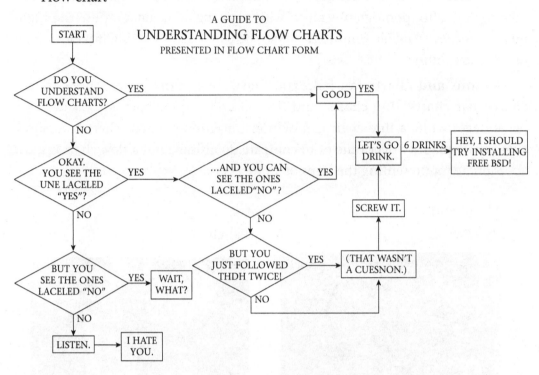

Tables are used for side-by-side comparisons of quantitative data. They are frequently used in research paper to present the research findings in a succinct way. A table can display much information in the form of numbers. However, if you want to display information in a more dramatic or impressive way, use a chart. When you present your research findings, it is quite vivid and impressive to demonstrate figures and tables from the results of your research paper. The following two pictures show the same data demonstrated in the form of a table and a bar chart respectively.

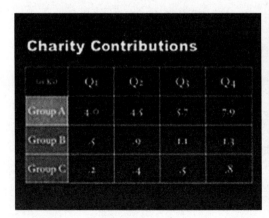
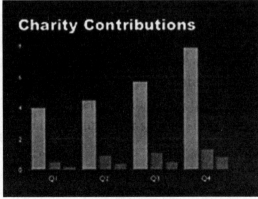

Video and audio clips are helpful for showing concrete examples. It will not only illustrate your ideas better, but also change the pace of delivery and thereby increase the interest of your audience and attract their attention.

The speaker and the audience can also be visual aids. You can ask volunteers from the audience to help you demonstrate a process or explain the process by doing something yourself.

Sensory aids are used when you want to arouse audience's senses of sight, smell, hearing, taste, or touch. This is most appropriate when your presentation focuses on topics related with your senses such as food, music, flower, etc.

PowerPoint is the most convenient and most frequently used visual aid. But when using PowerPoint, you need to pay attention to the following things:

—Limit the number of PowerPoint slides.

The number of PowerPoint slides is decided by the length of your speech. You'd better prepare neither too many slides and display them in a hurry during the speech, nor too few so that your speech seems not well-prepared. Generally speaking, about half a minute is appropriate for one slide.

—Avoid using complete sentences and paragraphs.

Don't put a whole paragraph on the same PowerPoint slide. This will only make the audience tempted to read rather than listen and make it hard for them to catch the main points immediately. Include just keywords or phrases to make them conspicuous.

—Try to avoid text-heavy slides.

A text-heavy slide contains too many words that appear quite small and illegible. Such slides do not make much sense because the audience can hardly get anything from them. Slides with only a few big enough words are appropriate.

—Do not put many ideas in one slide, try to share one idea per slide.

If you have several ideas, try to put them in different slides. This will keep the audience focused. Besides, you need some time to explain each of the ideas. Having all of them listed on the same page may make the talk sound a little hasty.

—Do not overuse special effects such as animation and sounds.

Using special effects such as animation and sounds will be a plus but overuse of them is not suggested. Two much animation and too loud sound will sometimes distract the audience's attention.

—Use appropriate font type and font size.

A sans serif typeface is normally preferred. You can use large fonts for the main idea and small ones for the subordinate content. But too many fonts in a single slide may make it look messy.

—Use parallel structure.

As has been detailed in the outline section of the book, the wording of items at the same level should be in a parallel structure, so should it be in PowerPoint slides.

—Use contrasting colors for text and background.

There should be sharp contrast in color between the background and the words. Choose light colored words against dark background or vice versa. It is also the case with a picture against the background.

—Use good quality images.

You cannot simply download a picture and paste it on the PowerPoint slide without considering its quality. Downloaded pictures are often of low quality and blurred, especially when enlarged. If you need a big picture, pay attention to its quality.

—Avoid errors.

You have to check your spelling and grammar. If you make mistakes in such a few words written in your PowerPoint, you will leave the audience a negative impression that you are a very careless person, that your speech is inadequately prepared, or that your research is not well-done.

—Use space effectively.

The space on the slides should be used appropriately and the words and pictures should be arranged in a balanced and charming manner.

—Use graphs and charts effectively.

Graphs and charts are very useful, especially in academic presentations. They are vivid and convincing, and can be attached to the PowerPoint slides to demonstrate research findings.

—Use visuals to increase emotional appeal.

If possible, try to show the content by using visual effect because it will be more impressive than the words or numbers.

Questions and answers

For many scholars, the Q & A session might be the most challenging part of the presentation. You are expected to improvise answers to the questions. Nobody is supposed to be knowledgeable about everything. It is quite normal that you cannot provide a satisfactory answer occasionally. You come to a conference to share what you know and to learn from others as well. The following are some tips for handling questions:

—Predict questions and prepare for them.

—Make clear your expectations about questions.

—Repeat the question aloud to the entire audience.

—Make sure you understand the question fully before answering it.

—Respond to the entire audience, not just to the questioner.

—Do not get into a one-to-one long conversation with a single questioner.

—Be brief, direct and courteous while answering the question.

—Check for satisfaction after answering a question.

—If you are not sure about the answer to the question, say so and suggest where to find the answer or contact the questioner later by email.

—Do not always say "that's a good question".

—Make a Plan B for a situation where no questions are raised and explain difficult points in that case.

18.3 In-Class Activities

Activity 1

Watch the video and summarize the key points for the presenter's effective use of her voice and gestures.

Effective use of her voice	1. 2. 3. ...
Effective use of her gestures	1. 2. 3. ...

Activity 2

Watch the videos clips. Find out what visual aids are used in the presentation and fill them in the table.

Presentation title	Visual aids
Maybe the Best Robot Demo Ever	
A Story of Mixed Emoticons	
The 8 Billion iPod	
Nature Beauty Gratitude	

Unit 18 Speech Delivery

(Continued)

Presentation title	Visual aids
The Brain Changing Benefits of Exercise	
Music and Passion	
Making Incredible Presentations	

Activity 3

Compare the following pairs of PowerPoint slides and tell which one is better in each of the pairs? Give your reasons.

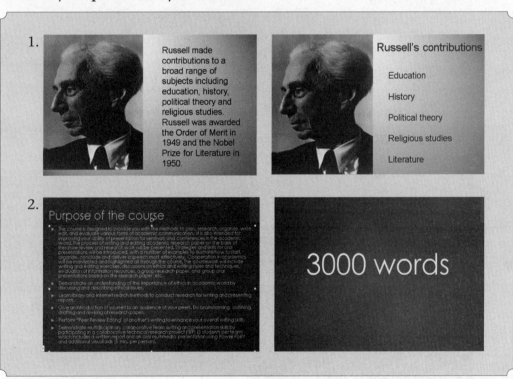

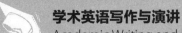

3.

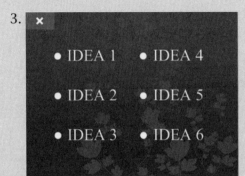

4.

| Why do people Make fonts **Too big** OR Too small | Size fonts appropriately use bigger font for the main idea use smaller font for the subordinate content |

5.

| ESSENTIALS IN A CONCLUSION • Repeat the topic, purpose and thesis • Summarize the main points • Extend your topic | ESSENTIALS IN A CONCLUSION • Repeat the topic, purpose and thesis • to summarize the main points • extending your topic |

6.

| This is hard to read | Can you see it clearly? |

Unit 18 **Speech Delivery**

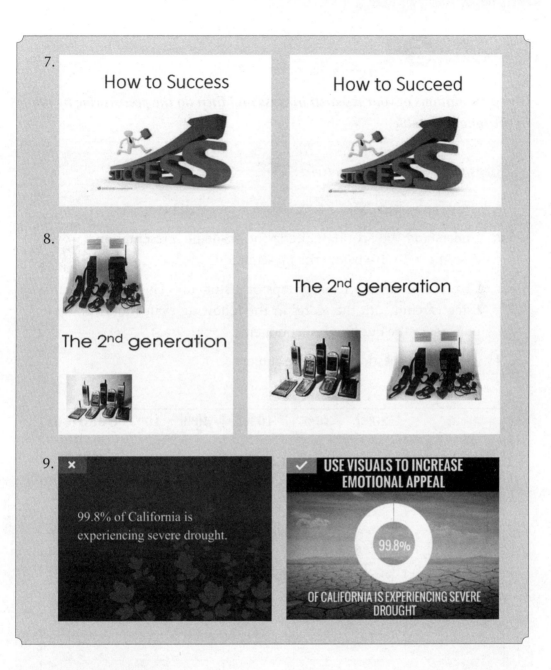

Activity 4

Watch the video and summarize the major points about how Steve Jobs gives a presentation.

Activity 5[1]

Give presentations of your research in class and then do the peer-scoring by filling in the following table.

Steps for organizing the activity:

1. Finish after-class Tasks 1 & 2. Get well-prepared before class.
2. Understand the Scoring Criteria for Academic Presentation (See Appendix 10) before the presentation.
3. Give the presentations in groups of 3 students. The other students listen carefully, fill the scores in the following evaluation form and prepare for the questions or comments.
4. Answer the questions from the audience.

No.	Names	20% Intro- duction	30% Body	10% Conclu- sion	30% Deliv- ery	10% Q&A	Questions or comments to the speakers
1							
2							
3							

---

1 This activity is performed in separate lessons from Activities 1–4. It can be arranged at the end of the course. It is actually the academic conference where students can report the research they have conducted in the semester.

Unit 18 **Speech Delivery**

(Continued)

No.	Names	20%	30%	10%	30%	10%	Questions or comments to the speakers
		Introduction	Body	Conclusion	Delivery	Q&A	
4							
5							

18.4 After-Class Tasks

Task 1

Design your PPT, prepare your presentation on the basis of your PPT, and rehearse until you are satisfied.

Task 2

Read your research paper again. Try to be familiar with your contents and be ready for the possible questions.

References & Example Sources

Abraham, R. R., Kamath, M. G., Vashe, A., Wong H. J., Tahrim, M., & Kasmuri, M. (2018). Factors influencing academic success of high achievers and low achievers in physiology. *Journal of Clinical & Diagnostic Research, 12*(7), 11–15.

American Psychological Association (2020). *Publication manual of the American psychological association* (7th ed.). American Psychological Association.

Attali, Y., & Burstein, J. (2006). Automated essay scoring with e-rater® V.2. *Journal of Technology, Learning, and Assessment, 4*(3). http://www.jtla.org

Bridgeman, B., Trapani, C., & Attali, Y. (2009, April). *Considering fairness and validity in evaluating automated scoring.* Paper presented at the annual meeting of the National Council on Measurement in Education (NCME), San Diego, CA.

Burstein, J., Chodorow, M., & Leacock, C. (2004). Automated essay evaluation: The Criterion online writing service. *AI Magazine, 25*(3), 27–35.

Carlson, J. M., Schaefer, M., Monaco, D. C., Batorsky, R., Claiborne, D. T., Prince, J., Deymier, M. J., Ende, Z. S., Klatt, N. R., DeZiel, C. E., Lin, T.-H., Peng, J., Seese, A. M., Shapiro, R., Frater, J., Ndung'u, T., Tang, J., Goepfert, P., Gilmour, J., ... Hunter, E. (2014). Selection bias at the heterosexual HIV-1 transmission bottleneck. *Science, 345*(6193), 1–13.

Chen, C. F. E., & Cheng W. Y. E. (2008). Beyond the design of automated writing evaluation: Pedagogical practices and perceived learning effectiveness in EFL writing classes. *Language Learning & Technology, 12*(2), 94–112.

Chen, D. F., & Zhang, L. 2017. A Study of formative assessment for academic English writing of Chinese EFL learners. *TESOL International Journal, 12*(2): 47–64.

Cotos, E. (2011). Potential of automated writing evaluation feedback. *Calico Journal, 28*(2), 420–459.

Chuchai S., Tassanee H., Pongchan P., Veerawan W., & Pimchanok, K. (2018). Factors influencing students' academic success: The mediating role of study engagement. *International Journal of Behavioral Science, 13*(1), 1–14.

Daniels, B. T., Human, A. E., Gallagher, K. M., & Howie, E. K. (2021). Relationships between grit, physical activity, and academic success in university students: Domains of physical activity matter. *Journal of American College Health.* https://doi.org/10.1080/07448481.2021.1950163

Davis, B. J. (2008). Resilience in African American youth: African American female single-parent perceptions of factors and causes of academic success [ProQuest Information & Learning]. In *Dissertation Abstracts International Section A: Humanities and Social Sciences, 69*(2–A), 501.

Donoso, M., Collins, A. G. E., & Koechlin, E. (2014). Foundations of human reasoning in the prefrontal cortex. *Science, 344*(6191), 1481–1486.

Ekwonye, A. U., & DeLauer, V. (2019). Exploring individual and interpersonal level factors associated with academic success of college students at a women's, faith-based higher institution. *Higher Education Studies, 9*(1), 86–99.

El-Ebyary, K., & Windeatt, S. (2010). The impact of computer-based feedback on students' written work. *International Journal of English Studies, 10*(2), 121–142.

Ge, Y., Xin, S., Luan, D., Zou, Z., Bai, X., Liu, M., & Gao, Q. (2020). Independent and combined associations between screen time and physical activity and perceived stress among college students. *Addictive Behaviors, 103.* https://doi.org/10.1016/j.addbeh.2019.106224

Graham, S. (2006). Listening comprehension: The learners' perspective. *System, 34*(2), 165–182.

Greenfield, D. H. (1998). Cognitive flexibility, communication strategy, and integrative complexity in groups: Public versus private reactions to majority and minority status. *Journal of Experimental Social Psychology, 34*(2), 202–226.

He, D. H., Lu, Y. B., & Zhou, D. Y. (2008). Empirical study of consumers' purchase intentions in c2c electronic commerce. *Tsinghua Science and Technology, 13*(3),

References & Example Sources

287–292.

Hepworth, D., Littlepage, B., & Hancock, K. (2018). Factors influencing university student academic success. *Educational Research Quarterly, 42*(1), 45–61.

Hyland, K. (1999). Academic attribution: Citation and the construction of disciplinary knowledge. *Applied Linguistics, 20*(3), 341–67.

Jaisoorya, T. S., Rani, A., Menon, P. G., Jeevan, C. R., Revamma, M., Jose, V., Radhakrishnan, K. S., Kishore, A., Thennarasu, K., & Sivasankaran N. B. (2017). Psychological distress among college students in Kerala, India—Prevalence and correlates. *Asian Journal of Psychiatry, 28*, 28–31.

Keck, C. (2014). Copying, paraphrasing, and academic writing development: A re-examination of L1 and L2 summarization practices. *Journal of Second Language Writing, 25*(1), 4–22.

Kraus, S., Sears, S. R., & Burke, B. L. (2013). Is truthiness enough? Classroom activities for encouraging evidence-based critical thinking. *Journal of Effective Teaching, 13*(2), 83–93.

Lan, Y. J. (2014). Does second life improve mandarin learning by overseas Chinese students? *Language Learning & Technology, 18*(2), 36–56.

Lisnyj, K. T., Gillani, N., Pearl, D. L., McWhirter, J. E., & Papadopoulos, A. (2021). Factors associated with stress impacting academic success among post-secondary students: A systematic review. *Journal of American College Health.* https://doi.org/10.1080/07448481.2021.1909037

McBride, C. S. et al. (2014). Evolution of mosquito preference for humans linked to an odorant receptor. *Nature, 515*(13), 222–227.

Merriam-Webster. (n.d.). Definition of plagiarize. In *Merriam-Webster.com dictionary*. Retrieved July 12, 2021, from https://www.merriam-webster.com/dictionary/plagiarize

Moriña, A., & Biagiotti, G. (2021). Academic success factors in university students with disabilities: A systematic review. *European Journal of Special Needs Education.* https://doi.org/10.1080/08856257.2021.1940007

Nguyen, V. A. (2017). A peer assessment approach to project based blended learning course in a Vietnamese higher education. *Education & Information Technologies, 22*(5), 2141–2157.

Powers, D. E., Burstein, J. C., Chodorow, M. S., Fowles, M. E., & Kukich, K. (2002).

Comparing the validity of automated and human scoring of essays. *Journal of Educational Computing Research, 26* (4), 407–425.

Rezaei, A., & Khosroshahi, J. B. (2018). Optimism, social intelligence and positive affect as predictors of university students' life satisfaction. *European Journal of Mental Health,13*(2), 150–162.

Saunders-Scott, D., Braley, M. B., & Stennes-Spidahl, N. (2018). Traditional and psychological factors associated with academic success: Investigating best predictors of college retention. *Motivation & Emotion, 42*(4), 459–465.

Schutte, N. S., & Malouff, J. M. (2020). Connections between curiosity, flow and creativity. *Personality and Individual Differences, 152*. https://doi.org/10.1016/j.paid.2019.109555

Stankovska, G., Dimitrovski, D., Angelkoska, S., Ibraimi, Z., & Uka, V. (2018). Emotional intelligence, test anxiety and academic stress among university students. *Bulgarian Comparative Education Society, 16*(1), 157–164.

Swales, J. (1990). *Genre analysis*. Cambridge: Cambridge University Press.

Swales, J. M., & Feak, C. B. (2004). *Academic writing for graduate students*. Ann Arbor: University of Michigan Press.

Talhelm, T., Zhang, X., Oishi, S., Shimin, C., Duan, D. Lan, X., & Kitayama, S. (2014). Large-scale psychological differences within China explained by rice versus wheat agriculture. *Science, 344*(6184), 603–608.

Tilman, D., & Clark, M. (2014). Global diets link environmental sustainability and human health. *Nature, 515*(7528), 518–522.

Tin, T. B. (2006). Investigating the nature of "interest" reported by a group of postgraduate students in an MA in English language teacher education programme. *System, 34*(2), 222–238.

Vantage Learning. (2005). *How intelliMetric works*. http://www.cengagesites.com/academic/assets/sites/4994/WE_2_IM_How_IntelliMetric_Works.pdf

Web of Science Group. (2018). *EndNote X9 research smarter: Quick reference guide for Windows*. https://clarivate.libguides.com/ld.php?content_id=44898510

Weigle, S. C. (2010). Validation of automated scores of TOEFL iBT tasks against non-test indicators of writing ability. *Language Testing, 27*(3), 335–353.

Wilson., J., Olinghouse, N. G., & Andrada, G. N. (2014). Does automated

References & Example Sources

feedback improve writing quality? *Learning Disabilities: A Contemporary Journal, 12*(1), 93–118.

Yang, Y., Buckendahl, C. W., Juszkiewicz, P. J., & Bhola, D. S. (2002). A review of strategies for validating computer-automated scoring. *Applied Measurement in Education, 15*(4), 391–412.

Yin, H. Y., & Xu, L. Q. (2010). Measuring the structural vulnerability of road network: A network efficiency perspective. *Shanghai Jiao Tong Univ. (Sci.) 15*(6), 736–742.

Zeng, Q. F., Chen, W. B., & Huang, L. H. (2008). E-business transformation: An analysis framework based on critical organizational dimensions. *Tsinghua Science and Technology, 13*(3), 408–413.

Zhang, L. (2014). Review of handbook of automated essay evaluation: Current applications and new directions. *Language Learning and Technology, 18* (2), 65–69.

Zhang L. (2015, March). *Automated writing evaluation: Past, present and prospect.* Paper presented at TESOL International Convention. Toronto, Ontario, Canada.

Zhang, L., Beach, R., & Sheng, Y. 2016. Understanding the use of online role-play for collaborative argument through teacher experiencing: A case study. *Asia-Pacific Journal of Teacher Education, 44*(3), 242–256.

Zhang, L., Sheng, Y., & Li, L. (2014). Presenting and evaluating an academic writing course based on an integrated model. *The Journal of Asia TEFL, 11*(1), 71–96.